The House of El Shaddai

God's Dwelling Place Reconsidered

The House of El-Shaddai—God's Dwelling Place Reconsidered
Copyright © 2018 by Andrew L. Hoy. All Rights Reserved.

Conditions of Use

Permission is granted to make up to 14 paper copies of 16 individual pages from the book for classroom use only, three times per year. The pages must be complete and may not be modified in any manner. Permission is not granted to modify pages, reprint charts or images apart from the page setting, reprint groups of pages in bound form, either electronically or physically, or to offer copies for sale or donation either at cost or profit. These tables, images, and illustrations may not be used on web sites. No part of this publication may be stored in a retrieval system or transmitted in any form or by any means—electronic, mechanical, or recording without prior written permission from the publisher, except for the inclusion of brief quotations in a review. The round structure design shown herein is patent pending. All commercial use of this material is reserved by Andrew L. Hoy. Any other use must be approved in writing by Andrew L. Hoy. Graphical renderings included herein are for illustrative purposes only and are not intended to be used as fabrication drawings. Serious injury or death may result from misapplication of design information.

Photographs, Illustrations and Other Credits

Cover art, along with CGI imagery and diagrams of Tabernacle floor plans and components shown on pages i, vii, viii, 25-27, 29-36, 38, 40-49, 51-55, 57, 59-60, 62-65, 67-72, 74-80, 82-121, 124-130, 132-133, 135-136, 139-146, 148, 150-169, 171-174, 176-177, 179, 182-184, 196, and 198 are by Andrew Hoy, Copyright 2015-2018. Phillip Medhurst collection images are used in accordance with terms identified in https://creativecommons.org/licenses/by-sa/3.0/deed.en. All other credits are included in image captions and/or are materials from the public domain. PowerPoint® is a registered Microsoft trademark.

Unless otherwise specified, all Scripture was taken from the 1769 edition of the King James Bible.

For information about this title or to order other books and/or electronic media, contact:

    Project 314
    P.O. Box 1314
    Grafton, WI 53024
    elshaddai@project314.org

ISBN-13:	978-0-9911166-8-3 (Hardcover)
ISBN-13:	978-0-9911166-6-9 (Softcover)
BISAC:	REL006700—Religion / Biblical Studies / Bible Study Guides
	REL072000—Religion : Antiquities & Archaeology
	ARC005020—Architecture : History—Ancient & Classical

Table of Contents

~ Acknowledgment ~	IV
~ Foreword ~	VI
~ Preface ~	VII
Introduction	1
Part 1 — Tabernacle Coverings	26
~ Linen Curtains ~	28
~ Wool Curtains ~	37
~ Leather Covering ~	48
Part 2 — Tabernacle Frame	51
~ South Rib ~	56
~ North Rib ~	73
~ Ring Assembly ~	81
~ Tabernacle Bars ~	98
Part 3 — Tabernacle Internals	113
~ Holy of Holies ~	113
~ Tent Entrance ~	123
Part 4 — Roof & Courtyard Items	129
~ Tabernacle Roof ~	131
~ Courtyard Edge / Frame ~	137
~ Courtyard Gating ~	165
~ Copper Altar ~	174
~ Copper Basin ~	178
Part 5 — Transforming Ideas	181
~ Quality Review and Assessment ~	182
~ The Subjective Perspective ~	196

~ Acknowledgment ~

When I stop and ponder the uniqueness and significance of the material revealed herein, words alone cannot express my profound sense of amazement that I have been granted the privilege to be instrumental in this one-in-ten-billion discovery. That being said, I will begin this acknowledgment by giving thanks to El Shaddai, who is the God of Pi and the sustainer of all.

I hereby acknowledge my late father Harvey, who instilled the principle of "FDB with TLC". It is only because of his accomplishments and dedication that I was able to make this discovery, and it is only because of the faithfulness of my mother, Janet, that I am able to bring this Tabernacle discovery to light.

I would also like to express a special measure of gratitude to Eric G., Brian S., and Ali F., who were in a variety of different and unique ways able to make this book possible. Likewise, I would like to thank Eliyahu B., Rob S., Zen G., Jackson S., and Gene P., for their special ability to think outside the box, read between the lines, and even color off the page. For offering their insight, fiscal support, and faithfulness, I would like to extend my thanks to "everybody else" that have had a hand in or contribution to this project. Among them, I thank Abonni A., Abram F., Amanda G., Angie M., Anita J., Anthony W., Ariel C., Ariel E., Ashon S., Bernie M., Brian C., Brian M., Bruce B., Carolyn F., Charlie L., Cheryl G., Chris B., Chris D., Christian A., April T., Craig W., Daisy P., David F., Debi S., Doina L., Don O., Donald S., Dot G., Ed G., Edoardo R., Eric B., Gary P., Geo B., George G., Gershon S., Greg V., Hanock Y., Harold B., Heath T., Hector B., Henry J., Israel B., Isaac M., James H., James R., JCE., Jeff B., Jesse F., Jessee G., Joanne C., Joel C., Joseph D., Joshua R., Joey B., J.P.M., Julian K., Julie H., Justin F., Karen A., Karen B., Kent H., Ledonna S., Leah T., Linda C., Local M., Lowell C., M.J. A., Marco R., Mark J., Marty L, Marty W., Melinda D., Michael S., Michael T., Micheal D., Mike G., Mordechai P., Monty P., Natalie N., Pekka H., Philip P., Randy P., Reut B., Rod P., Scott O., Shayla N., Shelly G., Stephen B.., Steve K., Steve P., Todd S., Trill C., Tyler O., Valerie I., Ward G., Warren & Son, Weitzel B., Yitzhaq H., and Zoe C. Finally, I extend my deepest apologies to anyone that I have accidentally omitted in the above compilation. Without the support of the people like those mentioned above, I would have been compelled to abandon this work several years back.

"And let them make me a sanctuary; that I may dwell among them."
~ Exodus 25:8 ~

~ Foreword ~

Used primarily in religious contexts, the word "tabernacle" is seldom spoken or heard in daily conversation. On rare occasion, "tabernacle" might be used in the name of a local church or synagogue building, but in most cases, "Tabernacle" refers exclusively to the tent built at the foot of Mount Sinai following Israel's historic exodus from Egypt. Usually associated with bizarre religious jargon, ancient cultures, and enigmatic ritual, "Tabernacle" studies are consequentially few and far between. Being unfamiliar and detached from everyday human experiences, it thus stands to reason that God's "Tabernacle" scarcely comes to mind.

For several thousand years, overall public sentiment towards the Exodus wilderness Tabernacle might be described as indifference. While public opinion may be shaped by a variety of contributing factors, some conclude that the Tabernacle was nothing special based on the former Egyptian labor force used to construct it, who could be presumed to be unskilled slaves. Likewise, the Sinai wilderness conditions are not regarded to be conducive to industrial processes or works of any sort. Furthermore, even if the nomadic nation is regarded to be skilled and resourceful enough to overcome the environmental and technological challenges imposed by the desert wilderness, Solomon's Jerusalem Temple has since become a replacement benchmark for all subsequent religious buildings. Whereas the Exodus Tabernacle was a wilderness tent built from wood, fabric, leather, and tons of precious metals worth tens of millions of today's dollars, Solomon's Temple was a permanent structure built with enormous stones and with a budget perhaps in excess of 3,000 times of what Moses used. Thus, perceptions of Solomon's Temple typically diminish any public appreciation for the Exodus tent that was pitched for religious purposes centuries prior.

While manpower, money, and materials have been used since antiquity to determine prominence or value, such temporal metrics can hardly be compared or equated to things such as divine favor, revelation, or presence. In this regard, the ancient Hebrew Tabernacle was singularly unique and truly of special importance. After all, the Tabernacle was a structure that was conceived by God, the first house of worship to be commanded to be built by God, as well as a structure which God himself chose to inhabit. Unfortunately, these unique attributes have not been preserved or conveyed via religious "Tabernacle" connotations ever since the Bible was first translated into Latin. After all, the original Hebrew Bible term "mishkan" is more literally translated as "dwelling place", whereas the English "Tabernacle" term was derived from the Latin "taberna", which refers to a hut or booth. Thus, in the economy of language, the English "Tabernacle" has in effect reduced God's "dwelling place" to a mere hut.

God's Dwelling Place Reconsidered

The Traditional Rectangular Tabernacle: A Crude Hut?

Knowing that human thoughts are governed by language, and that language has morphed over the course of time, some of the historic indifference toward "God's Tabernacle" can be excused, or at least understood. After all, it's an arbitrary thing for a religious person to say, "the Exodus *Tabernacle* doesn't matter", but it's quite another thing to declare, "God's *dwelling place* doesn't matter." People might be comfortable in claiming the former, but would naturally be reluctant to profess the latter. Regardless, when the Tabernacle term is introduced, the "hut" construct is almost instantly established in the mind; and as such, it is difficult for people to think of God's dwelling place as anything but a hut.

In addition to the suggestive Tabernacle connotation, presumptive and erroneous religious artwork has likewise reinforced the notion that God's dwelling place was a shack. As the mind is under the spell of boxy Tabernacle images, numerous misinterpretations and compromised Bible translations are further reinforced. Nevertheless, when images are compared to Bible texts and speculative translations, it seems that God not only lived in a shack, but is also incoherent and incompetent.

Does challenging the longstanding "God in a box" version of the Exodus Tabernacle appear to be inflammatory? Is it irreverent to propose that widely accepted Bible translations have been mistaken for centuries? Is it inconceivable that popular religious traditions portray a substandard picture of God—as being incoherent and incompetent?

Make no mistake about it, there is more to this study than personal opinion; God's reputation is at stake here. In fact, the integrity of God's word and his credibility are exactly *why* his dwelling place

The Round Hebrew Tabernacle: God's Ancient Dwelling Place?

The House of El Shaddai

must be seriously reconsidered, especially in light of the recent discovery depicted and explained in pages to follow. The two choices left for the reader are distinctly different and abundantly clear: Either God gave Moses clear and straightforward instructions by which to build a technically sophisticated and magnificent dwelling place—or the Bible contains a record of cryptic, confusing, and irrational instructions to build a dysfunctional and unimpressive habitation.

"Why are so many Bible pages filled with so much meaningless detail?" When reading the ancient texts, it's tempting for people to breeze over the lists of names, places, or numbers in the text, but only those without understanding would presume that the details, like those in Exodus describing God's dwelling place, to be meaningless. Granted, it's sometimes hard for a person to "see the forest through the trees"; however, it is exponentially more difficult to explain a forest to a person who has never seen a tree. For this very reason, *The House of El Shaddai* is unique among all other works pertaining to God's Tabernacle, i.e., God's dwelling place, in that it offers a detailed explanation as to how God wanted his house to be built. From this material, may the reader come to appreciate that sometimes it's the small things that matter most, and that big ideas, e.g., God's dwelling place, will never be apparent to those who readily discount or are incapable of discerning meaning from details. Although the devil is known for hiding in the details, the greater truth is that God's creation is full of many details and his handiwork is made known by them.

Round Tabernacle Model Superimposed over Rectangular Tabernacle Model

~ Preface ~

"Never again." That's exactly what I said to myself after my first book publishing effort. The energy expended in writing, revising, publishing, and promoting did not result in the impact on the world in the way that I had hoped; neither did the sales revenue remotely compensate for everything invested along the way. After a weak public response and with great conviction, I concluded that writing a book was a bad experience, and I more or less swore that I'd never attempt writing another one.

But then it happened to me again. I was struck with that nagging sense of inspiration that kept me from falling asleep at night and preoccupied my mind with ideas that danced about in my head for what seemed to be every minute of the day. Convinced that my idea had little if any market viability, I ignored this urge to write to the extent that I could; although squelching it left me bearing a heavy load of guilt upon my shoulders. It was completely relentless, rebuking me outright as I flipped through the channels while looking for something that qualified as entertainment. I might liken the experience to picking up a newspaper after handling freshly cut pine branches. With sap on your hands, you can't just simply put down the newspaper. Like it or not, the paper is stuck to the sap, which is in turn stuck to your hands. After you've handled the pine sap and then the newspaper, personal preference is no longer a factor. Once you touch the two, they have become a part of you, at least for a while, and frustration eventually compels you to do whatever you can to resolve the situation. It was for this reason that I threw caution to the wind and I began writing again, hoping that doing so would remove this splinter from my mind.

The inspiration to write another book first struck me on an airplane back in January of 2013 as I was departing from an "Electric Universe" conference. At the conference, a number of eclectic scientists presented a series of unusual lectures, some of which were advocating the notion that electricity, as opposed to Newtonian gravity, was the driving force in the universe and throughout the nature. Others at the conference spoke about mankind's ancient encounters with electrical phenomenon, which intrigued me even more. Needless to say, subjects such as esoteric physics and ancient electricity do not readily lend themselves to everyday conversation, nor do you typically find this kind of material in print at the grocery store checkout between the *Reader's Digest* and the *National Enquirer*. So, when the conference left me compelled to write about the connections between esoteric electrical physics and the ancient Hebrew Bible, my reluctance to begin doing so was not without basis. Furthermore, I was unemployed, displaced, not very prosperous at the time, and not exactly in the best place to start chasing rainbows.

About a year and a half after the conference, my sense of inspiration to write another book had not diminished, and I submitted in part fearing that I could no longer suppress the urge to do so. Longing for closure and peace of mind, I began diligently researching and writing again, against daunting and perhaps even impossible odds, and to some degree, against my better judgment. Fortunately, after being engaged in research and writing for only about a month, things took a radical turn as I happened upon a description of Moses' ancient wilderness Tabernacle.

The House of El Shaddai

It seems fitting at this point to mention that before setting out in this new book endeavor, I had no intention to include the "Tent of Meeting" in my research. Furthermore, I had no interest in the Hebrew Tabernacle whatsoever. I had not studied the wilderness tent in the past in any detail, neither did I have intentions to do so; that is, until my Hebrew "cherubim" research put me on a collision course with Moses' Tabernacle narrative.

Although the cherub, occasionally translated as "angel", is not exactly central to my Tabernacle research, an in-depth study of the Hebrew word did put me in the vicinity of where I needed to be. While the first cherub reference is found in the book of Genesis, the second mention is in Exodus, where the cherub is described in the context of the Tabernacle curtains. Literally pulling on a Tabernacle / cherub curtain thread, I continued on my research tangent, being both curious and determined to see how the cherubim related to the Tabernacle and its curtains. So, I did what any expert researcher would do; I entered the key search terms into Google's image search engine to see what I might find.

If I could use one word to describe what my Internet inquiry found, that one word would be "inconsistency". After surveying perhaps a few dozen images, it became clear that some of the Tabernacle curtains were depicted in a similar fashion; but in most cases, those who produced more specific details in their illustrations were almost never in agreement. But in my quest for understanding, I would not be easily discouraged.

Not ready to surrender, and by now more curious than ever, I set out to see what Bible texts said for themselves. After all, if there was one thing that I was able to glean from my first book experience, it is that many religious ideas that people advocate come from English Bible translations, and that translations are simply not to be trusted. Period. I say this from personal experience, as I had to rewrite my first book multiple times over a five year period because I set out with misunderstandings derived from Bible mistranslations and translator biases, many of which became more evident after I went to Israel to study Hebrew. While learning the truth about the translations came at great cost, my "Hebrew-first", and eventually my "Hebrew-only" paradigm shift left me with a healthy skepticism and awareness of the extreme limitations of Bible translations.

As I began to survey the Exodus texts, I also put on my engineering hat, following the advice of my father, who was not just an engineer, but also an engineering professor. In teaching his courses, he used to tell his students to draw a "FBD with TLC", which simply translates to "Free Body Diagram with Tender Loving Care". While this phrase may sound strange to most people, a "free body diagram" is used to summarize a problem by depicting a physical object and all of the forces that act upon it. As I sought to understand the cherubim relative to the Tabernacle curtains, I began sketching the layout. I even put the data into a spreadsheet, citing all of the dimensions and details that were in the Exodus text.

Not long after entering the data in the spreadsheet, I started to look at the numbers, which is where I made my discovery. I noticed that eleven wool curtains were specified for the Tabernacle, each measuring 30 cubits in length. Having a subconscious tally on the numbers, I came to Exodus 26:12, which described the last curtain as being folded in half. I realized that if connected end-to-end via the short edges, the eleven curtain assembly would measure 315 cubits, which struck me as interesting, as I realized immediately how close the number was to 100 times Pi, the ratio describing the relationship between a circle's circumference and its diameter. For a brief moment, I thought little of my incidental observation, thinking of it as a numeric anomaly and having no reason to believe the Tabernacle as round at that point. But then I read the next verse, which shook me to the core of my being. In English, Exodus 26:13 reads, "And a cubit on the one side, and a cubit on the other side of that which remaineth in the length of the curtains of the tent, it shall hang over the sides of the tabernacle on this side and on that side, to cover it." If this single cubit was deducted from the 315 cubit tally of the curtains, the adjusted length would amount to 314, which is a near perfect multiple of the π constant. Within seven verses of the Exodus account, I had discovered, or shall I say rediscovered, the most accurate approximation of π ever recorded by the ancient world. I wasn't exactly sure what it meant at that point in time, but I intuitively understood somehow that what I had discovered was of great significance; and I strongly suspected the Tabernacle to be round.

The months that followed my initial 314 or π discovery I can only compare to drinking from a fire hose, as I would need to produce much more than a single number in order for the discovery to be meaningful. The rest of the Exodus account had to also describe that which was round. Thus, in order to test a round Hebrew Tabernacle hypothesis, another technically viable model would need to be proposed, which coincides with the description provided in the original Hebrew narrative. For the round Tabernacle theory to be validated, all specifications, including material type, material size, material weight, fabrication processes, arrangement, interconnection, relative positioning, functions, etc., must coincide with the Hebrew Exodus texts, and must yield a viable structure as well. Being a real-world physical structure, the Tabernacle is much more than a Sunday school study or a Jewish fable; it's a case where etymology and engineering must dwell together in perfect harmony.

Within a few short months, the engineering calculations and the Hebrew language research did more than validate the round Tabernacle hypothesis; it became clear that an elegant and majestic yurt-like structure has been hidden in plain sight in the Hebrew text for thousands of years. But it was obvious that publishing an engineering analysis or computer model and even disclosing a thorough verse-by-verse Hebrew exegesis would not be enough; for tradition and translation bias still rules supreme—as does the human mind's affinity to images. To that end, this book was written and illustrated—so that the reader might see the glory of God's dwelling place.

Is your God a talented engineer and designer? I know that mine is... because he gave me the plans to build his dwelling place.

-Andrew Hoy

"And I will sanctify the tabernacle of the congregation...

And I will dwell among the children of Israel, and will be their God.

And they shall know that I am the LORD their God,
that brought them forth out of the land of Egypt,
that I may dwell among them: I am the LORD their God."

~ Exodus 29:44-46 ~

God's Dwelling Place Reconsidered

God's Dwelling Place

"...there were thunders and lightnings, and a thick cloud upon the mount...and Moses brought forth the people out of the camp to meet with God..."

~ Exodus 19:16-17, KJV ~

Israel at Mt. Sinai - Providence Lithograph Company, 1907

What if God gave you a complete set of the original plans to his house? Would you look at them with great interest, or would you instead dismiss them as being of no significance?

What if God gave the entire nation of Israel detailed plans to his house thousands of years ago, but the plans have since been lost in translation and obscured by tradition? Would you want a way to decipher the original plans to his house?

Introducing God's House

Nearly 3,500 years have passed since liberated Egyptian slaves built God's "Tabernacle", or "dwelling place", in the Sinai wilderness. According to Bible accounts, this famous Tabernacle was unique, in that it was not conceived by man or constructed arbitrarily; the book of Exodus describes how Moses received special plans for the unique tent directly from God on Mount Sinai.

Constructed at the beginning of Israel's wilderness wanderings using only wood, fabric, leather, and precious metals, the Tabernacle is usually perceived in this context: as a portable tent and temporary worship center. However, this special tent easily outlasted all of its builders. The Tabernacle served as God's house for nearly five centuries after the Mount Sinai revelation. Yet, the tent's lifespan should come as no surprise, especially as the Tabernacle plans were given to Israel as part of an everlasting covenant.

Unfortunately, centuries after the Israelites settled in the Promised Land, the Tabernacle was eventually forgotten. As Israel demanded a monarchy in place of their theocratic system of government under God's law, with God as their king, government reforms resulted in religious transformations, at which point the Tabernacle was discontinued. The exact year and circumstances under which the Tabernacle was no longer used might be subject to debate; some presume it may have been result of Philistine invasion, others believe it was due to natural disaster, still others might speculate that it was simply dismantled to reclaim its precious metals, which would be worth tens of millions in today's dollars. Regardless of which event prompted the Tabernacle's downfall, it is clear that during this period of political turmoil and religious upheaval, the Israelites lacked the conviction to either maintain or restore God's original dwelling place. Whatever the case, the fact remains that the tent that was once known to host God's presence would not be experienced by future generations. In effect, the Tabernacle would be reduced to legend, relegated to ancient history and distant memories. But this is not to say that Israel had just given the Tabernacle up for nothing—they would come to yearn for something else to fill the void.

The New House Conceived

Perhaps surviving a generation of turmoil and war during the reign of King Saul, it seems that the condition, or perhaps the humble nature of God's dwelling place, came to be at the forefront of David's mind. Acquiring massive wealth, power, and affluence over the course of his lifetime, David began to lament what he perceived to be misappropriated blessings, saying to the prophet Nathan, "Lo, I dwell in an house of cedars, but the ark of the covenant of the LORD remaineth under curtains" (1 Chronicles 17:1). While Nathan's initial response was to encourage David in his building vision, Nathan received a different—and probably unexpected—message from God, which he delivered to David the following day (1 Chronicles 17:4-6, 10-15).

It might have been hard for David to hear God's objection to his Temple building plans, given his personal passion and the mixed messianic overtones scattered throughout the revelation, but Nathan's remarks should have absolved David of any guilt or sense of obligation that he apparently developed in the climax of his reign. Regardless of Nathan's assurance that God was content with his tent, it seemed that David's inspiration and sense of duty towards God's house did not diminish.

House of God, or House of David?

Despite God's rejection of David's Temple construction ambitions, David remained steadfast in his vision in many ways. While David did not go so far as to break ground for Temple construction, it would seem that he staged everything he could up unto the point he charged his son Solomon

House of David

"Go and tell David my servant, Thus saith the LORD, Thou shalt not build me an house to dwell in: For I have not dwelt in an house since the day that I brought up Israel unto this day; but have gone from tent to tent, and from one tabernacle to another. Wheresoever I have walked with all Israel, spake I a word to any of the judges of Israel, whom I commanded to feed my people, saying, Why have ye not built me an house of cedars?

Furthermore I tell thee that the LORD will build thee an house. And it shall come to pass, when thy days be expired that thou must go to be with thy fathers, that I will raise up thy seed after thee, which shall be of thy sons; and I will establish his kingdom. He shall build me an house, and I will establish his throne forever. I will be his father, and he shall be my son: and I will not take my mercy away from him, as I took it from him that was before thee: But I will settle him in mine house and in my kingdom for ever: and his throne shall be established for evermore."

~ 1 Chronicles 17:4-6, 10-15, KJV ~

God's Dwelling Place Reconsidered

David's Plans

"Then David gave to Solomon his son the pattern of the porch, and of the houses thereof, and of the treasuries thereof, and of the upper chambers thereof, and of the inner parlours thereof, and of the place of the mercy seat, And the pattern of all that he had by the spirit, of the courts of the house of the LORD, and of all the chambers round about, of the treasuries of the house of God, and of the treasuries of the dedicated things..."

~ 1 Chronicles 28:11,12, KJV ~

David's Temple pattern revelation is never recorded in Bible texts, even though a physical description is given.

House of Glory

"And when all the children of Israel saw how the fire came down, and the glory of the LORD upon the house, they bowed themselves with their faces to the ground upon the pavement, and worshipped, and praised the LORD, saying, For he is good; for his mercy endureth for ever."

~ 2 Chronicles 7:3, KJV ~

with building the Temple. According to the Bible accounts, David not only staged massive amounts of wealth for Temple construction, but he also directed all of his subordinates to assist Solomon in his future Temple project. Although it is clear that Solomon was eventually to be endowed with special wisdom at the onset of his reign, it is also of note that the plans for the Temple—that would ultimately come to be known as "Solomon's Temple"—didn't actually come from or through Solomon; the Temple plans came from David, who passed his vision for "God's house" along to his son (1 Chronicles 28:11, 12). Granted, Jerusalem's first Temple is usually attributed to Solomon by name; but in reality, Solomon's Temple was made possible because of David's dreams and ambitions.

First Temple Dedication - W. Hole, 1910

As Solomon's Temple was put into service before hundreds of thousands of people, it seems that the original Tabernacle was either decommissioned or had fallen with minimal national concern. While there is no hard evidence indicating that either David or Solomon were directly involved in decommissioning the original Tabernacle, it is probably safe to say that the great zeal that David and Solomon had for the replacement Temple may have created a climate, or reflected a climate, whereby God's earlier dwelling place was quickly forgotten. Furthermore, the public manifestation of the divine presence, also known as the "Shekinah glory", during Solomon's commissioning ceremony (2 Chronicles 7:3) is likely to have suppressed any reservations toward the replacement Temple in the event that they existed among even the most skeptical people.

While the divine presence appeared in public at the commissioning of both the wilderness

Tabernacle and Solomon's Temple, this is not to say that the plans or written records describing the facilities are equally created or preserved. Apart from the various dimensions and features, it is clear that the Bible descriptions of Jerusalem's first Temple read distinctly different from those which were received by Moses on Mount Sinai during the Exodus. For example, the Exodus account begins with a complete list of raw materials, describes each and every Tabernacle part, and perhaps most importantly, is a listing of divine commandments which are preceded by authoritative pronouncements. In contrast, the accounts of Solomon's Temple (1 Kings 6 and 2 Chronicles 3) are not on par with the standards set in Exodus. Solomon's Temple descriptions are only recorded in the past-tense, post-construction, as-built state, and any plans or instructions that came from David's mouth or pen were not recorded in Bible texts as inspired writ, or for that matter, backed by a "Thus saith the LORD" introduction. In other words, with Moses being the greatest among the prophets and speaking to God face-to-face, it stands to reason that the "plans to God's house" which were given for the Tabernacle are not only more concise and complete, but also better represent the expressed will of God in its construction. In this regard, comparing the Tabernacle to Solomon's Temple might be likened to comparing God's preferred will to his consented will. While Solomon's house is generally considered to be greater than the one built under Moses, it is clear that reverence for the two buildings was not the same—with Solomon's Temple eventually being filled with unclean things and even an idol (2 Chronicles 29:16, 33:7).

The Next Temple - A Different Pattern?

Subsequent to the destruction of Solomon's Temple and the return of the exile from Babylon, a second Temple was built in Jerusalem. However, the second Temple texts are unusual in that they include no record of a Temple commissioning ceremony marked by a public witness of the divine presence. Furthermore, the records that have survived from the Temple construction period are relatively vague. Apart from citing Cyrus' overall sizing specifications of the wood and stone temple, neither Ezra, Nehemiah nor the prophet Haggai seem to offer a useful Temple description.

Although Ezra offers no technical details in his narrative, he did record an interesting public reaction, which took place during the initial stages of the Temple building. According to Ezra, after seeing the Temple foundation, the elders began to weep, while the younger people shouted for joy (Ezra 3:12-13). This brings about an interesting question. Based on the mixed reaction

Temple Defilement

"And the priests went into the inner part of the house of the LORD, to cleanse it, and brought out all the uncleanness that they found in the temple of the LORD into the court of the house of the LORD. And the Levites took it, to carry it out abroad into the brook Kidron."

~ 2 Chronicles 29:16, KJV ~

Temple Idolatry

"And he set a carved image, the idol which he had made, in the house of God, of which God had said to David and to Solomon his son, In this house, and in Jerusalem, which I have chosen before all the tribes of Israel, will I put my name for ever."

~ 2 Chronicles 33:7, KJV ~

The nations of Judah and Israel and their kings permitted and practiced idolatry over the course of the first Temple period. In contrast, there is no Bible record of idols in the Tabernacle.

God's Dwelling Place Reconsidered

Bad Foundations?

"But many of the priests and Levites and chief of the fathers, who were ancient men, that had seen the first house, when the foundation of this house was laid before their eyes, wept with a loud voice; and many shouted aloud for joy: So that the people could not discern the noise of the shout of joy from the noise of the weeping of the people: for the people shouted with a loud shout, and the noise was heard afar off."

~ Ezra 3:12-13, KJV ~

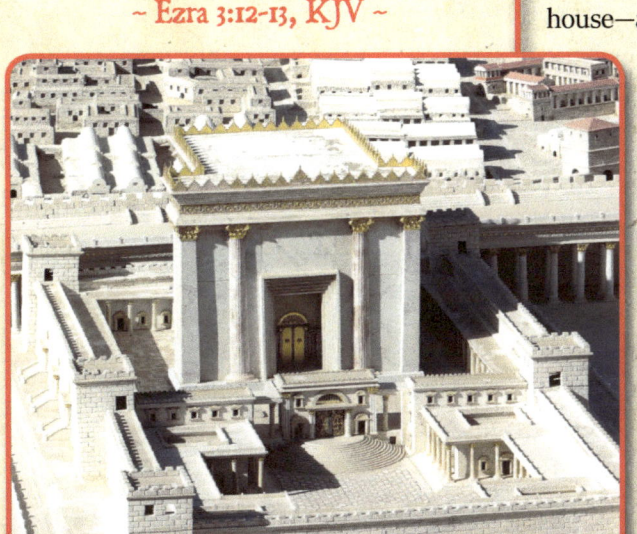

Second Temple Model - Jerusalem, Israel

to seeing the Temple's foundation, is it possible that returning exiles had in effect lost the "plans to God's house"? According to Nehemiah's record, this "lost plans" hypothesis seems plausible, as it seems that half of the exiles had no command of the Jewish tongue, which was the Hebrew language (Nehemiah 13:24). While the scope and scale of the second Temple's transformation between the time of Ezra and Herod is not fully known, it seems logical to suspect—based on eyewitness accounts—that the second Jerusalem Temple was significantly different than the first one that had endured for four centuries after David and Solomon. This curious account begs a simple question: *Did the elders weep because the shape of the Temple's foundation was wrong?*

Be they called temples, churches, synagogues, or mosques, it seems that there is by no means a shortage of religious shrines and edifices throughout the world today. But how do these compare to the first known plans of God's house—namely those as recorded by Moses in Exodus? A survey of the present day religious landscape and associated traditions seems to indicate that people have forgotten not only *what* they were first instructed to build, but perhaps more importantly, *why* they were supposed to build it. In order to comprehend these distinctions, it seems appropriate to return to Exodus, which is where the plans to God's house—and the reason for making God's house—are first recorded.

Returning to the Exodus

The Egyptian Exodus has been a story familiar to countless generations all throughout the world. This is even true among biblically illiterate people and those living outside of Judeo-Christian religious traditions, as fragments of the narrative are likely to have passed along through incidental exchanges, religious culture, and secular history, even if it has only been introduced by the likes of Charlton Heston.

It is only logical that people will recall the Exodus account in a way that is particular to themselves or unique to their experiences as individuals. Whether the subject matter is the liberation of oppressed slaves, the devastating Egyptian plagues, the Passover, the plundering of the Egyptians, the parting of the Red Sea, the Mount Sinai encampment, the wilderness wanderings and miracles, the Ten Commandments, the manna bread from heaven, the Ark of the Covenant, or the Wilderness Tabernacle, everyone is bound to relate to different aspects of Exodus history, and for different reasons. Obviously, responses will vary from person to person based upon tradition, education, or culture; for a Hebrew is likely to voice a radically different opinion of the Exodus events than that of an Egyptian.

Given the vast scope of Israel's Exodus and its extensive impact on all of humanity, to say that the Egyptian Exodus all boils down to a single question or central idea might rightfully be regarded to be ambitious—or even a bit foolish. But this is not said to undermine exhaustive inquiries or discourage the deduction of pointed conclusions. Beginning by presuming that God is not only sovereign over his creation, but also personally involved with it, it may make sense to begin by asking, "Why did the Israelites suffer as slaves?", and subsequently, "Why were the Israelites brought out of Egypt?"

Moses before Pharaoh - Robert Leinweber, 1850

"Let My People Go!" - The Story of Exodus

As a story of miracles and of transformation, the Exodus account universally speaks to all those who struggle, offering hope for those who dream of a day whereby they have a chance to start anew. While the pages to follow are not intended to serve as an explanation for suffering or as any sort of guidebook to personal liberation, such human elements help make the Exodus story timeless—transcending generations. The Exodus is a story juxtaposing prosperity and misfortune, oppression and liberation, drudgery and adventure, cruelty and justice, and heroes and villains—eventually concluding with a happy ending. This happy ending, however, was part of a large cycle of smaller stories, and a small part of a larger story. As for Israel's destiny and one of the happy endings, it was declared at the very onset of the struggle between God and Pharaoh. As Moses issued his first mandate to Pharaoh to free the Israelites, Moses concurrently expressed God's future expectations for Israelites (Exodus 5:1).

In addition to saying, "let my people go", Pharaoh not only received the clear mandate to send out the people, but also an explanation as to why they were to be released—which was for the sake of festive religious celebration! As Moses warned Pharaoh six more times (Exodus 7:16, 8:1, 8:20, 9:1, 9:13, 10:3), the Israelites were not to remain Pharaoh's servants any longer or to be liberated

"And afterward Moses and Aaron went in, and told Pharaoh, Thus saith the LORD God of Israel, Let my people go, that they may hold a feast unto me in the wilderness."

~ Exodus 5:1, KJV ~

> "...that they may hold a feast unto me...."

"Let my people go" is a familiar phrase frequently quoted from the Exodus account. However, the reason for Israel's liberation from Egypt is seldom, if ever, recalled in citations.

God's Dwelling Place Reconsidered

> "And the Egyptians were urgent upon the people, that they might send them out of the land in haste..."
>
> ~ Exodus 12:33, KJV ~

Wilderness Freedom Festivals

Only after ten devastating plagues, including the death of all firstborn Egyptians, did Pharaoh allow Moses to take Israel out into the wilderness to hold their feasts. The Feast of Unleavened Bread was observed after the Passover en route to Sinai.

*Moses and Israel at the Red Sea
Providence Lithograph Company, 1907*

that they might live without mission or purpose – they were being called to serve God instead. This service was to begin with a wilderness feast.

Israel in Egypt - Sir Edward John Poynter, 1867

Wilderness Feasts with the Divine Presence

Despite Moses' demands to Pharaoh, it seems to be a little ironic that Israel's departure from Egypt didn't immediately culminate with some great religious festival. After all, one might expect that following all of the trouble and miracles that Israel experienced that they might have stopped as they reached a critical milestone at Egypt's outskirts and set apart some time to have an "out of Egypt feast" to celebrate their newfound freedom—or perhaps an official "Red Sea liberation party" after reaching the threshold of safety. To the contrary, the only "feast" that Israel would experience would be that of fast food and unleavened bread, which the Israelites baked just before they abandoned the land of their captivity (Exodus 12:39).

Strange as it may seem, the Bible makes no mention of Israel observing any legitimate religious feast for an entire year after they abandoned Egypt. Immediately after leaving Egypt, the first Exodus Sabbath of record was defined by the supernatural provision of manna, which arrived despite Israel rising up and complaining in unison (Exodus 16:3-31). Moreover, the next "feast" of record was even more problematic, in which case the Israelites practiced idolatry and feasted in the presence of a golden calf idol (Exodus 32). Even after Israel was informed of a number of other religious feasts (Exodus 23:14-17), it would appear that the first religious feast which Israel observed according to divine mandate was the Passover commemoration (Numbers 9:1-3), which took place on the one year anniversary of their liberation from captivity. The amount of time that had elapsed between the Exodus and evidence of Israel's feast seems to beg a number of questions. First of all, why did Israel wait so long before the first religious feast? Second, and perhaps more to the point, why did it seem that God had Israel wait so long before the first religious feast? Finally, what was Israel supposed to do in the meantime as they waited to have the religious festival in the wilderness?

Fast Food Feast

"And they baked unleavened cakes of the dough which they brought forth out of Egypt, for it was not leavened; because they were thrust out of Egypt, and could not tarry, neither had they prepared for themselves any victual."

~ Exodus 12:39, KJV ~

Aaron and Israel Worship the Golden Calf
Providence Lithograph Company, 1901

The second half of the book of Exodus seems to offer some explanation as to the amount of elapsed time between the Exodus and the Israelites fulfillment of God's explicit feast request. Apart from the Ten Commandments and the introduction to the other basic laws that were established for community governance, the vast majority of the latter half of Exodus is dedicated to specific instructions detailing how they were to build God's dwelling place, which is commonly translated as "sanctuary" or "Tabernacle".

While "Let my people go" is a popular refrain that is to this day echoed and even sung among those who are feeling enslaved, it seems that the latter half, namely, "that they may hold a feast unto me in the wilderness" is all but omitted from clichés and pop culture. Lest it be forgotten, the construction of the Tabernacle—explicitly created to host God's presence—was a prerequisite to all of the feasts. To have a feast dedicated to God in the wilderness, it seems, was to also have God's presence manifest. His presence in the midst of the congregation was an integral part of the holiday experience!

Handmade Unleavened Matza Bread

In remembrance of the Egyptian Exodus, Israel was commanded to bake matza every year after the Passover holiday.

God's Dwelling

"And let them make me a sanctuary; that I may dwell among them."

~ Exodus 25:8 ~

God's Dwelling Place Reconsidered

The Tentmaker

"See, I have called by name Bezaleel the son of Uri, the son of Hur, of the tribe of Judah: And I have filled him with the spirit of God, in wisdom, and in understanding, and in knowledge, and in all manner of workmanship, to devise cunning works, to work in gold, and in silver, and in brass, and in cutting of stones, to set them, and in carving of timber, to work in all manner of workmanship."

~ Exodus 31:3-5, KJV ~

Desert Nomad Circular Tent, 1867

A Father of Tents and House in God's Image

Given God's intention to dwell among the nation of Israel, God wanted Israel to build a house for him—and in a very specific way. Although it was Moses who received the instructions for God's house, Moses was not appointed to personally oversee every aspect of its construction. Instead, Tabernacle construction was delegated to a man named "Betzalel", or "Bezaleel", who was evidentially born for the very purpose of building God's house.

However unusual the name "Betzalel" might sound to western ears, the meaning of the name is of great significance and suggestive of his mission. In Hebrew, the name Bet-zal-el might be parsed and understood to mean, "house in God's image". Based on the description of the talents endowed to Betzalel (Exodus 31:3-5), it seems as if he was the primary architect, as he specialized in metalwork, woodwork, and stone cutting. The text also describes Betzalel as being the son of Uri and the son of Hur, or "Ben Uri" and "Ben Hur" in Hebrew. These

The Creation of Adam - Michelangelo, 1512

names obviously did not originate with the Charton Heston character, but might be literally translated as, "son of my light" and "son of white", or "son of my flame" and "son of white linen". As such, it seems that even Betzalel's heritage was alluding to his role in Tabernacle construction, as after its construction, the tent would host a light or fire overhead by night and a cloud over it during the daytime.

In addition to Betzalel, Exodus identifies a man named Aholiab as being anointed to oversee various aspects of fabrication of the Tabernacle and its furnishings. Introducing another name that has minimal use among western cultures, the Hebrew named Aholiab was also appointed work in the Exodus texts in accordance with his namesake. With "Aholi-ab", or "Aholi-av" being comprised of two words, "av" being "father" and "Aholi" being "tents" or "my tent", it seems fitting that the "father of tents", or "my tent-father", would be specialized in the work of fabrics—which is the material that is perhaps most definitively associated with tents. Moreover, it would seem that Aholiab would assume the responsibility of making "tents", or garments, for Aaron. In this regard, it is fitting that Aholiab was assigned to do his work, as he was descendant of the tribe of Dan, and as the name Dan is referring to a judge or ruler. Thus, Aholiab would make not only the garments of the priest who was appointed to serve in various judicial and ruling functions, but also the fabrics which would surround the holy courtyard, which is where the judgments would often be decided.

With one of the Tabernacle builders descending from Judah and the other from Dan, two powerful themes are conveyed concurrently, namely *praise* and *judgment*. For just as the name Dan is referring to a judge or judgment, so too is the Hebrew name of Judah rooted in praise or thanks. As such, God's house would be constructed for the sake of these two very things—thanksgiving and righteousness. After all, without judgment, a community will be deprived of justice and righteousness; likewise, without gratitude, a community will be devoid of joy. Thus, it was for these reasons that these two specific men were appointed to build the Tabernacle, and it was because of these very things that they were to have this house in God's image erected in their midst.

Restoring the Image

After briefly surveying the origins and history of Israel's religious worship facilities, it would appear that mans' perceptions of God's dwelling place have changed radically and repeatedly throughout the years. The materials of construction have changed, as have the perceived size and shape. Likewise, the motive for building and the purpose it is associated with seems to have changed. But do any of these changes or details actually matter?

The answer to this question is probably entirely dependent upon a person's perception of God. Is God careless? Is he arbitrary? Is he indifferent? Is he fickle? Is he inconsistent? Is he incompetent? Obviously, to respond with a "yes" answer to these questions is to stand on a slippery slope—as is undermining the Exodus texts which meticulously describe God's dwelling

---

The Tentmaker's Helper

"And I, behold, I have given with him Aholiab, the son of Ahisamach, of the tribe of Dan: and in the hearts of all that are wise hearted I have put wisdom, that they may make all that I have commanded thee; the tabernacle of the congregation, and the ark of the testimony, and the mercy seat that is thereupon, and all the furniture of the tabernacle, and the table and his furniture, and the pure candlestick with all his furniture, and the altar of incense, and the altar of burnt offering with all his furniture, and the laver and his foot, and the cloths of service, and the holy garments for Aaron the priest, and the garments of his sons, to minister in the priest's office, and the anointing oil, and sweet incense for the holy place: according to all that I have commanded thee shall they do."

~ Exodus 31:6-11, KJV ~

Although the ancient tent of meeting is most often associated with Moses, the implementation of the design and the manufacturing oversight became the responsibility of two men purposefully named Betzalel and Aholiab.

God's Dwelling Place Reconsidered

Bibles of Babel?

"God is not a man, that he should lie; neither the son of man, that he should repent: hath he said, and shall he not do it? or hath he spoken, and shall he not make it good?"

~ Numbers 23:19, KJV ~

The Tower of Babel - Pieter Bruegel the Elder, 1563

place in God's own words. To say that "the size and shape of God's house do not really matter" is clearly a sentiment rooted in ignorance—or perhaps arrogance. Moreover, it is equally absurd to assert that the size and shape of God's house never did matter. Since he is a God who says, "I change not", it is probably worthwhile to try to think of things from his perspective, wondering not only what he wanted, but also why he wanted things the way that he specifies them. After all, the commandment to build the structure was given for a clear reason—and that commandment was never rescinded. To undermine the details pertaining to God's house is to deny or discount the possibility that the ancient Tabernacle dwelling place was actually a house in God's image.

Lost in Translation

Following an act of ignorance, arrogance, and rebellion, humanity continues to suffer from the Tower of Babel aftermath. As humanity united together in an effort to build their own tower or house into heaven, God not only dispersed them, but he confused their languages as well. In Hebrew, Babel means "confusion", and to this day, even modern believers continue to live under the influence of Babel's shadow, as second-hand languages and confusion taints every page of every Bible translation. Ironically, it is this same Tower of Babel curse that confounds the narratives which describe God's dwelling place.

Unfair as it may seem, the unfortunate reality is that no Bible translation is capable of expressing the exact same message as conveyed in the original. In fact, even in translation, it is of note that the Bible issues a number of warnings and commandments to not change the texts. The book of Deuteronomy, for example, instructs to not add to the word or take away from it (Deuteronomy 4:2) – which is something that any Bible translation inherently requires. Nehemiah's frustration (Nehemiah 13:24) is also noteworthy, as he was frustrated by the fact that the returning exiles had lost their knowledge of the original Bible language.

Jeremiah also warned his readers about the "lying pen of the scribes" and the twisting of texts (Jeremiah 8:8). Finally, Matthew's gospel makes a point to underscore the significance of the original language, as the world's most famous Jew warned that not one "jot or tittle" would be stricken from Moses' writings (Matthew 5:17). As jots and tittles refer to Hebrew particulars which are not translated into English, it follows that the notion of producing a translation that is equal to the original is a fantasy, and might be likened unto drawing a square circle.

As most Jews and Christians consider Bible texts to be divinely inspired writ, most serious students and scholars likewise seem to agree that the Bible texts are only considered to be divinely inspired in the original language. Nevertheless, a sizable contingent of English speaking believers promote the notion of the King James translation being a divinely inspired source. Unfortunately, the majority of people who are of this persuasion are not sufficiently equipped to test such a claim. After all, substantiating an English equality or even English adequacy view of the King James Bible texts isn't something that can be done on faith alone, it requires a measure of intellectual curiosity to compare the version's italic insertions to the ancient language. Given the King James Bible revision history, the reams of criticisms brought about the translations, and aforementioned precedents and literal warnings about changing the word as even preserved in translations, to question the translation is more than an act of academic honesty, it is an obligation of sorts. Conversely, those espousing the equality or sufficiency of Bible translations seldom do so from a position of knowledge or strength, but instead assume a dogmatic stance, as they are generally insecure in their faith. While some aspects and elements of God's "living word" are bound to survive the translation process, readers should not assume a sense of entitlement—thinking that God has or is somehow obligated to perfectly preserve his word in their own native tongue.

Regardless of problems or confidence in various Bible translations, *The House of El Shaddai* is written to an audience likely to be familiar with only English Bible translations. As such, the King James texts are cited as a familiar point of reference, along with pointed criticism where warranted. However, criticisms are common to all English Bibles in most cases, as other versions are strongly influenced by the King James translations, with minor changes made for the sake of copyright claim or avoidance of copyright violation. While the only way to truly step beyond translation contradictions and variants is to defer to the Hebrew texts, detailed Hebrew

Lost Jots & Tittles

Moses Smashing the Tablets of the Law
Rembrandt, 1659

"For verily I say unto you, Till heaven and earth pass, one jot or one tittle shall in no wise pass from the law, till all be fulfilled."

~ Matthew 5:18, KJV ~

Even after smashing the first set of tablets in anger, Moses received a second set containing the exact same content.

Subtle Changes

"Ye shall not add unto the word which I command you, neither shall ye diminish ought from it, that ye may keep the commandments of the LORD your God which I command you."

~ Deuteronomy 4:2, KJV ~

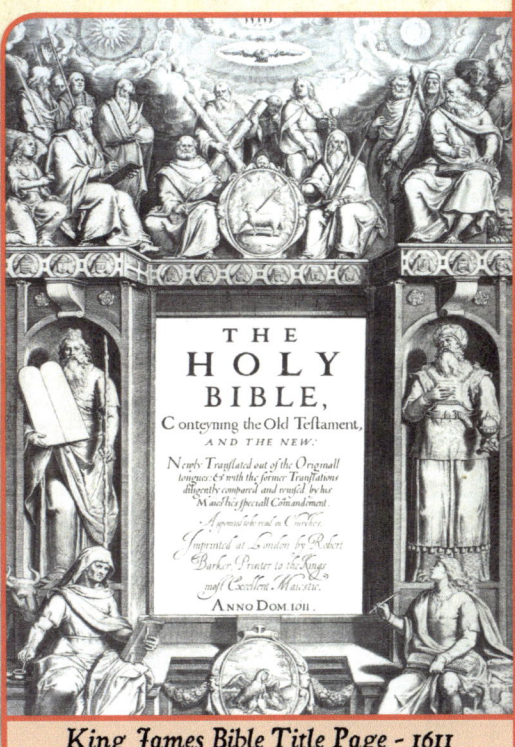

King James Bible Title Page - 1611

exegesis is not included within the scope of this work. Instead, detailed illustrations and English commentary are provided in order to help contextualize Exodus translations. In cases where translations are incorrect, Hebrew texts are paraphrased and explained alongside illustrations, helping restore that which has been otherwise lost in translation for centuries.

Obscured by Tradition

Tradition, of course, can profoundly influence translation. Reciprocally, even the most obscure interpretation might even be perpetuated as tradition if it is encapsulated in translation, which lends it a special measure of credence. Tradition-based translations tend to feed into a vicious circle, introducing more confusion and ambiguity, which in turn invites new and additional interpretation. Thus, blame cannot be categorically ascribed to translators trying to reconstruct ancient thoughts with dictionaries that are also influenced by ancient traditions. In fact, Josephus Flavius' first century writings reinforce questionable Tabernacle traditions, even though the Tabernacle had not stood or been seen for a thousand years beforehand.

Josephus Flavius - W. Whiston, 1817

Granted, there is great potential danger in vilifying tradition unconditionally. After all, if tradition is condemned without cause, it inevitably results in the rejection of all authority—and with it, the rejection of all truth. Even words would lose all meaning if not for tradition. English speaking people understand what a wheel is because the term has been used consistently and its meaning has been successively passed down for generations, even though nobody is sure when the word was first used. Although English has evolved as some sort of post-Babel language, even timeless Hebrew Bible texts could be seen as being dependent upon tradition and be subsequently rejected on that basis alone. Without access to time travel technology in order to do independent verification of source material, it follows that it is necessary to put faith in both God and man and trust that open mindedness, a spirit of inquiry, and divine intervention are bound to yield positive results when earnestly and diligently seeking the truth.

While traditions can be good or bad, traditions cannot be established to be true based solely upon their existence. After all, it is possible for lies to be regurgitated for thousands of years, as tradition sometimes has a way of overshadowing translation. So how can a true tradition be distinguished from a false one? According to Bible texts, multiple witnesses or proofs must be consulted in establishing a matter as true. Since truth is absolute by nature, true traditions will always stand in agreement with multiple witnesses and stand steadfast under the scrutiny of false witnesses.

A House Filled with Images

Although no Tabernacle illustrations are known to date back to the time of Moses, later artistic renderings of the desert tent have wielded significant influence over public perception. Generally speaking, the older the images, the more credence they seem to lend to an idea, and the more they are assumed to be actual historical record. Just as simple icons barely decades old can convey meanings and ideas beyond the simple pictures, images dating back as little as a century likewise have a way of reinforcing traditions. Even without the aid of two-dimensional images, written commentary can implant images into the subconscious. For example, if people read about an object, whether it is a square, a circle, an apple, or a house, the mind will generally associate an object with the given word and will race to visualize such objects with little hesitation.

Perhaps it is because of the mind's affinity to images that artist renderings and commentaries can reinforce traditions, such that the image's perceived reality might supersede what is written content in Bible texts. While people say that "a picture is worth a thousand words", the problem with visual learning is that images can be quickly and subconsciously absorbed without the benefit of critical thinking. In the case of Tabernacle images, they are typically ingrained without any validation. Detailed Tabernacle pictures can easily convey more than 1000 words, but nobody makes time to compare them to the 655 Hebrew words used to describe the Tabernacle in Exodus 26 and 27, or for that matter the 1423 English words used by King James translators.

Image Recall

Icons and relatively crude images are not only capable of bringing basic objects to mind, but can also be used to convey simple ideas, actions, and even complex processes.

God's Dwelling Place Reconsidered

Traditional A-Frame Roof Tabernacle

Traditional A-Frame Roof style models assume a sharply sloped leather roof which is propped up by a long beam at the building's peak that runs the entire length of the building. However, Exodus texts offer no provisions for supporting tall or long elevated beams.

While not everyone has read the Tabernacle descriptions of Exodus 26 and 27, it is probably safe to say that the majority of Bible readers have at least seen images intending to depict the Tabernacle, be they artists' renderings or photos of real-life models. Of those who have read the written Exodus Tabernacle account, it is unlikely that many of them have done so without first encountering an image of the Tabernacle, which may have even been adjacent to the written description. Over the course of their lives, most religious people might see dozens of images perhaps dozens of times, whereas it is highly unlikely that they have read the Bible text description even once for every dozen images they have seen. Conversely, it is highly unlikely that anyone has made a point to read the Exodus text dozens of times while keeping their eyes from being exposed to any images, and it's probably safe to say that in this age of information and multimedia, it's unlikely that anybody has read the text without seeing at least one single Tabernacle illustration. If someone asked, "What is the Tabernacle like?" it is highly unlikely that the mind would defer first to the Bible texts before it instantly began to access familiar images retained in the brain.

Tabernacle Depicted with A-Frame Roof - German Bible, 1891

Upon surveying the various Tabernacle renderings, it becomes evident that not all artistic works are created equally. Looking from one Tabernacle image to the next, evidence of artistic latitude, or differing opinions, can be found at every turn. Different fabric color schemes are envisioned. Different post counts and arrangements are illustrated. Different frame and roof styles are depicted. Different shapes are employed in post and foundation design. Different frame stabilizing elements are used. Different plank sizes and types are assumed.

Confusion abounds all the more when comparing the Bible texts to Tabernacle images, especially as the referenced Bible translations are never in full agreement. After the different models and illustrations are strictly tested against English Bible specifications, it becomes clear that images might be created by designers or artists who are indifferent, illiterate, or working under incompetent authority. In other cases, it seems that many differences between artwork might be attributed to what appear to be shortcomings, ambiguities, or conflicts in Bible texts themselves. But to suggest that Moses' record is somehow inferior is even more illogical; for if the words therein are thought to be of supernatural origin, they should describe things clearly and beyond a reasonable doubt, and the end result should be one of harmony, uniformity, and consistency.

After a frustrating and thorough survey of Tabernacle images, the natural response is to stop searching—or, in other cases, to abandon the quest long before it's even begun. After being exposed to a handful of image conflicts, it's easier to just sit back, shrug the shoulders, and throw your hands in the air assuming that the contradictions in the imagery exist because the Tabernacle text is too enigmatic and the problem of deciphering it is therefore insurmountable. As people quit, they are likely to do so in conjunction with pessimistic thinking, perhaps reasoning, "if master theologians and professional linguists can't figure out exactly how the Tabernacle hardware goes or come to an agreement as to what it looks like, nobody can." But herein lies the problem—and the solution.

The Ancient Theologian's House

Having an appetite for the abstract and an affinity towards two-dimensional materials, e.g., books and scrolls, theologians and linguists are likely to be heavily exposed to and thus influenced by preexisting religious traditions, and statistically less likely to become skilled craftsmen with a mastery of materials in the three-dimensional realm. Contrary to Betzalel or Aholiab, many lack sufficient training in carpentry in order to build a basic bookshelf, or maybe even to build a simple birdhouse. Few would be experienced in butchering an animal or, more to the point, trained to process the animal's skin into something as practical as a simple leather belt or wallet. Only a fraction of theologians are likely to be even

Traditional Draped Roof Tabernacle

Traditional draped Tabernacle roof models assume a flat roof made with loose leather and fabric coverings that are not secured to ground or the frame (as they are not listed in Exodus). This tent design does not allow for proper watershed or wind protection, or include features for lateral stability.

The Tabernacle in the Wilderness - W. Dickes, 1815-1892

God's Dwelling Place Reconsidered

Tabernacle Model at Timna Park, Israel - © 2016 Andrew Hoy

Traditional Tethered roof Tabernacle models employ extrabiblical materials (such as galvanized steel stabilizers and deep underground anchors used in the Timna exhibit shown above) to keep the structure from collapsing.

Traditional Tethered Roof Tabernacle

remotely skilled in metalwork such as casting or forging. Most of them would have little personal experience with textile work or weaving, lacking the knowledge required to make a simple scarf. Likewise, the vast majority of them have never worked as architects, or have been trained in engineering disciplines. Yet ironically, despite this general lack of real-world material and construction experience, theologians are among the first inclined—and first solicited—to offer expertise on the configuration details of God's house.

Thousands of years ago, the patriarchs, priests, and prophets living in Bible times were all portrayed as being experienced in practical vocations. Adam was a gardener. Noah was a carpenter, shipbuilder, herdsman, butcher, grape gardener, vintner, and zoologist. Abel, Abraham, Isaac, Jacob, and all of Jacob's sons were shepherds, as was king David. While enslaved in Egypt, it is unlikely that any of the Israelites served the Egyptians in the capacity of clergy or theologian. In fact, long before theologians as we know them arrived on the scene, the Levites—the first appointed ministers who were called to erect, manage, and transport the Tabernacle—were described as part time shepherds, butchers, and leather workers.

While working daily in sheep pastures and under the night sky might have afforded the Levites some of the solitude and meditation time required to become deep thinkers and abstract philosophers, the entire Levite tribe was appointed to serve in a very hands-on capacity, dealing with the practical and mechanical aspects of the Tabernacle (Numbers 3-4). According to Bible records, the Levites were never officially assigned to teach Tabernacle typology. They did not write theses whereby they relegated the Tabernacle structure to symbolism—nor did they simply spiritualize their work experiences. Working as theologians who were cut from a very different cloth, the Levites were more inclined to tell people what things were from a hands-on and practical standpoint than what things meant in the world of the abstract and imaginary. Although the Levites were not credited for fabricating all of the Tabernacle hardware, their first-hand experience with the metal, wood, fabric, and leather that was used to make God's house made them intimately familiar with the image it formed.

Construction in Context

Moses may have first recorded the Tabernacle plans on a two-dimensional layer of sheepskin, but for the Israelites, building the Tabernacle was not a two dimensional exercise. For Israel, real-world construction demanded much more time than an afternoon to draft a sketch or even a month to make a painting, and it demanded that the physical construction was done precisely. After all, buildings in two dimensional paintings and sketches are not bound by laws of physics; if drawn incorrectly, they do not collapse and kill people. To the contrary, Israel's Tabernacle would be constantly subjected to three dimensional forces and elements, such as wind, sun, rain, and even the occasional earthquake.

With the massive amounts of manpower and materials required to make the Tabernacle, the Israelites could not build using a trial-and-error approach. The large wood beams would be heavy, probably exceeding one ton each. Even after they were cut from the forest and shaped by a team of carpenters, the amount of muscle and horsepower required just to transport each beam would be formidable. The large curtains would require thousands of pounds of wool and flax, which took countless hours of labor to spin, bleach, weave, and dye the fabric. Herds of animals would be slaughtered to harness thousands of square yards of leather, and vast quantities of natural resources would be required to treat and tan the hides. They would have built large furnaces in the wilderness in order to refine and cast metal. In short, the pictures of the wilderness

Raising the Tabernacle - Phillip Medhurst Collection Picture 491

God's Dwelling Place Reconsidered

God's Pattern

"According to all that I shew thee, after the pattern of the tabernacle, and the pattern of all the instruments thereof, even so shall ye make it."

~ Exodus 25:9, KJV ~

Contrary to religious tradition, Moses was not given artistic latitude to make the Tabernacle his own way; he had to follow God's instructions exactly (which excluded a wood roof).

Tabernacle Vellum Print - Gerhard Schott Circa 1723-1729

Tabernacle usually only depict a final product, but the Tabernacle fabrication would have been a large scale industrial project involving tens of thousands of people. To not soberly consider these many intermediate steps along the way is to lose sight of the final Tabernacle design.

Being no strangers to manual labor and large building projects, the Israelites who participated in the Tabernacle construction were not unskilled or inexperienced—they were professionally seasoned in Egypt. While most don't believe that the Egyptian pyramids were built by Israelite slaves, it should be obvious that the advanced Egyptian building capabilities, technologies, and engineering know-how would have rubbed off on the Israelites. While Hollywood and religious art might portray Israelites as working in Egypt as nothing more than brute force labor—pulling big stones with thick ropes, it is probably an oversimplified and unrealistic view. History suggests a cyclical progression of empires, where overlords and slave masters tend to rise to a point whereby they eventually delegate all matters of labor—including the bearing of heavy intellectual loads—to their workforce. Thus, if Israel is not perceived to be a skilled labor force—being literate, educated, masters of engineering and ancient technology, and capable of autonomously planning projects—depictions of the Tabernacle work are bound to remain desperately lacking.

Building False Images

While countless Tabernacle depictions have been conceived and expressed graphically or artistically on two-dimensional media, few images actually reflect a viable configuration of a real-world, three-dimensional, and functional Tabernacle model. Why is this? Apart from the previously discussed misappropriation of talent between artists, theologians, and builders, few full-size three-dimensional models of traditional Tabernacle replicas are even attempted, given the expense and manufacturing complexities involved. In fact, of the preexisting life-size Tabernacle models constructed, not a single one has been built literally according to the ancient Exodus specifications. All models created in recent decades are in effect mere mock-ups best resembling Hollywood movie sets, as a genuine full scale model construction has not only been proven to be cost prohibitive, but also an outright logical fallacy.

As for exorbitant Tabernacle model costs, precious metals are not the only financial deterrent to creating a viable Tabernacle replica. While it is fairly practical to substitute gold and silver with less expensive metal types, it is also cost prohibitive to use enormous timbers or to create large loom-woven fabrics. So, in hopes of reducing overall expense as well as overall weight, the substitutions commence. Single fabric or plywood sheets are conveniently substituted for multiple piece parts, which are described in Exodus. In some cases wood is substituted for metal and vice-versa. Hollow wood sections are painted to look like solid metal items, even though they do not remotely behave the same way or perform the same function. While the ends are often believed to justify the means, low-budget Tabernacle replicas do little more than reinforce a religious myth and propagate that which is ultimately a fake religion.

A casual review of architectural history throughout the world further underscores how the traditional Tabernacle model is a logical fallacy. Nomadic people living in portable shelters see to it that the framework is lightweight and easy to handle, which is a stark contrast to the traditional rectangular Tabernacle models, which propose a high density clustering of extremely heavy wood planks. Thinking above and beyond ancient nomadic people, the fact remains that no culture throughout the world has deliberately built a functioning tent that resembles the traditional rectangular Tabernacle model, even for purposes of nostalgia or for the sake of religious ambitions. Even royalty—being known for extravagance and eccentricity—has yet to create something as unusual, unintuitive, or impractical as a tent made with thick wood walls sitting on large silver blocks and topped by a flexible roof. With such a bizarre and inefficient utilization of materials, it should come as no surprise that no design principles evident in traditional Tabernacle models are transferred into other real-world designs. The rectangular models are not fit to serve as a house of God, and for this reason, they can only be found in modern times in religious theme parks.

After disregarding perhaps dozens of Tabernacle fabrication specifications that are defined in the Bible texts, it becomes clear that the life-size models serve to create a false image and sustain a false, albeit traditional, narrative. Eventually, what is built is nothing like what Moses actually described, but nobody is inclined or equipped to notice—so long as the overall shape of the three-dimensional model conforms to the images already constructed in the mind's eye. Extra materials not mentioned in the Bible texts are always added in order to keep the pseudo-models standing,

Mobile Materials

Nomadic Scandinavian Lavuu Dwelling

Tabernacle materials including wood, fabric, and leather have been used by nomadic tribes to make lightweight and portable tents for thousands of years. Precious metals are seldom employed.

Mobile Yurt - Turkestan Album, 1872

Raw Materials

"And the LORD spake unto Moses, saying, Speak unto the children of Israel, that they bring me an offering: of every man that giveth it willingly with his heart ye shall take my offering. And this is the offering which ye shall take of them; gold, and silver, and brass, And blue, and purple, and scarlet, and fine linen, and goats' hair, And rams' skins dyed red, and badgers' skins, and shittim wood... And let them make me a sanctuary; that I may dwell among them."

~ Exodus 25:1-5,8, KJV ~

Flax Plant used for Fabrics - Köhler, 1897

but seldom are they any point of concern for modern visitors, who more are likely to be more overwhelmed, entertained, and emotionally engaged than they are to be rationally inquiring or skeptical. Building with an imbalanced mindset of symbolism over substance, people cut corners without apology to save on time, money, or effort; but at what point do the traditional representations of the Tabernacle fail to remotely resemble God's dwelling place?

A Small Picture View

As the Tabernacle is introduced in the Exodus text, it is not first introduced as a finished product or from a standpoint of a "big picture" perspective; it begins with a listing of raw materials, and then follows with descriptive lists of Tabernacle hardware. Considering this progression of revelation, the only way to get a proper big picture view of God's house is to start with small pictures, proceeding with the assumption that there are no idle words in Scripture. No written description is superfluous and no specified quantity is without significance.

To start with small pictures is to consider every seemingly insignificant detail—down to the finest thread of fabric that is described. It is to consider and question every "what", "who", "when", "where", "how", and "why" along the path. What kind of fabric was specified? Was it made from animal or vegetable? Who gathered and processed the fabric? Was the fabric spun by Hebrews or already provided in finished form? When was the fabric harvested? Was the fabric acquired before or after the Exodus? Where did the fabric come from? Was the fabric native to the Sinai region or imported into Egypt? How much fabric was required? How was the fabric processed in the Sinai wilderness? What purpose did the fabric serve? Why was fabric selected for the Tabernacle instead of some other material? Did the fabric need to be shielded from inclement weather, or need to interconnect with adjacent Tabernacle hardware? Would the material need to be of a particular thickness or strength in order to perform its intended function?

Obviously, the small battery of questions posed above is not intended to be exhaustive, but each answer may have a bearing on the Tabernacle's final configuration. Conversely, not every question identified above has immediate relevance to the Tabernacle design, but many of the data points help in this enormous "connect the dots" exercise. The more small points there are to work with, the easier it is to begin to see the bigger picture.

Putting it Back Together

Deciphering the Tabernacle design from Exodus is a little like putting a jigsaw puzzle together; it requires a measure of patience, attentiveness, and systematic thought. Like a two dimensional jigsaw puzzle, each three-dimensional Tabernacle piece must be shaped in a way that it fits together with a corresponding piece, with the exception that each Tabernacle piece must also perform a special function. Ironically, solving the puzzle isn't always made easier by looking at the outside of the box, especially in the case where the puzzle pieces were carelessly put into the wrong box with the wrong image on the exterior.

Fortunately, the Exodus Tabernacle plans are not given in a state of total disorder or in a random pile like a jigsaw puzzle; the Exodus text lists the pieces in a very deliberate order, but in hopes that the reader is paying attention such that the Tabernacle hardware is not misappropriated or force-fit together. For this reason, the Tabernacle assembly sequence described herein coincides with the basic Exodus text progression, proceeding step by step, just as Moses instructed. In accordance with hardware group, chapters are divided into general sections as follows:

English Flax for WWI - H. Nicholls, 1914

- Part 1 – Tabernacle Coverings (Exodus 26:1-14)
- Part 2 – Tabernacle Frame (Exodus 26:15-28)
- Part 3 – Tabernacle Internals (Exodus 26:29-37)
- Part 4 – Tabernacle Courtyard (Exodus 27:1, 9-19)

Before embarking on the Tabernacle discovery journey, it is important to first understand that not all Tabernacle "puzzle parts" are described in a consistent manner. Typical jigsaw puzzle parts are simple, in that each piece is consistent and in predictable arrangements, having a part of a picture on one side and usually up to four irregular edges that need to be matched with an adjacent unit. However, being a three-dimensional structure comprised of different materials, Tabernacle parts must be designed with greater distinction, as their shapes must perform mission-critical functions and work in concert with other parts to create structural stability. Further complicating Tabernacle hardware definition, sometimes only names or functional descriptions are given in Exodus; and other hardware attributes such as shapes, sizes, weights, colors, features, and

French Shepherds Spinning Wool

God's Dwelling Place Reconsidered

Hewn Ontario Lumber - W.D. Watt, 1913

Beginning with the Basics

Understanding the Exodus Tabernacle begins with an understanding of raw materials and ancient technologies.

Metal Smelting - Georg Bauer, 1556

orientation are not always specified in their entirety. Thus, some parts are more completely specified by the Exodus texts, whereas others can only be determined by means of deductive reasoning.

In order to satisfy all requirements of this unique Exodus puzzle, many traditional Tabernacle parts need to be radically transformed and reallocated. In numerous cases, this requires massive shape, weight, or size changes to traditional Tabernacle hardware—both to make them fit and to bring them back into Exodus specifications. In several cases, this is obligatory, as traditional models assume material sizes or inventories which are orders of magnitude greater than what is allowed in Bible texts.

Richard Buckminster Fuller, the revolutionary 20th century architect, once said, "You never change things by fighting the existing reality. To change something, build a new model that

German Leather Skudding - Nuremberg, 1609

makes the existing model obsolete." While this book was not exactly written to introduce a new model, it is written with the ironic intent of replacing the existing model with an older one. In order to do this, Parts 1-4 begin with the dismantling of existing misconceptions that are familiar, which are replaced with familiar concepts that have been forgotten. Illustrations are used to depict the Tabernacle hardware as it is reallocated, reoriented, and/or transformed. Upon the completion of the transformation, Part 5 is included to compare and contrast the rectangular Tabernacle model relative to the ancient Hebrew Tabernacle model. Within these pages, it should become apparent that the traditional right-angled model doesn't stand a chance, because the rediscovered round Hebrew model is—and always was—built upon God's word.

The House of El Shaddai

Quality Control
REJECTED
TEXT REFERENCE: Exodus 26:1-14
BASIS FOR FAILURE: Many Tabernacle models assume roof layers are tethered to the ground, but no features or joints are specified for anchoring the fabrics or leather.

Traditional Rectangular Tabernacle
East Side View - Roof Coverings Tethered to Ground

Covering Materials

- Linen
- Gold
- Wool
- Copper
- Leather

Part 1 – Tabernacle Coverings

If people are to believe that the word of God and his dwelling place of are importance, they must first come to terms with an unusual section of Exodus text describing several layers of Tabernacle coverings. While overlooked and benign to even the most seasoned Bible scholars, upon further examination, these descriptions prove to hold the key to deciphering the Tabernacle's secrets.

Unfortunately, mastering Bible facts and digesting data in raw form usually isn't regarded to be a high priority when it comes to just about anyone's Bible study agenda. Given that the Tabernacle topic seems as mundane as genealogies, census data, or the counting of animals, few strive to find meaning therein. Consequently, in Bible texts where underlying purposes are not openly identified, underscored, or understood, it is only rational for people to question what they are reading and wonder if it is just an arbitrary collection of meaningless ramblings or actually divinely inspired writ. The Tabernacle coverings under consideration might be summarized as follows:

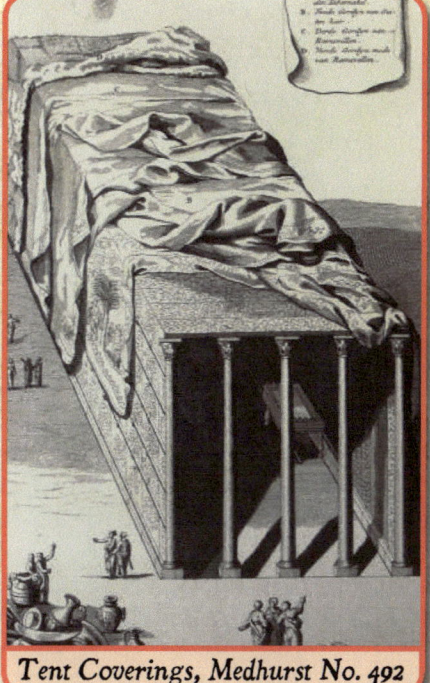

Tent Coverings, Medhurst No. 492

a. Linen Curtains w/Gold "Taches" (Ex. 26:1-6)
b. Wool Curtains w/Copper "Taches" (Ex. 26:7-13)
c. Leather Roof Lower Section (Ex. 26:14a)
d. Leather Roof Upper Section (Ex. 26:14b)

At first glance, the disproportionate amount of attention that Moses allocates to different materials might seem strange. Altogether, thirteen consecutive verses are dedicated to two sets of fabric, whereas there is only a single verse dedicated to two leather Tabernacle coverings. Moses even dedicated more ink to the Tabernacle fabrics than he did in describing the Ark of the Covenant! How can this obsession with Tabernacle fabrics be explained?

The House of El Shaddai

Quality Control REJECTED

TEXT REFERENCE: Exodus 26:1-6

BASIS FOR FAILURE: Traditional models assume a single rectangular 40x28 covering is made from multiple smaller curtains, but dimensions do not correspond to other hardware sizes or quantities. This leaves no basis for making ten 4x28 cubit curtains.

Traditional Rectangular Tabernacle
Linen Curtain Assembly (40x28 Cubits) over Wood Tent Frame

Why are Curtains "Cunning Work"?

"Moreover thou shalt make the tabernacle with ten curtains of fine twined linen, and blue, and purple, and scarlet: with cherubims of cunning work shalt thou make them. The length of one curtain shall be eight and twenty cubits, and the breadth of one curtain four cubits: and every one of the curtains shall have one measure."

~ Exodus 26:1-2, KJV ~

The Thinker - Musée Rodin, Horne 2010

~ Linen Curtains ~

When first surveying the texts describing the Tabernacle's ten linen curtains, it would appear that the Exodus writings (Exodus 26:1-6) are replete with trivia. The details seem to be arbitrary and largely inconsequential in the scheme of the overall Tabernacle design. Traditionally, and in accordance with Bible translations, the ten linen curtains measuring 4 x 28 cubits are assumed to form a single multi-colored sheet measuring 40 cubits long by 28 wide, which is to be draped over the Tabernacle frame. But is this a reasonable way to construct a tent?

Decorative or Functional?

As Moses' Tabernacle is first introduced, Exodus 26:1 describes linen curtains as "cunning work". Several translations suggest that the work is "skillful" or "artistic", as if the structure's beauty was of foremost concern. However, this aesthetic objective, as proposed by translators and echoed within numerous Tabernacle models and renderings, is worthy of serious scrutiny. This should be intuitively obvious based upon the arrangement of the linen curtain in traditional models, which presume that the linen layer is directly covered by larger wool and leather layers above, such that the decorative linen curtains are completely concealed by the upper and outer layers.

While some may insist that the colorful linen curtains were woven for the sake of artistically decorating the Tabernacle's fully shaded and poorly illuminated interior ceiling, few go so far as to provide an explanation as to why curtains are created in a given quantity and size before they were assembled, or why they employ blue loops, which are included at opposite curtain ends. These details collectively point to a different reality—that the curtains were indeed a "cunning" or perhaps a "clever" or "thoughtful" work, and that they are engineered Tabernacle hardware.

Curtain Loop Joints

Given that the ten linen curtains were created as long and narrow strips, they were also made with blue loops on opposing ends (Exodus 26:4), whereby they might be joined one to another. For those believing the Tabernacle fabrics to be of no significance, these loop-joint details are of even lesser significance, but for those aspiring to hold Bible texts literally, this blue-loop-end-

The House of El Shaddai

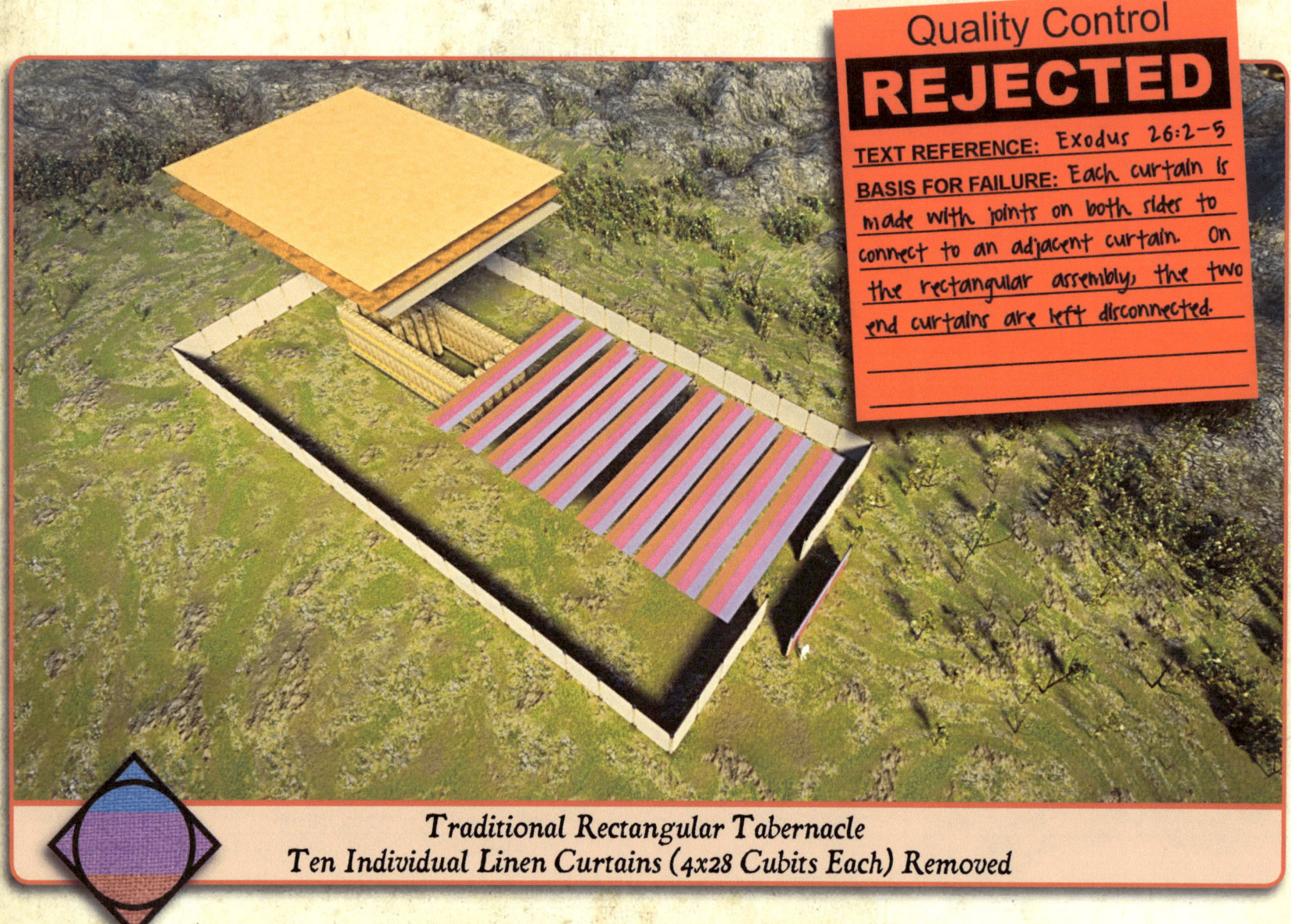

Quality Control REJECTED

TEXT REFERENCE: Exodus 26:2-5

BASIS FOR FAILURE: Each curtain is made with joints on both sides to connect to an adjacent curtain. On the rectangular assembly, the two end curtains are left disconnected.

Traditional Rectangular Tabernacle
Ten Individual Linen Curtains (4x28 Cubits Each) Removed

God's Dwelling Place Reconsidered

Quality Control: REJECTED
TEXT REFERENCE: Exodus 26:4,5
BASIS FOR FAILURE: Loops for joining curtain ends are blue, presumably extending from blue fabric. Curtain connections must be made from from blue-end to blue-end.

Traditional Rectangular Tabernacle
Two Sets of Five Linen Curtains Connected on Long Edges

joint detail is of paramount importance. On a rectangular curtain assembly arrangement, this blue-loop-joint detail makes little sense, as it would leave open or unconnected loops at the two opposing edges at the front and back sides of the Tabernacle, as the Exodus text would literally demand. If a rectangular arrangement is assumed, only eight of the ten curtains would be joined as Exodus specifies, and there would remain no provisions for connecting the linen curtains to the frame beneath.

Moreover, curtain quantities and dimensions also implicitly challenge the rectangular subassembly of the ten long and narrow strips of fabric. In particular, why make ten long and narrow strips of fabric (10 x 4 cubits x 28 cubits) if the end goal is really one large rectangular assembly measuring 40 x 28 cubits? And why use fabric loops to join single sheets into two subassemblies 2 x (5 x 4 cubits x 28 cubits) = 2 x (20 cubits x 28 cubits), only to add fifty gold clasps (Exodus 26:6) to join the two subassemblies of five sheets together into a single large 40 cubit x 28 cubit unit? Why not specify the final size and allow it to be made at the craftsmen's discretion?

Finally, there is the matter of loop-joint location. The Exodus text is not indifferent as to where loop-joints are located; verse 4 appropriates loops to the ends where the threads are cut (mistranslated as "selvedge"), which would be the "uttermost" edges or those being "outermost" with the farthest reaches. Although the Hebrew text doest not refer to the farthest reaches, it does refer to the cut fabric ends. As the curtains are woven on a loom, the threads in the longer dimension (warp) would be cut, whereas woven threads (weft) would remain uncut to the extent possible. Provided that each curtain is the same size, and that all curtains are connected with blue loops on opposing edges, a rectangular arrangement is just not viable. Instead, the two linen sheet subassemblies would form long strips, measuring 5 x 28 x 4 or 140 x 4 cubits each. When connected by the remaining blue loop joints and fifty gold latches, a ring would ultimately be formed as the ten curtains were joined end-to-end, either in a circular or decagonal arrangement.

Blue Loop Joints on the Cut Curtain Ends

"The five curtains shall be coupled together one to another; and other five curtains shall be coupled one to another. And thou shalt make loops of blue upon the edge of the one curtain from the selvedge in the coupling; and likewise shalt thou make in the uttermost edge of another curtain, in the coupling of the second. Fifty loops shalt thou make in the one curtain, and fifty loops shalt thou make in the edge of the curtain that is in the coupling of the second; that the loops may take hold one of another."

~ Exodus 26:3-5, KJV ~

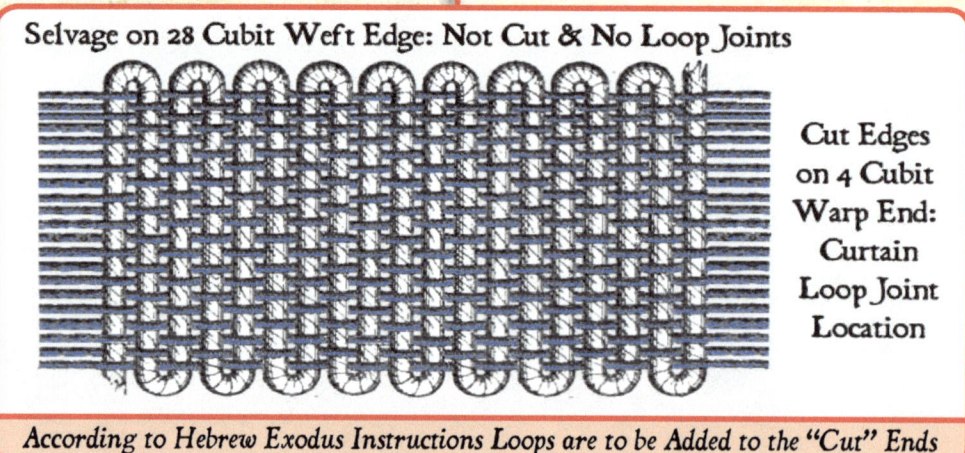

Selvage on 28 Cubit Weft Edge: Not Cut & No Loop Joints

Cut Edges on 4 Cubit Warp End: Curtain Loop Joint Location

According to Hebrew Exodus Instructions Loops are to be Added to the "Cut" Ends

God's Dwelling Place Reconsidered

Quality Control REWORK

TEXT REFERENCE: Exodus 26:4,5

CORRECTIVE ACTION: Curtain loop joints must be on "cut" edges, not on long 28 cubit curtain edges. Cut edges are defined by standard loom layout and operation. Long 28 cubit edges are uncut as thread is woven back and forth across a short 4 cubit span.

Tabernacle Material Transition
Linen Sheets Modified to Include Blue Loops on Short Edges

The House of El Shaddai

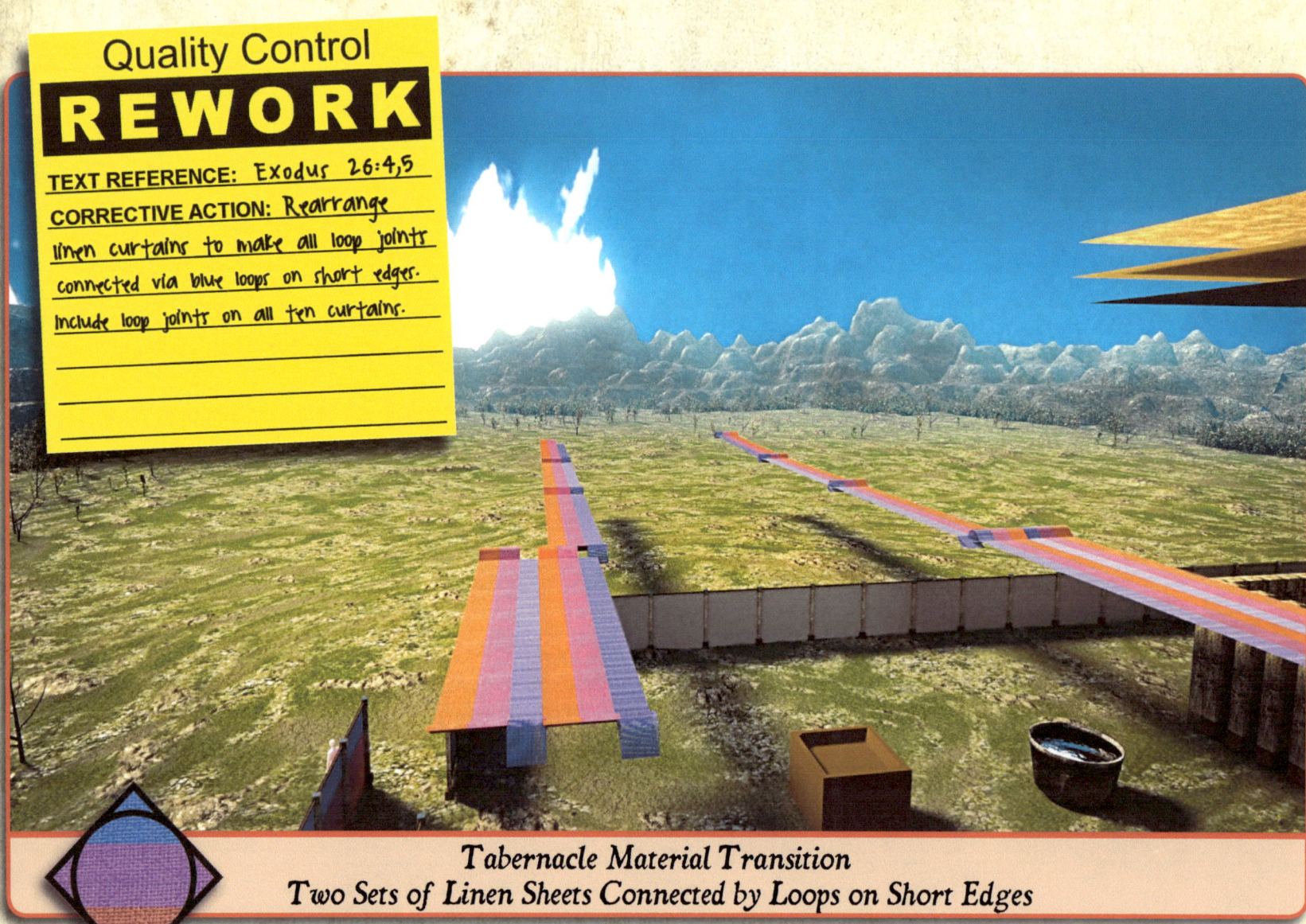

Quality Control

REWORK

TEXT REFERENCE: Exodus 26:4,5

CORRECTIVE ACTION: Rearrange linen curtains to make all loop joints connected via blue loops on short edges. Include loop joints on all ten curtains.

Tabernacle Material Transition
Two Sets of Linen Sheets Connected by Loops on Short Edges

God's Dwelling Place Reconsidered

What are Gold Taches?

"And thou shalt make fifty taches of gold, and couple the curtains together with the taches: and it shall be one tabernacle."

~ Exodus 26:6, KJV ~

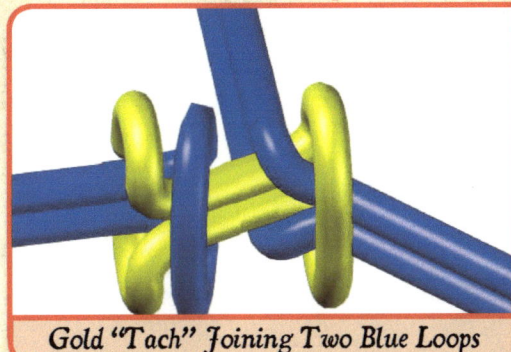

Gold "Tach" Joining Two Blue Loops

Fifty gold taches are used for joining the last set of the Tabernacle curtain end loop joints. Taches could assume a variety of different shapes (perhaps resembling a button with hooks), provided that the gold hardware pieces are capable of joining two rope loops and carrying a small tension load.

Linen Curtain Assembly Arrangement

From Exodus 26:1, it is clearly understood that the Tabernacle or "dwelling place" is made with ten linen sheets. However, from subsequent verses describing these curtains, it is not completely clear how they are being connected or employed as a Tabernacle covering. Just as the Exodus text never describes these sheets to be arranged overhead as a "covering", the text also seems to refrain from describing how these curtains are held in place. This is evident in variations of the rectangular Tabernacle model; some suggest they used ropes tied to stakes in the ground to hold the curtains in place, despite the fact that such hardware or corresponding curtain features are never mentioned in Exodus whatsoever. As such, many loosely drape the large rectangular swatch over the wood frame without offering any means of securing the fabric assembly.

Although Exodus suggests that the dwelling place either consists of or is bound by ten linen sheets, it is not entirely clear from the Exodus 26:1-6 texts how they might function as a boundary. If fabric curtains are intended to create a barrier—as opposed to a shelter, it would stand to reason that curtains would need to be arranged in a vertical plane, as opposed to the traditionally assumed horizontal and sloped orientation. Furthermore, assuming individual curtains are rectangular (i.e., two parallel edges with adjacent edges at right angles), logic would also demand that they be spanned horizontally lengthwise in order to make loop-to-loop connections with adjacent curtain units, and such that loops have equal engagement in the vertical direction.

Finally, there is the matter of curtain loop-joint interconnection or curtain support apparatus. How is one loop intended to "receive" another loop as the Exodus texts stipulate? Magicians are known for creating the illusion that two loops or metal rings can be joined by intersecting the rings when concealed skillfully manipulated, but logic dictates that two opposing circular loops are not able to interlock with another—unless they are cut and retied. At this point, it seems clear that the text indicates that all curtains are joined via loops end-to-end, or more specifically, short-edge-to-short-edge, forming a round or decagonal perimeter, but how are the curtains held in place, and how do they form the dwelling place perimeter and interface? How do the loops interface with other Tabernacle hardware, and how is the receiving of one loop into another loop accomplished? To what end are the ten linen sheets being used?

The House of El Shaddai

Quality Control APPROVED

TEXT REFERENCE: Exodus 26:1-5
VALIDATION BASIS: Ten long and narrow curtains (28 x 4 cubits) are joined together into two sets of five.

Round Hebrew Tabernacle
Two Sets of Five Linen Sheets

God's Dwelling Place Reconsidered

Quality Control APPROVED

TEXT REFERENCE: Exodus 26:1-6

VALIDATION BASIS: Ten long and narrow (28x4 cubit) linen curtains are joined together using blue fabric loops and gold clasps or buttons. The *intermediate* ten curtain layout assumes the shape of a decagon.

Round Hebrew Tabernacle
All Ten Linen Sheets Connected End-to-End via Blue Loops

~ Wool Curtains ~

After going through great lengths to describe the Tabernacle's first set of ten linen curtains, Moses' subsequent writings introduce a similar set of eleven curtains, which are larger and made of wool (Exodus 26:7-13). Again, this is not a collection of superfluous detail; each parameter described in the Exodus text has a meaningful impact upon the overall facility design. For purposes of comparison, particulars of the linen and wool curtain sets are summarized in the table below:

Tabernacle Curtain Comparison

Specification	Linen Curtain Set		Wool Curtain Set	
Material	Ex 26:1	Linen	Ex 26:7	Wool
Color	Ex 26:1	Yes	n/a	No (Bleached)
Quantity	Ex 26:1	10	Ex 26:7	11
Length	Ex 26:2	28	Ex 26:8	30
Width	Ex 26:2	4	Ex 26:8	4
Subassembly Group	Ex 26:3	5 + 5	Ex 26:9	5 + 6
Folded Curtain	n/a	n/a	Ex 26:9	Yes
Loop Quantity	Ex 26:4	50	Ex 26:10	50
Loop Placement	Ex 26:4	Short / Cut Edges	Ex 26:10	Short / Cut Edges
Loop Color	Ex 26:4	Blue	n/a	n/a
Taches	Ex 26:6	50 Gold	Ex 26:11	50 Brass
Remnant Position	n/a	n/a	Ex 26:12	Defined
Measured Overlap	n/a	n/a	Ex 26:13	1 Cubit
Final Assembly Size	n/a	Not Listed	n/a	Not Listed

Traditionally, as has been the case for the ten colored linen curtains, the eleven bleached wool curtains—each measuring 4 x 30 cubits—are assumed to connect via the long edges of the fabric,

---

314 Cubits of Wool?

"And thou shalt make curtains of goats' hair to be a covering upon the tabernacle: eleven curtains shalt thou make. The length of one curtain shall be thirty cubits, and the breadth of one curtain four cubits: and the eleven curtains shall be all of one measure. And thou shalt couple five curtains by themselves, and six curtains by themselves, and shalt double the sixth curtain in the forefront of the tabernacle. And thou shalt make fifty loops on the edge of the one curtain that is outmost in the coupling, and fifty loops in the edge of the curtain which coupleth the second. And thou shalt make fifty taches of brass, and put the taches into the loops, and couple the tent together, that it may be one. And the remnant that remaineth of the curtains of the tent, the half curtain that remaineth, shall hang over the backside of the tabernacle. And a cubit on the one side, and a cubit on the other side of that which remaineth in the length of the curtains of the tent, it shall hang over the sides of the tabernacle on this side and on that side, to cover it."

~ Exodus 26:7-13, KJV ~

God's Dwelling Place Reconsidered

Traditional Rectangular Tabernacle
Eleven Wool Curtains over Linen Curtains and Wood Frame

Quality Control: REJECTED

TEXT REFERENCE: Exodus 26:7&13

BASIS FOR FAILURE: Eleven wool curtains measuring 42x30 cubits do not cover all sides of the Tabernacle, (verse 7 and 13) have no provisions for securing them to other hardware, and would sag in the center and bunch up on the back end.

thus forming a single sheet measuring 42 cubits long by 30 wide, after the end curtain is folded in half lengthwise. Again, this single large wool curtain assembly has also been assumed to be draped over the Tabernacle frame and over the smaller 40 x 28 cubit fabric layer formed by the ten linen curtains. But given the Bible description, along with precedents established by earlier linen curtain analysis and evidence of translation bias, is this a reasonable assumption?

Wool Curtain Arrangement, Placement, and Purpose

Traditional rectangular Tabernacle models assume that the wool sheet assembly is literally "on top of" the tent. While "upon" or "over" translations in Exodus 26:7 seem to reinforce this "up-above" paradigm, it is of note that these simple relational prepositions are not exclusively used in reference to the vertical direction (in Old English, in Merriam-Webster English shown in margin, or in Hebrew forms). Apart from conveying a relative elevation relationship, "upon" or "over" prepositions also can convey "around", "against" or "on" relationships, as in a covering capacity (e.g., to apply wax "upon" a car, to have rust "on" a nail, or to wear a coat "over" a shirt).

Given the possible latitude of the Hebrew preposition that is translated "upon" or "over", the context must be examined to determine relative placement of the wool barrier. This barrier is described relative to the "Tabernacle", or more literally the "dwelling place", which is established by ten linen curtains (of Exodus 26:1-6). Thus, if the ten linen curtains are arranged in a ring configuration and a person standing at ground level is used to define the meaning of "upon" or "over", it is quite reasonable to consider that the eleven longer wool curtains are also arranged in a similar cylindrical fashion in order to form a larger lateral barrier "over" the smaller one.

Subtle Exodus terms also testify to this "over" or "around" relationship between the curtain sets. Exodus 26:1 first describes the ten linen curtains as being for the "dwelling place", whereas verse 7 of the Hebrew text describes the eleven curtains as being used "to tent" (or arguably "to wall") over the "dwelling place". Measuring about twice the length of a football field, the long assembly made from joining 11 wool curtains—each measuring 30 cubits in length—would easily encircle the smaller linen ring formed by 10 curtains measuring 28 cubits in length. Assuming a cylindrical shape, wool curtains measuring 4 cubits high would completely cover the sides of the entire dwelling place, blocking wind, limiting physical access, as well as obstructing line of sight.

"And thou shalt make curtains of goats' hair to be a covering upon the tabernacle: eleven curtains shalt thou make."

~ Exodus 26:7, KJV ~

upon / on
[uh-pon, uh-pawn / on, awn]

1c —used as a function word to indicate position in close proximity with

1d —used as a function word to indicate the location of something

Curtains "Upon" or "Over" Sides?

over
[oh-ver]

1a—across a barrier or intervening space

3b—so as to cover the whole

"And a cubit on the one side, and a cubit on the other side of that which remaineth in the length of the curtains of the tent, it shall hang over the sides of the tabernacle on this side and on that side, to cover it."

~ Exodus 26:13, KJV ~

God's Dwelling Place Reconsidered

Quality Control
REJECTED
TEXT REFERENCE: Exodus 26:7-8,10-11
BASIS FOR FAILURE: Eleven wool curtains are connected on long (uncut) edges contrary to verse 10. Also, curtains are to be one measure with loops on both sides (verse 8 & 10) so all curtains (including the first and last) should be connected by end loops.

Traditional Rectangular Tabernacle
Wool Curtains Joined into a Set of Five and Set of Six

The House of El Shaddai

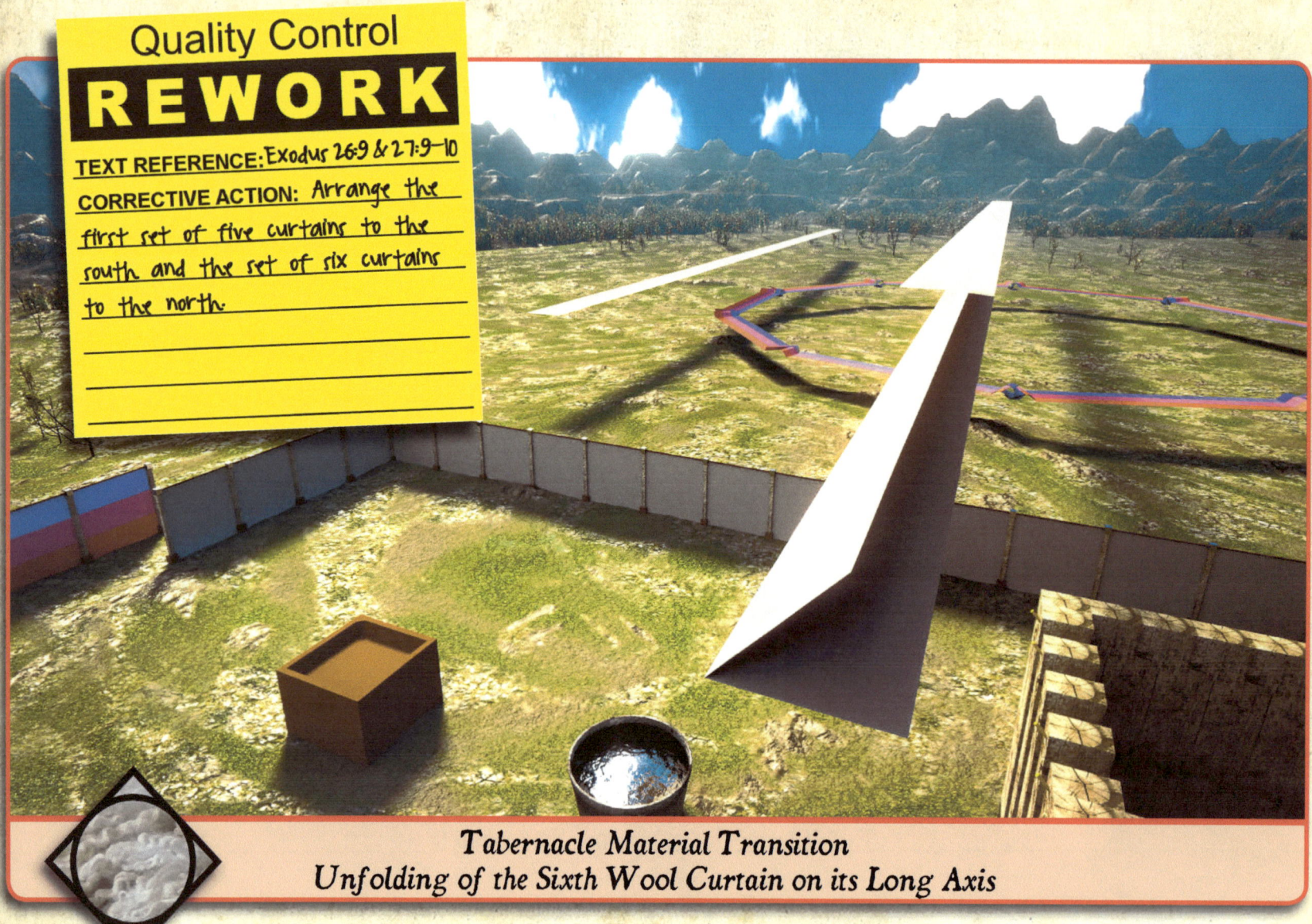

Quality Control
REWORK

TEXT REFERENCE: Exodus 26:9 & 27:9-10
CORRECTIVE ACTION: Arrange the first set of five curtains to the south and the set of six curtains to the north.

Tabernacle Material Transition
Unfolding of the Sixth Wool Curtain on its Long Axis

God's Dwelling Place Reconsidered

Quality Control
REWORK

TEXT REFERENCE: Exodus 26:9&10
CORRECTIVE ACTION: All wool curtains are to be rearranged and connected in two sets (one set of 5, and one set of 6) on the short ends of the wool curtains.

Tabernacle Material Transition
Eleven Wool Curtains in Two Sets Joined at the Short Edges

In contrast to a round arrangement, a large rectangular wool curtain assembly would be of marginal use if placed overhead or sandwiched between other layers of leather and fabric. Installed between layers, it could not serve as a rain barrier; and the extra layer would add insulation to the structure, often times retaining the desert heat. Furthermore, a large 42 x 30 rectangular wool curtain assembly does not lend itself to proper fitting over a rectangular frame with three-dimensional, 90 degree corners any more than a rectangular linen curtain assembly would; the slack fabric from both layers would be awkwardly arranged and irregularly bunched up on the west side and the corners, or folded like gift wrap around a shoe box, thereby complicating installation and creating a is clumsy final configuration that is far from being elegant or divine.

Odd Wool Sheets and Overlapping Ends

Beyond simple curtain end, curtain loop, and curtain positioning detail, the curtain quantities, dimensions, and assembly instructions of Exodus also offer hints to their overall configuration and purpose. Why specify a curtain set to be assembled from odd part quantities, which are made to such exacting dimensions? Because the curtain sizes, quantities, and assembly directions ultimately speak to a very specific geometric configuration. How so?

When eleven sheets measuring 30 x 4 cubits are joined on their short edges (a set of five sheets measuring 150 cubits long and a set of six measuring 180 cubits long), it creates an assembly measuring 330 cubits long. This length is reduced by "doubling" the sixth curtain—folding the end curtain in half—resulting in a final length of 315 cubits. However, the 315 cubit total is further reduced by a cubit, as loops on the curtain ends must ultimately overlap (for them to receive one another), thereby reducing the assembled length by another cubit, just as instructed in Exodus 26:13. Thus, the final assembly dimension measures 314 cubits, which is a near perfect multiple of π—the mathematical constant used to convey the ratio between a circle's circumference and its diameter.

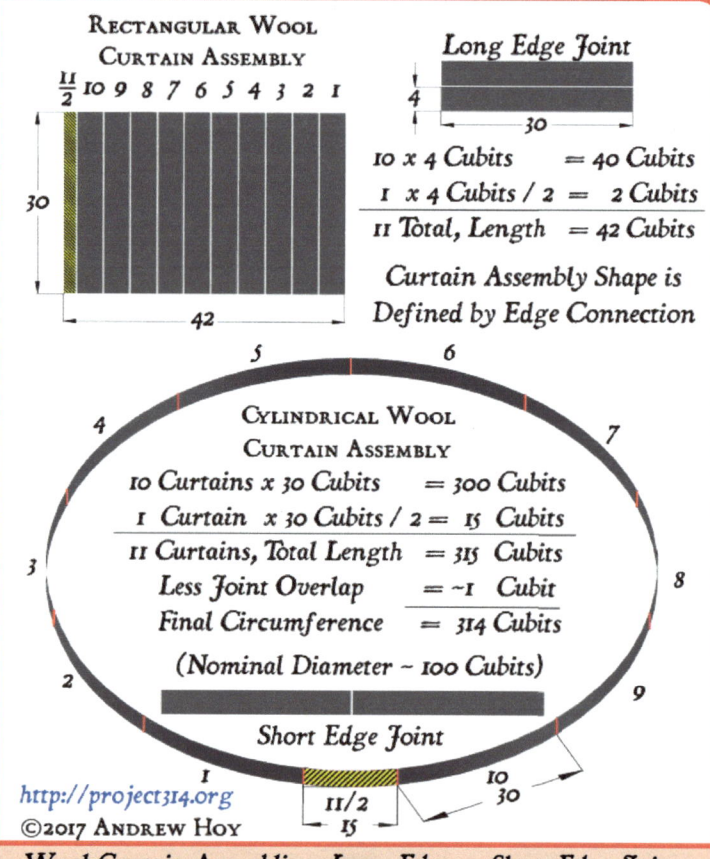

Exodus 26 specifies eleven curtains at 30x4 cubits (v7-8), with loop joints on each end (v9-10), with one sheet folded in half (v12), overlapping 1 cubit (v13). By joining all curtains at the short edges, a circular assembly is created.

God's Dwelling Place Reconsidered

Quality Control REWORK

TEXT REFERENCE: Exodus 26:9 & 27:9-10

CORRECTIVE ACTION: Arrange the first set of five curtains to the south and the set of six curtains to the north.

Tabernacle Material Transition
Two Wool Curtain Subassemblies - Set of Five and Set of Six

The House of El Shaddai

Quality Control APPROVED

TEXT REFERENCE: Exodus 26:7-13

VALIDATION BASIS: Eleven wool curtains (v7) measuring 30 cubits (v8) joined into two groups (v9) are connected by loops on short edges (v10) to cover all Tabernacle sides (v7&13), with the latter (sixth) curtain (v12-13) folded in half.

Round Hebrew Tabernacle
Folding the Sixth Wool Curtain on its Short Axis

God's Dwelling Place Reconsidered

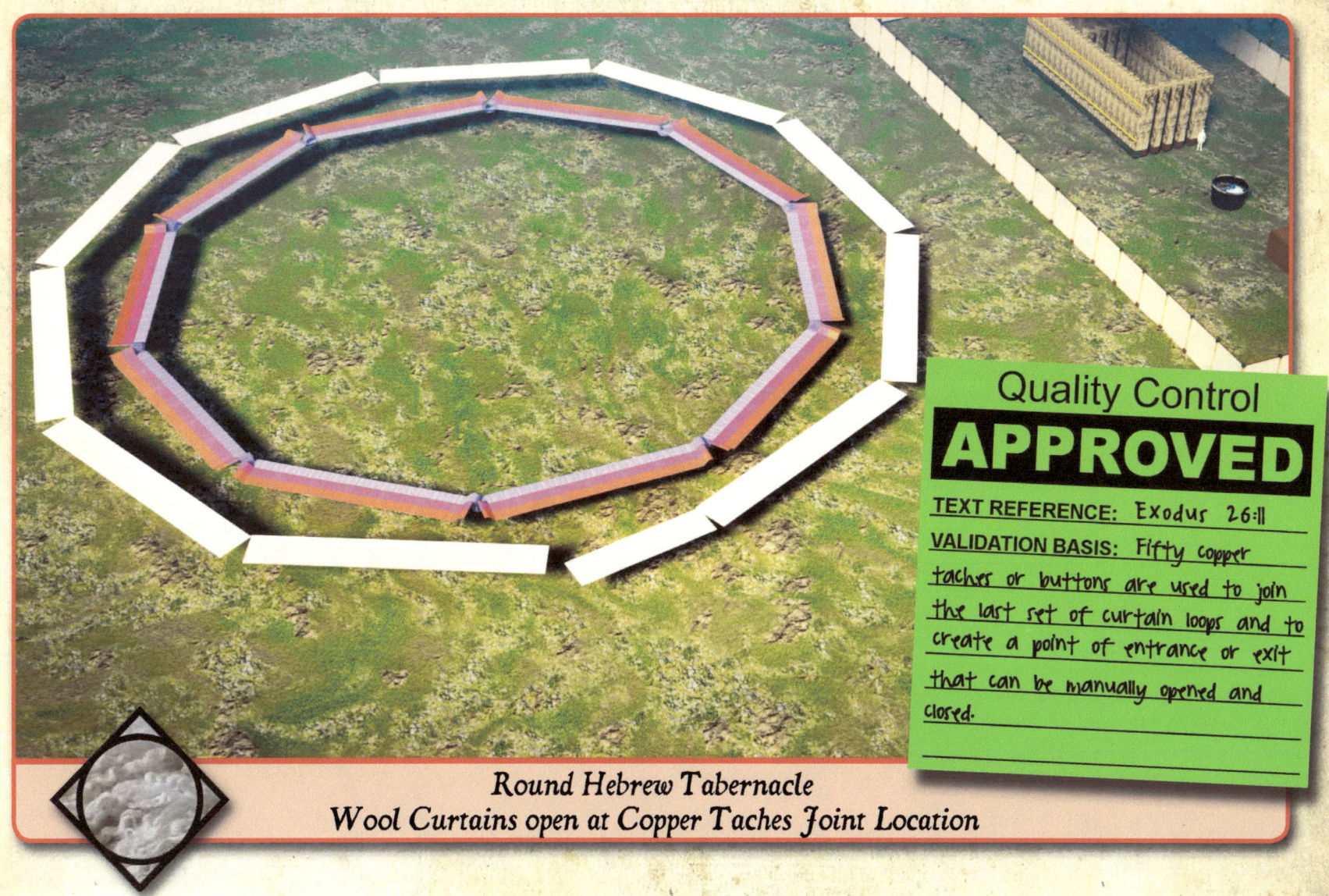

Round Hebrew Tabernacle
Wool Curtains open at Copper Taches Joint Location

Quality Control APPROVED

TEXT REFERENCE: Exodus 26:11

VALIDATION BASIS: Fifty copper taches or buttons are used to join the last set of curtain loops and to create a point of entrance or exit that can be manually opened and closed.

While it should come as no surprise to those accustomed to looking to Bible texts for esoteric knowledge that Moses recorded the closest approximation to the π constant known to the ancient world (within 0.05% error), this discovery also testifies to the Tabernacle's divine and round arrangement. After all, the Exodus specifications already imply a circular wool curtain arrangement given the fact that all curtains are fitted with loops on opposite sides for interconnection with adjacent units. Given that the curtain ring was fabricated with such deliberate intentions, the 314 cubit circumference measurement would be so exact, assuming a circle with a diameter of 100 cubits, that the difference between the 3.14 approximation inferred from Exodus and the actual π constant would amount to an error as little as 2 inches when measuring something as long as an entire football field. Thus, the 314 value for π that Exodus conveys demonstrates that the Hebrews had an outstanding grasp on mathematics long before the Greek letter π became synonymous with the mathematical constant, making Moses the ancient world record holder up until the second century Greco-Roman mathematician Claudius Ptolemy. Moreover, the 314 expression is a clear analogy for a circle—which is without beginning or end—like an eternal Hebrew God named *El Shaddai*—who put his mark on his dwelling place (see Part 5).

Ptolemy - 16th Century Engraving

What is π?

The π ratio is a mathematical constant based upon the relationship of a circle's circumference and its diameter. As an irrational number, π cannot be exactly expressed as a fraction or decimal but is often approximated at 22/7 or 3.14.

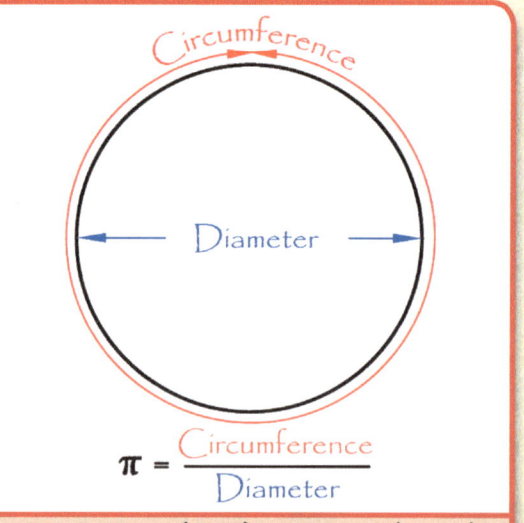

$$\pi = \frac{Circumference}{Diameter}$$

The Pi Ratio (C/D) is Constant (~3.14:1)

Overlapping Mixtures and Buttons

Finally, with respect to the wool curtain configuration, there is the matter of wool curtain-ring-assembly closure. As in the case of the linen curtains of Exodus 26:1-6, the wool curtains of Exodus 26:7-13 also employ fifty loops on the ends of the curtains to serve as joints. However, the single set of fifty "taches" used to join the two sets of wool curtains in conjunction with fifty fabric loops was specified to be copper, as opposed to the gold used for the linen curtain set.

In the case of the cylindrical wool curtain assembly, it is reasonable to surmise the copper taches would also be used in a gate or access capacity, joining the set of five curtains to the set of six

Copper Taches

"And thou shalt make fifty taches of brass, and put the taches into the loops, and couple the tent together, that it may be one."

~ Exodus 26:11, KJV ~

Hook-and-Loop Design
Photo by Lilly / Naturebeads.com

The Tabernacle taches probably featured some sort of hook and loop design. Alternatively, buttons with a head and hook could have also been used to make a loop-to-loop connection.

curtains at the end after the fold, and also in close proximity to the fifty gold taches used to close off the set of linen curtains.

Although this curtain-over-curtain arrangement works well with two concentric rings, further difficulties emerge in the event that curtains are connected on long edges and laid one on top of the other. First, there is the Biblical prohibition pertaining to mixing of two dissimilar fabrics (Leviticus 19:19, Deuteronomy 22:11), which should be given due consideration. Some may argue that this prohibition is to be limited to clothing, or that the prohibition is to be applied only to things that are "common" (i.e., not holy), as the Tabernacle's coverings are considered to be. Others might propose that the overlay really doesn't qualify as "mixing" of fabrics. But irrespective of these possible contradictions, there is the matter of the fifty brass "taches". If equidistantly spaced across the 28 cubit-wide linen and the 30 cubit-wide wool curtain assemblies, taches intervals would be highly irregular—about 28/50 or 0.56 cubits apart for the linen, compared to 30/50 or 0.6 cubits for the wool. Provided that curtains are aligned at the front of the Tabernacle, the taches would be prone to snagging with one another and with the loops above or below as the joints of the two curtain assemblies overlap. Also, with such large spaces between the assemblies, large air gaps (about 10 to 15 inches) between buttons wouldn't leave a contiguous connection between curtain edges. Finally, the curtains are not provided with any features or hardware for securing them to each other, to the frame beneath, to the ground below, or to anything else.

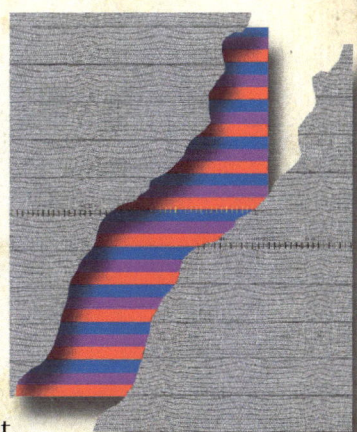

~ Leather Covering ~

Unlike the detailed curtain descriptions, Exodus texts seem to offer little indication as to how the leather skins for the Tabernacle roof were sized or assembled (Exodus 26:14). In fact, the single Exodus verse pertaining to the leather focuses on the animal species, skin or leather treatment type, and relative position, while not giving any indication whatsoever as to the leather dimensions or quantity of skins required. Why would the Exodus texts provide exacting Tabernacle fabric sizing details while leaving the leather covering or roof detail almost completely undefined?

The House of El Shaddai

Quality Control
REJECTED

TEXT REFERENCE: Exodus 26:14
BASIS FOR FAILURE: Two layers of leather (one laying upon the next) would trap moisture and mildew. Also, there is no reason to treat lower layer of leather if it is protected and not visible.

Traditional Rectangular Tabernacle
Tanned (Lower) Leather Roof with Upper Leather Layer Removed

Tanned Hides

"And thou shalt make a covering for the tent of rams' skins dyed red, and a covering above of badgers' skins."

~ Exodus 26:14, KJV ~

Moroccan Leather Tannery

For thousands of years, vegetable-based solutions have been used to transform animal skins into leather. After the hides are cleaned of hair or fur and treated with salt and potash solutions, hundreds of different roots, wood, bark, leaves, and fruit might be used to make the acidic solutions used for treating and coloring the leather. The leather tent roof would have been required a massive tanning operation.

Two-Tone Two-Layer Roof

While it is clear that four different coverings are specified over the course of the Exodus Tabernacle introduction (Exodus 26:1-14), it is evident at this point that Bible texts are not describing a four layer roof. After all, common sense and historical precedence demonstrate that a four-layer tent roof is simply not practical, and as a result, is not employed by nomadic cultures. Perhaps more importantly, this can be demonstrated not only by the Exodus descriptions of the linen and wool curtain assemblies, but also by the words used to describe each of the different materials. The linen curtains are described as making a "dwelling place" (often translated as "Tabernacle"), the wool curtains are used "to tent" around the "sides" of the linen "dwelling place", whereas only the two layers of leather are used as roofs. Of course, it makes little sense to dye the lower leather covering red in the event that it is concealed from view and protected from the elements.

As for leather roof materials, it is plausible to assume that Israelites collected and tanned ram skins; however it is completely unreasonable to assume that a "badger"—as known in today's English—would be employed in the capacity of a covering for the divine dwelling place. Why is badger forbidden? Because biblical hygienic law forbid the Israelites from harvesting carcasses of carnivorous mammals as they are listed as "unclean" animal types. The same principles would apply to the use of "dolphin", "porpoise", or "sea cows" for roof leather, albeit some animal species names have assumed radically different associations over the course of many centuries.

Although there is enough information to speculate about the arrangement and orientation of linen and wool curtains given within the first portion of Exodus 26, the same cannot be said of the leather configuration at this point. After all, if the leather is used for a tent covering, as Exodus indicates and as is consistent with nomadic tent building practices, it is not possible to determine the shape of the roof, as the details of the frame of the building have yet to be disclosed. One thing about the roof, however, is certain; it would not employ a double layer of leather as the traditional level-roof rectangular models propose. For good reason, the Law of Moses required the destruction of tents infested by mold or mildew, and a large double-layer of leather without much pitch would provide conditions of low light, moderate heat, and entrapped moisture, which are ideal for fungi colonization, but not so good for a divine dwelling place!

Part 2 – Tabernacle Frame

Nomadic dwellings need not be elaborate or sophisticated in order to provide basic shelter. At a minimum they must be designed to withstand year-round environmental conditions, and if they are used by migrating tribes, they should also be as lightweight as practical for ease of transport. With this criteria, the overall approach to tent making has remained virtually unchanged for thousands of years: span as much canvas as possible with as little frame as possible.

Following the tent covering narrative, the Exodus account continues by describing tent frame hardware. Comprised of a combination of wood ("shittim" wood, generally accepted to be of the acacia species) and metal (silver), the Bible specifically describes materials in accordance with composition, relative location, as well as function. Tabernacle frame is summarized as follows:

a. South Rib
   1. South Wood Planks (Exodus 26:15-19)
   2. South Silver Controllers (Exodus 26:19)
b. North Rib
   1. North Wood Beams (Exodus 26:20)
   2. North Silver Controllers (Exodus 26:21)
c. Ring Parts
   1. Six "Westward" Wood Braces (Exodus 26:22)
   2. Two Wood Ring "Corner" Sections (Exodus 26:23-24)
   3. Sixteen Silver Controllers (Exodus 26:25)
d. Wood Bars
   1. South Wood Bars (Exodus 26:26)
   2. North Wood Bars (Exodus 26:27a)
   3. West Wood Bars (Exodus 26:27b)

As is the case with modern tents, it stands to reason that the Tabernacle frame components are numbered, sized, and shaped to interface with the quantities, sizes, and features of the coverings

Frame Materials

Wood   **Silver**

Typical Yurt Tent Frame - Turkestan, 1872

For thousands of years, nomadic tribes have been using wood to build yurt frames, teepees, and other circular tents. To this day, wood remains a popular building material throughout the world as it is a renewable resource with a reasonable strength-to-weight ratio.

God's Dwelling Place Reconsidered

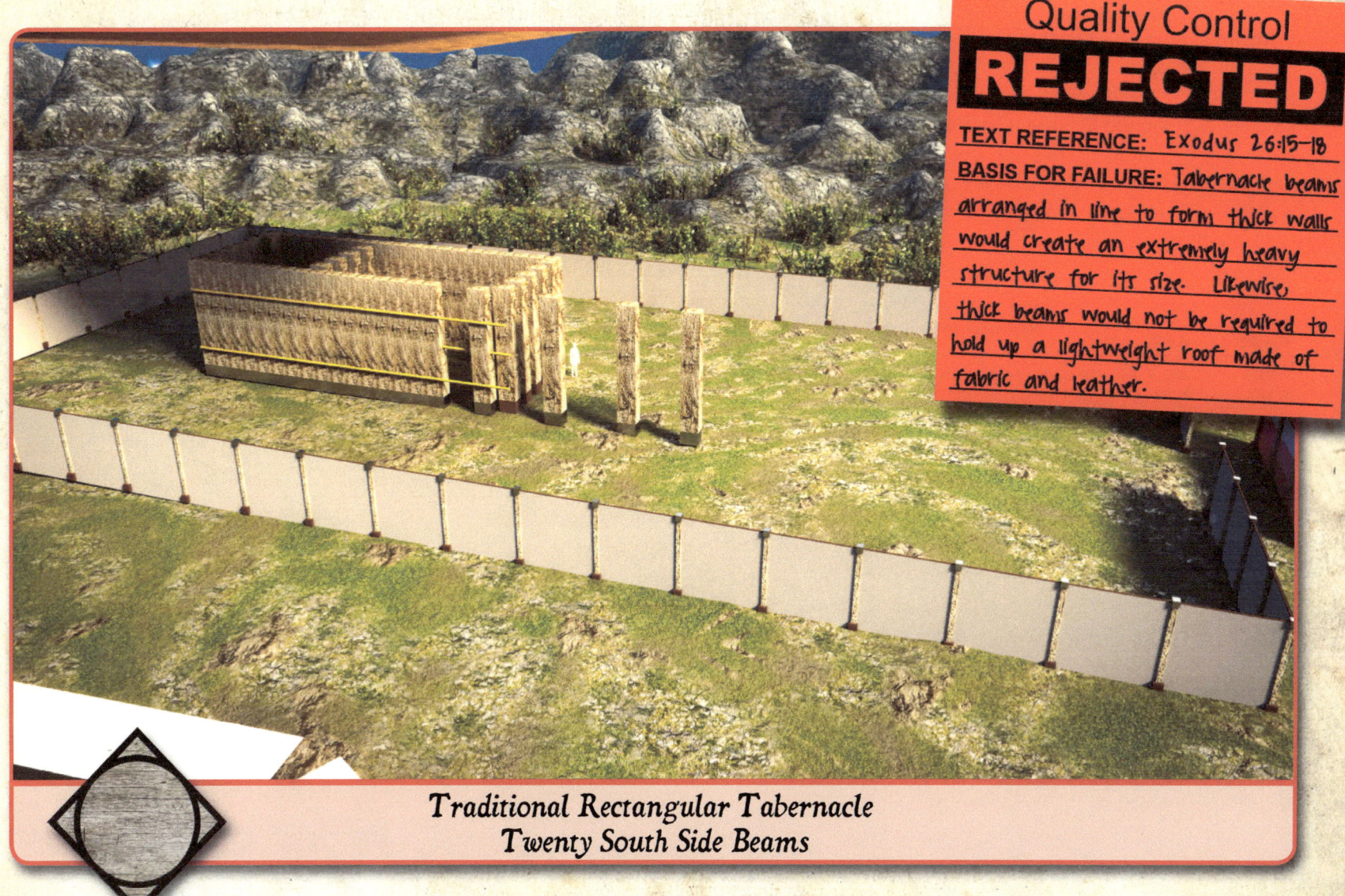

Quality Control REJECTED

TEXT REFERENCE: Exodus 26:15-18

BASIS FOR FAILURE: Tabernacle beams arranged in line to form thick walls would create an extremely heavy structure for its size. Likewise, thick beams would not be required to hold up a lightweight roof made of fabric and leather.

Traditional Rectangular Tabernacle
Twenty South Side Beams

or fabrics provided (with leather sizes and shapes being undefined), being erected within a footprint as established by the fabric materials.

Traditional rectangular models presume the Tabernacle tent "frame" is made of tall wood plank sections forming three sides aligned in three of the four cardinal compass directions—south, north, and west Exodus 26:15-22). But is it reasonable to once again assume that the beams are to be butted together via the long edges, as traditional models assume? Furthermore, is it practical to arrange wood beams to form three solid walls, which are offset 90 degrees from one another? How does this approach compare with tents and other structures, be they of ancient nomadic cultures, or even modern construction?

Tabernacle "Side" Plank Sizes

When evaluating the Exodus description of the ancient Tabernacle model, the wood planks used in its construction cannot be taken lightly. Measuring between 15 and 20 feet in length (Exodus 26:15), the massive beams would require large teams of men and/or animals to transport or erect.

While all traditional rectangular Tabernacle models consistently depict similar S/N/W wall arrangements, it is not uncommon for models and commentaries to propose different plank sizes. First, there is the matter of the cubit size used, which is understood to vary between cultures and eras (typically 18 inches, but sometimes 21 inches to 25 inches). However, apart from differing standards used in unit conversions, there is also a matter of Hebrew language translation and assumed dimensions. There are two primary schools of thought when it comes to the beam descriptions. Some believe that the original text is describing the beam in three dimensions, proposing a beam that measures 10 x 1½ x 1 cubits (which might weigh between 1000 lbs and 4500 lbs, depending upon cubit size and wood species). Presuming that the wood thickness is left undefined in the Bible text, others propose hewn planks measuring 10 x 1½ cubits, thereby drastically reducing plank weight – but leaving the carpenter with the dilemma of only having two of three dimensions specified and thus unable to proceed with confidence in fabrication.

However, in the tradition of tent making, perhaps it's prudent to reconsider the wood beam size description given the application. Understanding that tents typically employ rigid frames which

Tabernacle Beam Size

"And thou shalt make boards for the tabernacle of shittim wood standing up. Ten cubits shall be the length of a board, and a cubit and a half shall be the breadth of one board. Two tenons shall there be in one board, set in order one against another: thus shalt thou make for all the boards of the tabernacle."

~ Exodus 26:15-17, KJV ~

Perceived Beam Sizes - Exodus 26:15
A - 10 x 1-1/2 cubit diameter
B - 10 x 1-1/2 x 1 cubits
C - 10 x 1.5 cubits (thickness undefined)
D - 10 x 1 x 0.5 cubits

Traditional models need wide beams and depict profiles B or C. The round model could use A, B, or D profiles, but D is the most practical and literal interpretation.

God's Dwelling Place Reconsidered

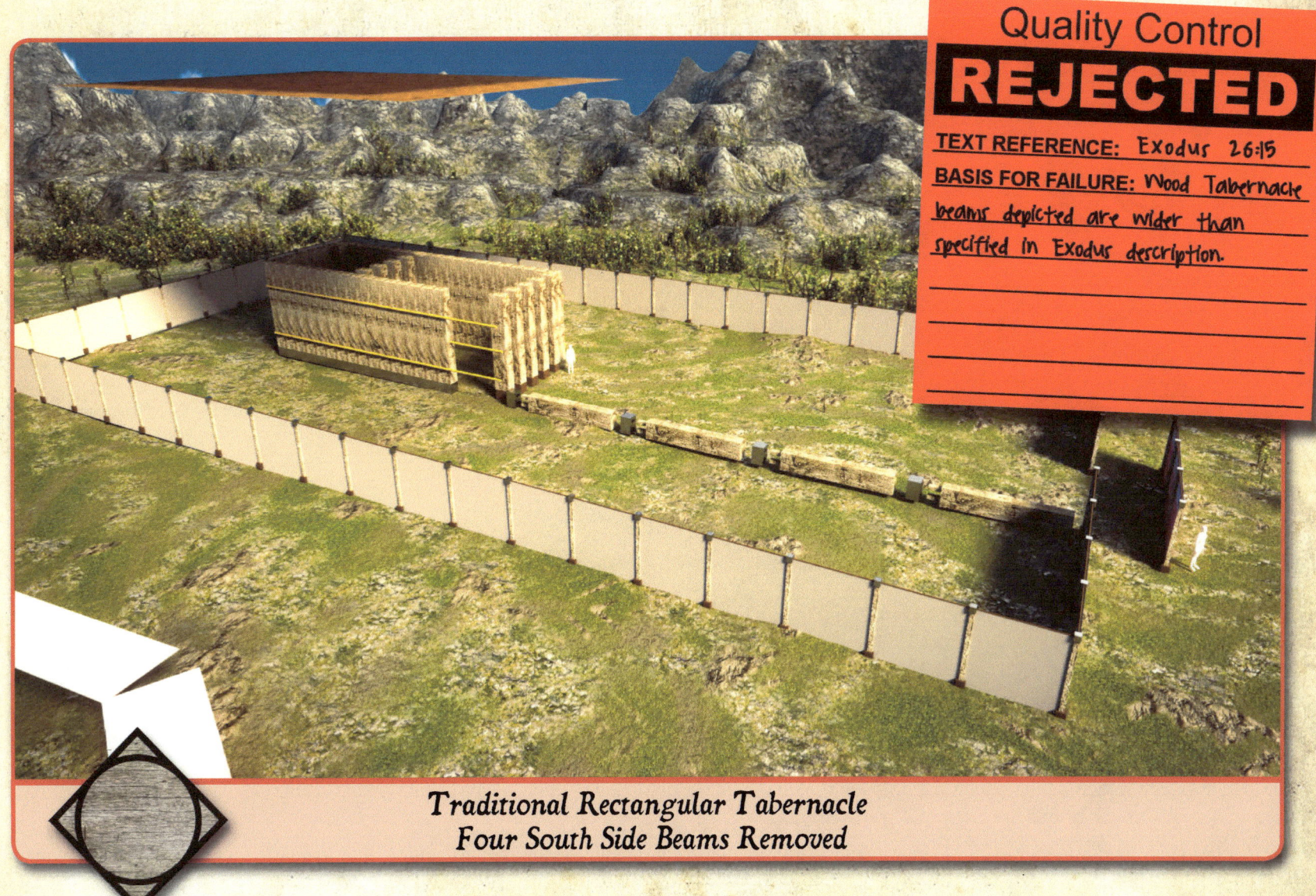

Quality Control REJECTED
TEXT REFERENCE: Exodus 26:15
BASIS FOR FAILURE: Wood Tabernacle beams depicted are wider than specified in Exodus description.

Traditional Rectangular Tabernacle
Four South Side Beams Removed

THE HOUSE OF EL SHADDAI

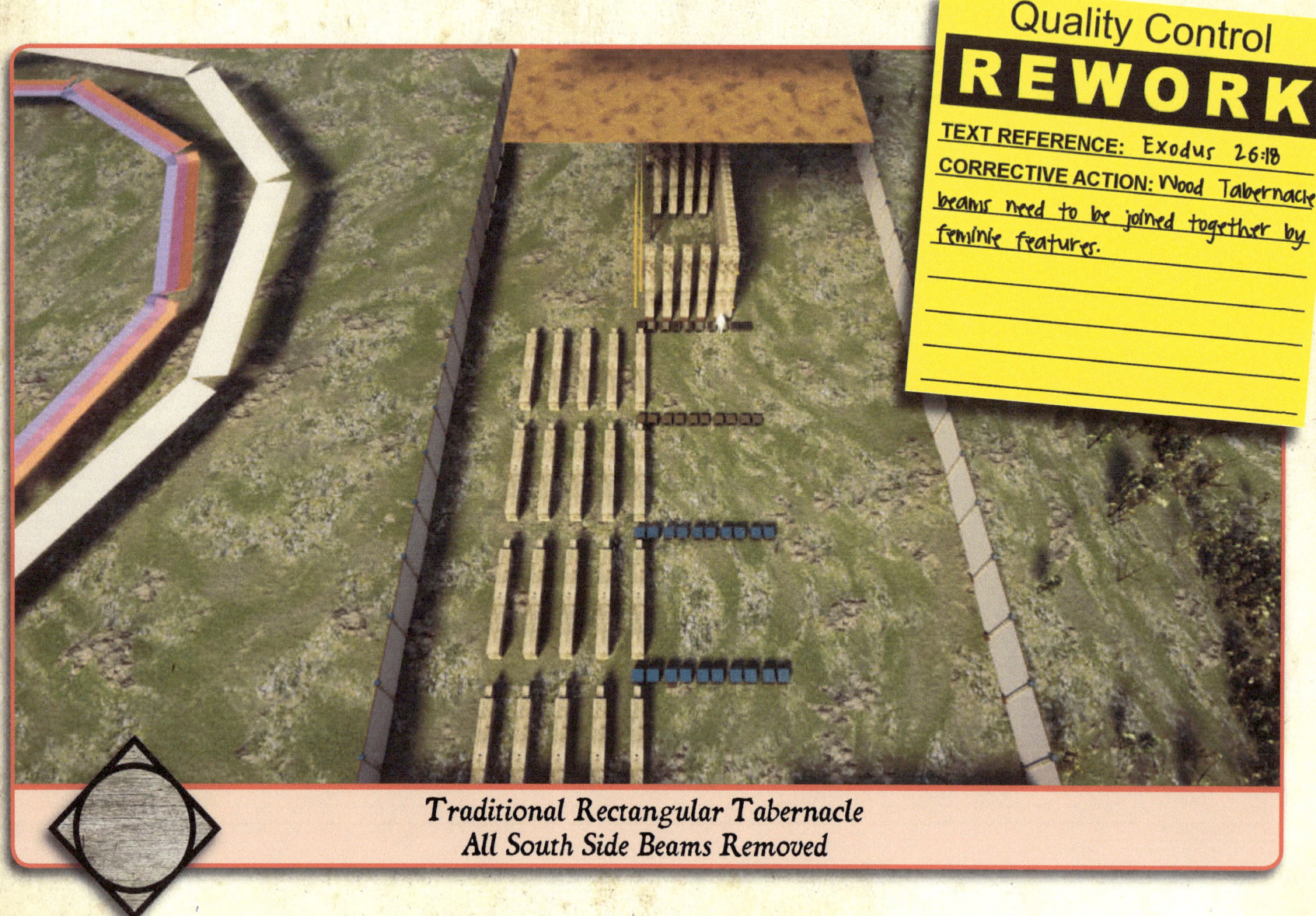

Traditional Rectangular Tabernacle
All South Side Beams Removed

Quality Control REWORK

TEXT REFERENCE: Exodus 26:18
CORRECTIVE ACTION: Wood Tabernacle beams need to be joined together by feminine features.

Beam Layout: South & Rightward

"And thou shalt make the boards for the tabernacle, twenty boards on the south side southward."

~ Exodus 26:18, KJV ~

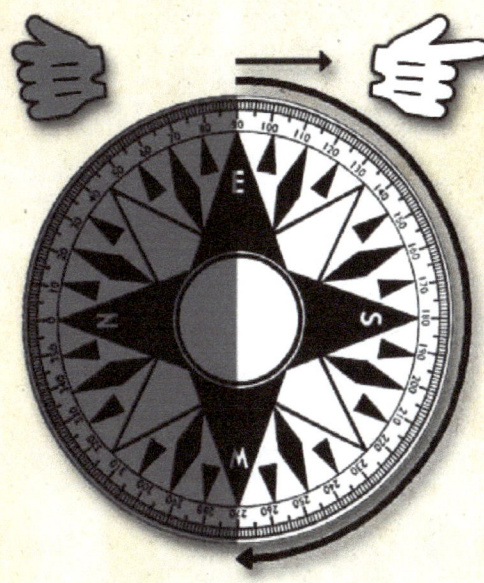

Rather than using north, Hebrews associated east with an origin, and would use it as a starting point. Facing east, south is toward the right. Tabernacle beams were to be placed toward the south and toward the right.

span thin flexible canvas-like materials to create roofs and walls, is it reasonable to assume that massive beams are stood vertically and butted together side-by-side? Not only is this approach completely without precedent throughout the history of tent making, but it's even impractical to apply this technique in permanent structures. Where tents use poles and fabric, typical houses use 2 x 4 studs spaced at some distance in order to span the drywall or paneling. Acknowledging universal construction precedents, it makes more sense to take the text literally and at face value as it reads, "the beam ten cubits length, and (a) cubit, and half the cubit wide" as 10 x 1 x ½ cubits, not 10 x 1½ x 1 cubits. After all, a three-dimensional beam would require measurements in three dimensions, in this case one length measurement and two width measurements. Nevertheless, by dropping the third "cubit" reference that is present in the Hebrew, translation bias (i.e., dropping the second of three cubit references, as does as the KJV) encourages the use of a beam measuring three times wider—which also means the beam is three times heavier than need be.

~ South Rib ~

While increasing beam weight provides no benefit, it becomes apparent that rectangular Tabernacle models greatly benefit from wider wood beams, assuming that the beams sit beneath large fabric coverings, which they assume to be rectangular swatches measuring 42 cubits in length. By supposing beams measuring 1½ cubits in width, the south wall is calculated to span at least 30 cubits, as 20 wood beams are allocated to the south side. Without expanding the individual beam size from 1 cubit to 1½ cubits by means of interpretation, the rectangular Tabernacle's wall measurement would be reduced from 300 to 20 cubits, thereby making it difficult to correlate the fabric roof assembly above, which measures 42 cubits with a building frame beneath measuring only 20 cubits. But does the text even call for vertical abutting beams?

Beams to the South Side Southward

Along with what often appears to be obscure information, such as curtain quantities, ancient units of measure, and specified lengths, sometimes English Bible language seems… odd. In particular, these twenty Tabernacle beams are to be arranged "on the south side southward". What does this exactly mean? According to the Hebrew, the boards are not placed "on the

The House of El Shaddai

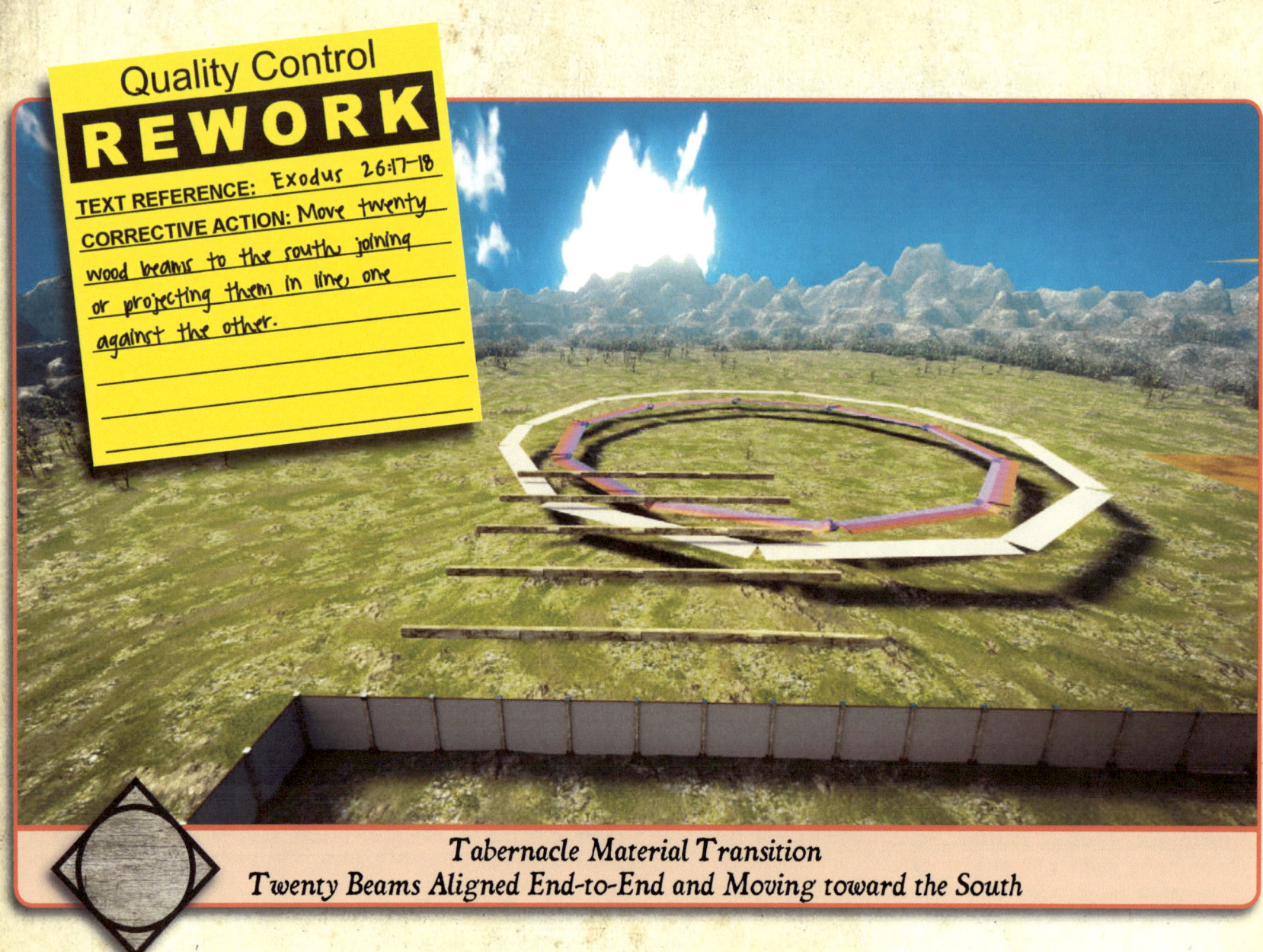

Quality Control REWORK

TEXT REFERENCE: Exodus 26:17-18

CORRECTIVE ACTION: Move twenty wood beams to the south, joining or projecting them in line, one against the other.

Tabernacle Material Transition
Twenty Beams Aligned End-to-End and Moving toward the South

God's Dwelling Place Reconsidered

Clockwise is Rotation Rightward of Center

Hand Fan - Wood Braces Spanned Radially

Australian Sundial - Counterclockwise Markings

south side southward, but rather, "to edge toward the south and toward the right". Of course, this description requires further explanation, as it demands a point of reference or origin.

While most modern maps and navigation gear use magnetic north as the primary point of reference (perhaps as a result of the advent of the compass in navigation) it is of note that the ancient Hebrews used the east—the direction of the sunrise—as their principal point of reference. Given this orientation standard, it is of significance that the first time the Tabernacle was erected, it was in the springtime, probably during the solar equinox when it is simple to determine due east. These correlations further underscore the literal rendering of the Hebrew—"to edge toward the south and toward the right"—in favor of the "south side southward" translation. As the Tabernacle was first erected, the morning shadow could be used to define cardinal compass points, and beam alignment would be accomplished by sweeping an arc through the entire southern compass circle in a clockwise direction. Of course, it would be absurd to expect for a culture that is unfamiliar with clocks as they are known today to use a term like "clockwise", but it is perhaps more absurd to say that ancient Israelites did not know how to comprehend or express something as simple as direction of rotation. Even to this day, people understand what it means to turn valve knobs and wheels "to the right", which is universally understood in English dialects to mean in a clockwise direction.

Why Twenty Planks?

Along with the clockwise and fanned out orientation of southern beams, there is the issue of the southern plank quantities. Why twenty planks? On a rectangular model, the reasons for using exactly twenty planks to create a Tabernacle side seem to be virtually nonexistent. After all, it

The House of El Shaddai

Quality Control APPROVED

TEXT REFERENCE: Exodus 26:17-18
VALIDATION BASIS: Twenty beams are placed clockwise and toward the south. Beams are grouped in 5 sets of 4 to correspond with the linen curtain quantities (Exodus 26:3).

Round Hebrew Tabernacle
Twenty Beams Placed Clockwise on the South Side

Round Hebrew Tabernacle
Twenty South Side Beams Stood Upright

is apparent from literal Exodus descriptions that the joined curtains were not intended to form rectangular assemblies; it is apparent that no curtain feature or apparatus has been identified for attaching the fabrics to the Tabernacle wall planks; and it is apparent that the southern beams do not form a wall measuring 30 cubits if the wood beams were stacked side-by-side.

What if the beams were rearranged into five sets, which were stacked vertically and joined end-to-end? While it might be perceived to be arbitrary to rearrange the twenty south beams into five groups of four, it is of note that the ten linen curtains were configured with blue loops at both ends, and of equal relevance, were joined together in two sets of five.

South Silver Controllers

In addition to arranging twenty beams "toward the south and toward the right", the Exodus text calls for forty silver parts to be created, which were to be placed "underneath" the twenty wood beams. Biased by bad curtain and wood beam assumptions, rectangular models depict silver hardware as being installed "under" the twenty beams (Exodus 26:19), that is, employing silver parts (translated as "sockets" or "bases") to position or anchor the beams, which are assumed to be oriented in perfect vertical alignment. But does this configuration and translation make sense from a physical construction standpoint, much less from a linguistic or anatomical standpoint?

Traditional "Socket" Talents

While the "socket" or "base" terminology is used to describe silver parts in English Bible translations, to really appreciate the disconnect between the translation language and the real-world application, the silver must be quantified and its proposed purpose or function must be reexamined. First of all, a quick but careful study of the Bible's material inventory specifications (Exodus 38:25-27) reveals a stark contrast between the silver allocated in the texts (1 Kikar [a.k.a., "Talent"] per piece, about ~75 pounds / 34 kg) and that which is described in commentaries or depicted in traditional rectangular Tabernacle model illustrations. Although silver part weights are clearly given, there are no corresponding physical dimensions listed in Exodus texts to describe the size or shape of these silver pieces. Despite the lack of size and shape specifications, traditional sources typically portray these silver "sockets" or "bases" as being shaped to match the footprint of

"And of the hundred talents of silver were cast the sockets of the sanctuary, and the sockets of the vail; an hundred sockets of the hundred talents, a talent for a socket."

~ Exodus 38:27, KJV ~

How Heavy are Silver Talents?

The Hebrew kikar is associated with the ancient talent measurements used elsewhere. Generally thought to weigh 70 or 75 lbs, some ancient talents were as light as 46 lbs and as heavy as 130 lbs.

"And thou shalt make forty sockets of silver under the twenty boards; two sockets under one board for his two tenons, and two sockets under another board for his two tenons."

~ Exodus 26:19, KJV ~

God's Dwelling Place Reconsidered

Quality Control REJECTED

TEXT REFERENCE: Exodus 26:19
BASIS FOR FAILURE: Forty south silver sockets far exceed silver allotted in Exodus 38:27. If reduced to the specified size, sockets would not be capable of standing beams upright.

Traditional Rectangular Tabernacle
Forty South Silver "Sockets" or "Bases"

The House of El Shaddai

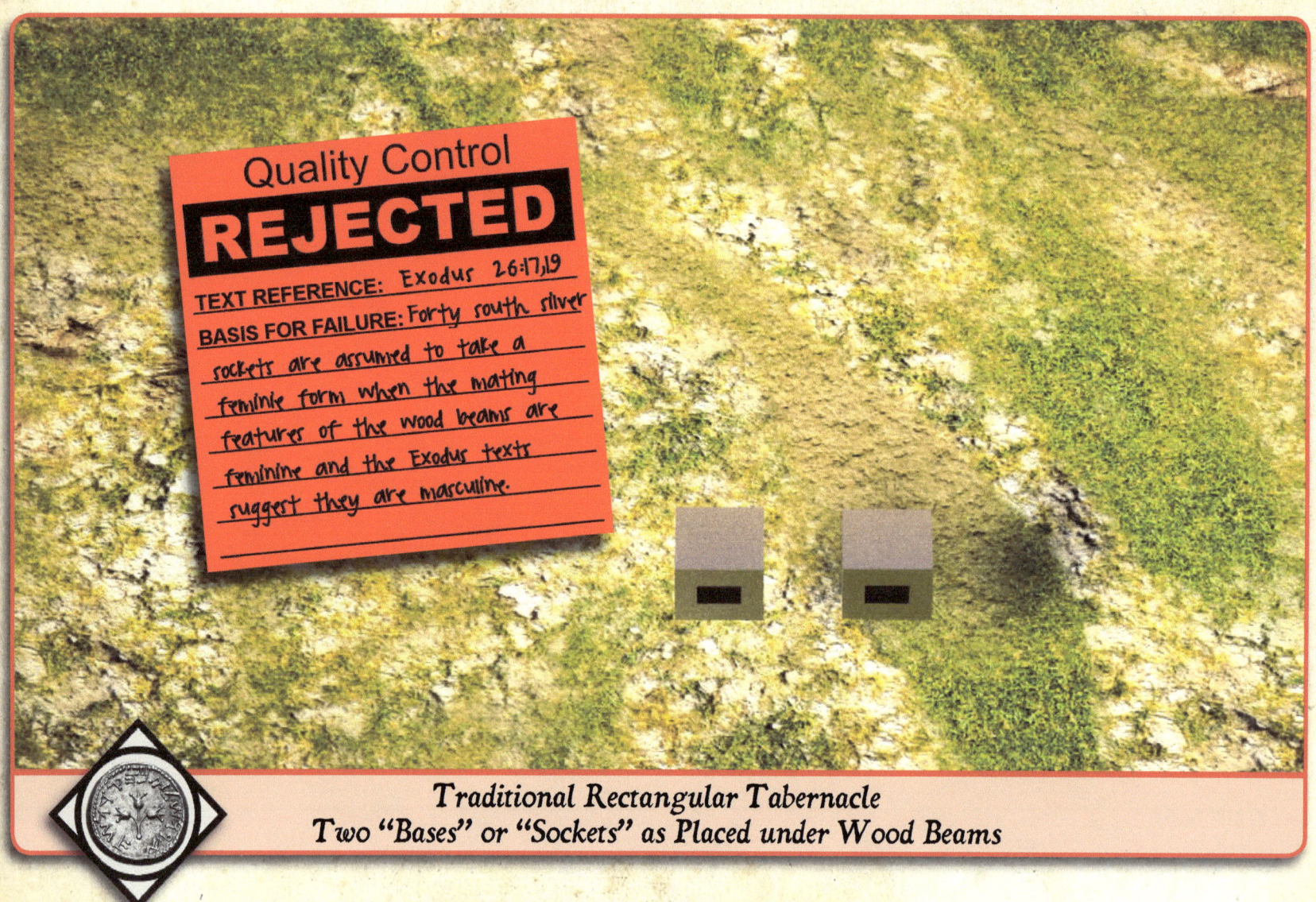

Quality Control
REJECTED

TEXT REFERENCE: Exodus 26:17,19

BASIS FOR FAILURE: Forty south silver sockets are assumed to take a feminine form when the mating features of the wood beams are feminine and the Exodus texts suggest they are masculine.

Traditional Rectangular Tabernacle
Two "Bases" or "Sockets" as Placed under Wood Beams

Talents Grossly Exaggerated

Silver Socket Size Assumed by Rashi		Common	Egyptian	Sacred	Units
Body	H	1	18	21	25	in
Body	W	1	18	21	25	in
Body	L	0.75	14	16	18.8	in
Socket	H	1	18	21	25	in
Socket	W	0.5	9	11	12.5	in
Socket	L	0.25	4.5	5.3	6.25	in
Volume		0.625	2.1	3.3	5.65	ft³
			60	95	160	liters
Weight		75	1383	2196	3704	lbs
		34	628	998	1684	kg
Sizing Error			18.4	29.3	49.4	times

Many Tabernacle models depict massive silver "sockets" or "bases" holding wood beams upright. Irrespective of nominal cubit size (between 18 and 25 inches), the assumed hollow block dimensions as shown above far exceed the silver quantity allotted. Only 1 talent (or 1 Hebrew kikar, approximately 75 lbs) is allotted for each piece per Exodus 38:27.

the wood beams above, externally measuring 1 H x ¾ W x 1 D, with internal holes measuring 1 H x ¼ W x ½ D. Assuming these dimensions, the silver that would occupy this space could weigh approximately 3,700 pounds, depending on the cubit and talent standards assumed. Putting this into perspective, each of the one hundred silver "sockets" depicted in traditional models would each weigh as much as an average car. Not only would such heavy pieces seriously compromise the tent's mobility, but more importantly, each "socket" might weigh almost 50 times more than what was specified, thus grossly exaggerating the talents described in Bible texts (Exodus 38:27).

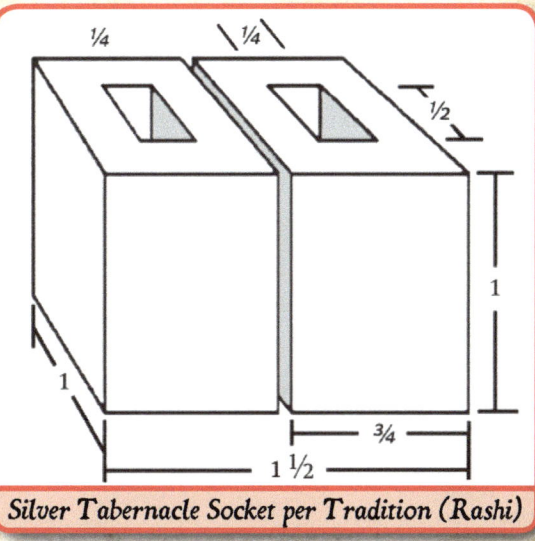
Silver Tabernacle Socket per Tradition (Rashi)

Although some rectangular models incorporate silver limitations as imposed by Bible texts, the purpose of silver "bases" beneath the large wood planks seems to remain enigmatic for proposed rectangular models. Usually, massive silver blocks are thought to anchor the large wood beams in place, offering vertical support for the planks through a tenon and socket approach. However, assuming a more accurate silver ingot size, it becomes clear that the two "bases" with a combined weight of about 150 lbs are simply not capable of keeping large wood beams—measuring 15 to 20 feet high and weighing as much as 4,500 lbs each—from toppling over. In other words, there is no way that the specified silver quantity could help retain the beams in an upright or vertical

Traditional Sockets Far Exceed 1 Talent

The House of El Shaddai

Tabernacle Material Transition
One of Two Silver Sockets Transformed into a Controlling Pin

orientation. Given a rectangular tent arrangement, the bases beneath the beams might be assumed to be used as aligning apparatus or equipment pads—marginally elevating part of the beam off the dirt floor. This, of course, is hardly a fitting use for a precious metal like silver, not to mention a relatively ineffective method of protecting the wood beams from the elements below or uniting the large beams above, given the minimal thickness of the silver base.

Gender Confusion

Unlike English, the Hebrew language is very gender-specific; genders are ascribed to all objects, and the Tabernacle description is no exception. However, in the case of the Tabernacle, it seems that the Hebrew-based gender relationships are not consistently conveyed or preserved in English translations. For example, the Hebrew noun for "arm" or "hand", which is usually used in masculine form, is uniquely used in the Hebrew Exodus Tabernacle texts in the plural feminine form to describe features in the wood beams. Likewise, the Hebrew noun used to describe the silver parts is found in the masculine form in the Hebrew texts.

Nevertheless, despite the deliberate linguistic nuance, gender relationships seems to be inverted in both traditional models and translations. Traditional models seem to universally employ a pair of "tenons", which are customarily depicted as protruding fingers on the bottom of the beam, i.e., male elements. Likewise, traditional wood beams employ two silver female "sockets" beneath, which are thought to receive the two "tenons" of the beam above. Assuming this, traditional models and English translation fit "hand-in-glove". But are they reasonable or accurate as they handle such seemingly trivial details without deference to Hebrew gender distinctions?

What if the wood beam and silver elements were shaped according to gender, as specified in the Hebrew texts, and correlated to genders, as is customary in modern-day English hardware connotations? The wood beams, for example, are not described in Hebrew as having protruding arms (which are male) but rather something more like gloves (i.e., housings or sleeves equipped to receive protruding fingers or arms). Likewise, the word almost universally translated as "socket" or "base" actually is a masculine term and spelled the same as the Hebrew word for "lord", which does not convey a feminine thing, but rather something that governs or controls another thing; or, like a judge, as something capable of opposing strong forces in order to keep things in balance. From these

"Male and Female He Created Them"

Male and Female are Distinct Forms

Tradition and mistranslation result in the inversion of Tabernacle hardware genders relative to the Hebrew terms.

Tabernacle Hardware Genders

	Item Description	Source	Gender
S I L V E R	Lords	Hebrew Bible	Male
	Sockets or Bases	Traditional Model	Female
	Controlling Pins or Rods	Round Model	Male
W O O D	Gloves or Sleeves	Hebrew Bible	Female
	Tenons	Traditional Model	Male
	Holes or Facets	Round Model	Female

~ 66 ~

The House of El Shaddai

Quality Control
REWORK
TEXT REFERENCE: Exodus 26:19
CORRECTIVE ACTION: Change shape of silver socket base to a masculine object weighing only 1 talent and capable of controlling beam motion and balancing lateral loads.

Tabernacle Material Transition
Silver Socket Transformed into Controlling Rod

Gender Identities Restored

Male Electric Plug and Female Socket

Hebrew Exodus texts use descriptive and gender-specific terminology to describe male and female Tabernacle parts. Gender-specific terminology is also used to identify parts in English.

Male Pipe Thread and Female Pipe Elbow

combined descriptions, it stands to reason that the wood beams would be fashioned with holes, as is consistent with a feminine object, whereas the male silver hardware would be designed to protrude and be inserted into the feminine hardware.

Finally, there is the matter of the beam orientation and the shapes of the silver "controllers" as they are placed beneath or inserted into the wood beams. The Exodus

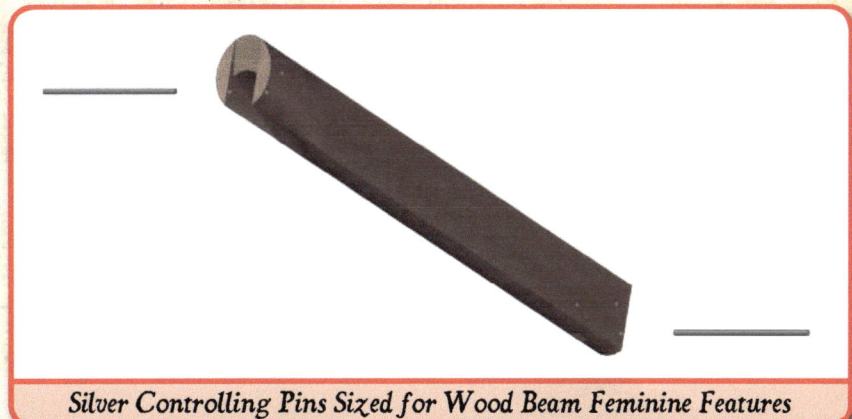

Silver Controlling Pins Sized for Wood Beam Feminine Features

text describes feminine features at both ends of the beams, but it also describes how two silver controllers are installed "under" the beams. How is it possible to use such a small amount of silver in conjunction with such large beams in a meaningful way, whereby the purpose of the silver hardware (i.e., as "controllers") is realized? With the small amount of silver provided for each part, there is hardly enough silver to form some sort of exterior coupling that is large enough or strong enough to join abutting beam ends, but there is enough to create a silver pin.

Presuming that the beams are arranged in an orientation described in the Hebrew texts, that is, "toward the south and toward the right", as well as "to the edge" of the Tabernacle, as the text indicates (Exodus 26:18), it stands to reason that the silver controller must be shaped in a way that it may join one plank to the next one which projects from it (Exodus 26:17). As proposed above, a simple way to accomplish this task would be to form the silver into the shape of a pin and place it in the hole which is in effect "under" the bottom of each beam. As for the remaining controlling silver element that is also to be placed beneath each beam, it stands to reason from texts that follow that it could be shaped into a long rod in order to maintain the form of the wood beams assembly, which has yet to be addressed as it is as described in the next verse of Exodus.

The House of El Shaddai

Quality Control REWORK

TEXT REFERENCE: Exodus 26:19
CORRECTIVE ACTION: Change shape of all 40 silver bases or sockets to pairs of pins/rods.

Tabernacle Material Transition
Twenty Silver Controlling Pins and Twenty Controlling Rods

God's Dwelling Place Reconsidered

Quality Control
REWORK
TEXT REFERENCE: Exodus 26:19
CORRECTIVE ACTION: Move 40 silver controllers so they are under 20 wood beams joined together.

Tabernacle Material Transition
Forty Silver Controllers Moved South toward Round Model

The House of El Shaddai

Quality Control
REWORK
TEXT REFERENCE: Exodus 26:17-19
CORRECTIVE ACTION: Align silver pins to sleeves in wood beams.

Round Hebrew Tabernacle
Silver Controlling Pins and Rods Elevated to Join South Side Beams

God's Dwelling Place Reconsidered

Quality Control APPROVED
TEXT REFERENCE: Exodus 26:17-19
VALIDATION BASIS: 40 silver controllers are installed under 20 south wood beams and joined together via sleeves in wood beams.

Round Hebrew Tabernacle
Two Silver Controllers Placed Beneath Each Wood Beam

~ North Rib ~

After describing twenty beams "toward the south and toward the right", the Exodus text continues by describing the second "side" of the Tabernacle (Exodus 26:20-21). The Bible doesn't exactly continue by describing the west side, or by specifying how to make the Tabernacle wall "to the north side northward", but it does use a special term to articulate the frame's overall shape. More specifically, the term that is often translated as "side" is actually referring to a "rib" in Hebrew.

This Exodus reference to a "second rib" is not only instrumental in defining equipment on the north side of the Tabernacle, but it is also key in conveying configuration information about the southern "side" of the Tabernacle. Clearly, the preceding southern frame section would logically be identified as the "first rib"; after all, both the north and south assemblies are comprised of the same number of wood and silver pieces, implying frame symmetry.

Finally, the two curved south and north tent "ribs" are designed to work with previously identified hardware. The linen curtains are joined into two sets of five; similarly, the forty wood beams would be ganged into two sets of five ribs. Also, the silver controlling pins and rods are ideal for shaping wood beams into curved rib assemblies, as the pins would be used to join wood beams end to end, and the rods would be used for keeping the rib beam ends in position and counteracting compressive rib beam loads. As such, Exodus specifies south and north "ribs" instead of "walls", "planes", or even "sides".

Two Balanced Tabernacle "Ribs"

"And for the second side of the tabernacle on the north side there shall be twenty boards: And their forty sockets of silver; two sockets under one board, and two sockets under another board."

~ Exodus 26:20-21, KJV ~

The Making of the Tabernacle (North Side Shown), Jan Luyken 1649 – 1712

God's Dwelling Place Reconsidered

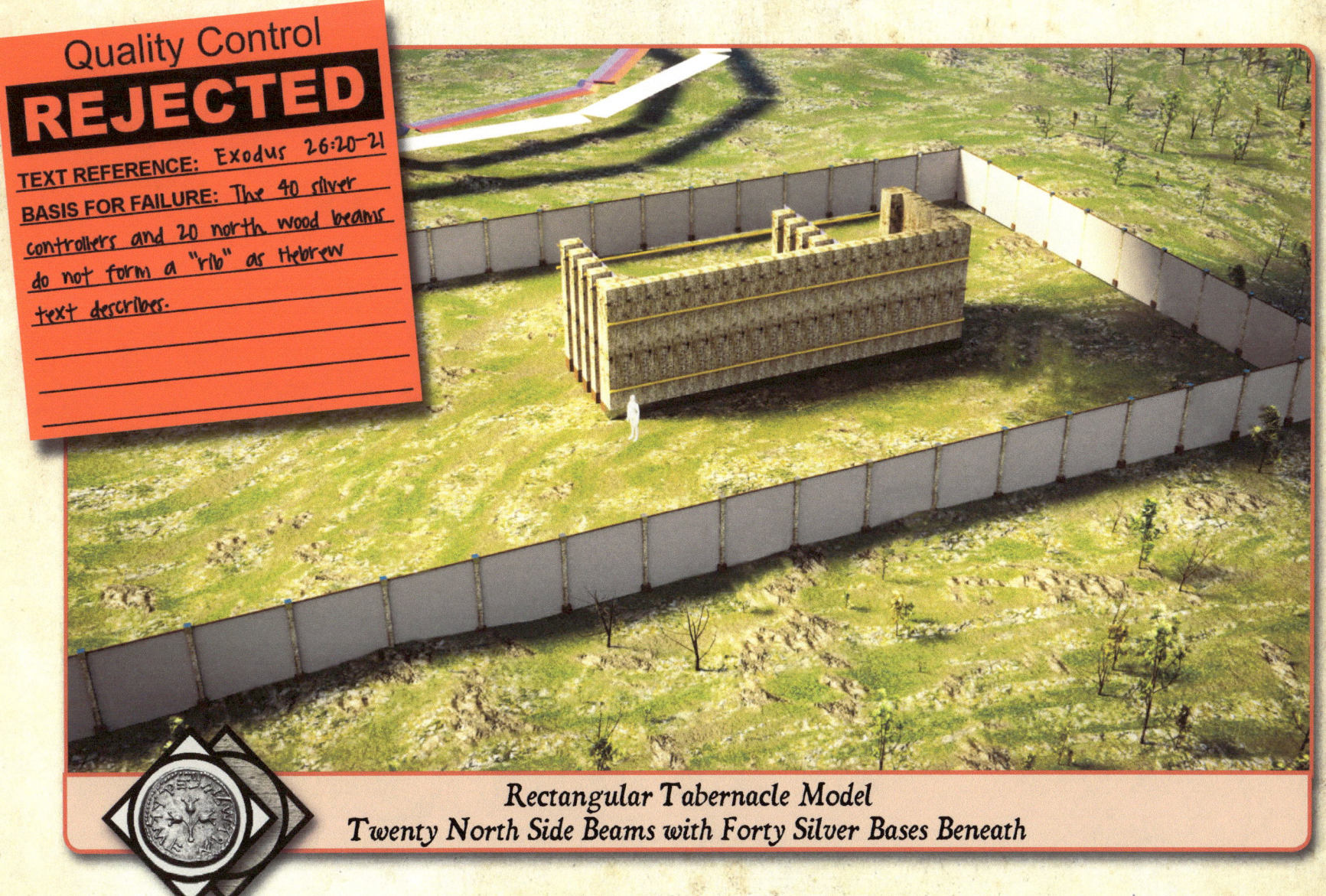

Quality Control
REJECTED
TEXT REFERENCE: Exodus 26:20-21
BASIS FOR FAILURE: The 40 silver controllers and 20 north wood beams do not form a "rib" as Hebrew text describes.

Rectangular Tabernacle Model
Twenty North Side Beams with Forty Silver Bases Beneath

The House of El Shaddai

Tabernacle Material Transition
North Wall Beams and Silver Removed

Quality Control REWORK
TEXT REFERENCE: Exodus 26:20-21
CORRECTIVE ACTION: Remove North wall as created by wood beams and silver controllers.

God's Dwelling Place Reconsidered

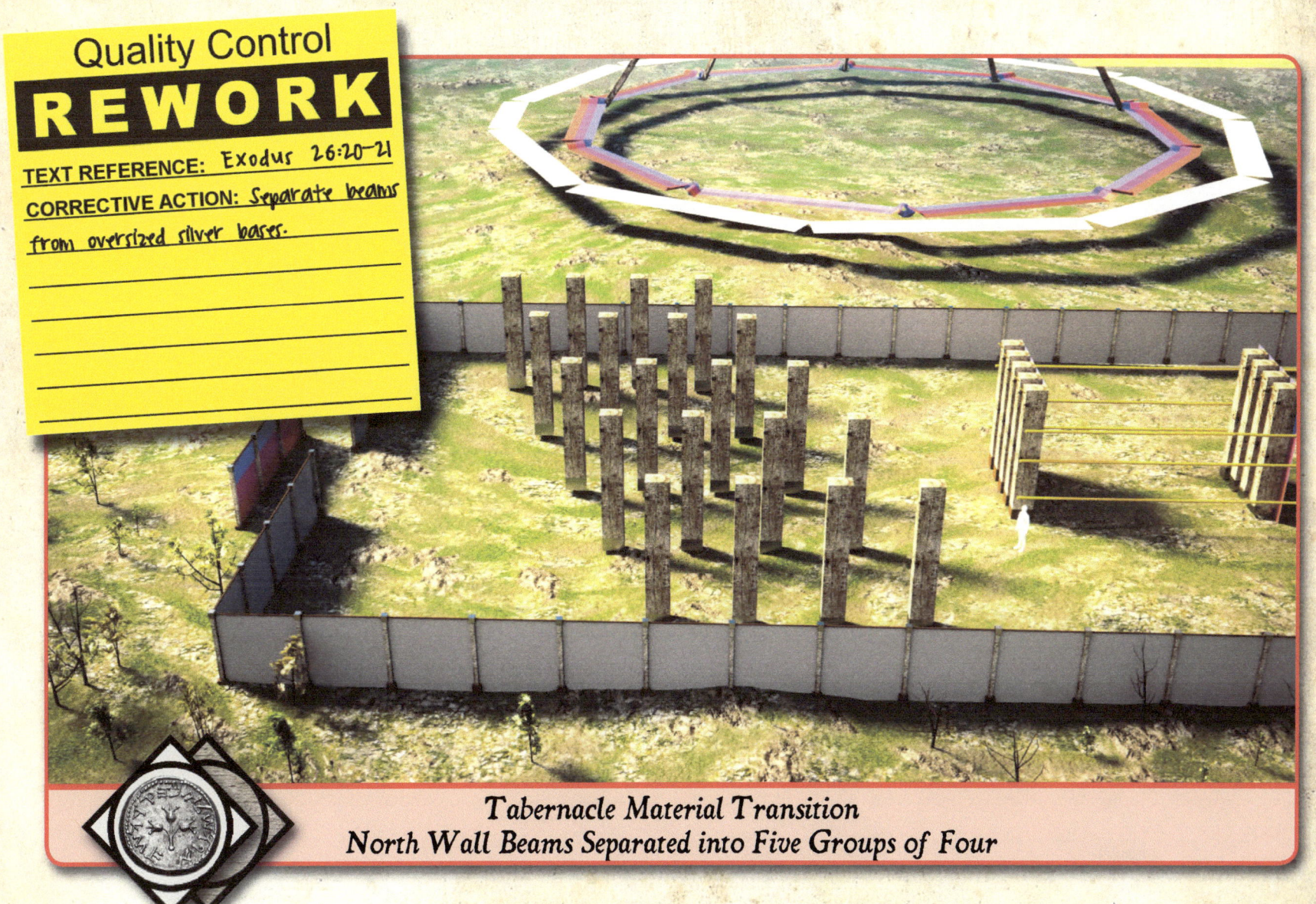

Quality Control REWORK
TEXT REFERENCE: Exodus 26:20-21
CORRECTIVE ACTION: Separate beams from oversized silver bases.

Tabernacle Material Transition
North Wall Beams Separated into Five Groups of Four

The House of El Shaddai

Quality Control
REWORK

TEXT REFERENCE: Exodus 26:20-21
CORRECTIVE ACTION: Reshape north beams and silver bases to match corresponding hardware created for the first / south rib.

Tabernacle Material Transition
North Beams and Silver Parts Aligned End-to-End

God's Dwelling Place Reconsidered

Tabernacle Material Transition
North Beams and Silver Parts Shaped into Five Rib Assemblies

Quality Control REWORK
TEXT REFERENCE: Exodus 26:20-21
CORRECTIVE ACTION: Join north beams and silver bases together to form 5 rib elements to correspond with linen curtain set and opposing southern rib assemblies.

The House of El Shaddai

Quality Control APPROVED

TEXT REFERENCE: Exodus 26:20-21
VALIDATION BASIS: Install north rib assemblies in continued clockwise fashion opposite of south rib assemblies.

Round Hebrew Tabernacle
Rib Assemblies Placed on North Side

God's Dwelling Place Reconsidered

Round Hebrew Tabernacle
Five North Rib Assemblies Installed

Quality Control APPROVED

TEXT REFERENCE: Exodus 26:20-21

VALIDATION BASIS: North side is complete with 20 beams and 40 silver controllers, assuming the shape of a curved rib.

~ Ring Assembly ~

Following Bible descriptions of two opposing Tabernacle rib halves, the Exodus text introduces descriptions of what is traditionally presumed to be the third or western wall of the Tabernacle (Exodus 26:22-25). While traditional Tabernacle models generally seem to agree upon this third or western wall arrangement—presuming west beams and silver hardware to be almost identical to those used on the south and north sides—this "west wall" paradigm is simply taken for granted and never seriously challenged. Nevertheless, as other traditional model assumptions now appear to be suspect, the arrangement, location, and purpose of "west" wood beams are also subject to question, especially as hardware etymology and relative position descriptions are reconsidered.

"Westward" Braces

Ironically, understanding the six "westward boards" (Exodus 26:22) from the standpoint of a circular model isn't intuitive for people living in so-called "western" cultures. As indicated previously, Hebrews were not accustomed to using magnetic north as a primary reference direction, but rather thought of east as a point of origin. The sun marks the beginning of daylight as it rises in the East, and likewise, the Tabernacle frame assembly begins in the east. Wood beams are arranged "toward the south and toward the right" or clockwise, forming the first or southern rib, which ultimately concludes in the west. However, following through with northern rib construction, beam layout would logically progress in the clockwise direction, continuing from the west back to the eastern point of origin. Thus, the placement of "westward" boards would be relative to the extreme eastern edge. However, the question, "How far westward?" remains undefined by verse 22 and is not further quantified or qualified by other Exodus texts.

Although all traditional rectangular models assume a west wall comprised of solid wood beams, this is not to say that the "westward" term is consistently applied to rectangular models. For example, some models depict westward boards as being spanned in between the south and north walls, with the west wall's exterior being flush with the west ends of the south and north wall. Others presume that the westward boards create a wall to the west of the ends of the south and north walls. While the different schools of thought may offer what seems be good reason for the

"Westward" is a Relative Location

And for the sides of the tabernacle westward thou shalt make six boards.

~ Exodus 26:22, KJV ~

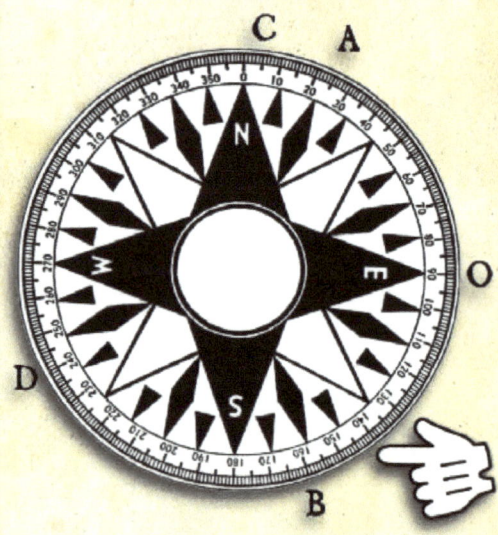

Points A, B, C, and D are all west of O, the eastern point of origin. Likewise, B is west of A, and C is west of B and A, even though Points A, B, and C are all east of the center. Westward is a general or relative direction, and not always a final destination or boundary extremity, as is customarily assumed in rectangular Tabernacle arrangements.

Rectangular Tabernacle Model
Six Bracing Beams on West Side

The House of El Shaddai

Quality Control
REWORK

TEXT REFERENCE: Exodus 26:22
CORRECTIVE ACTION: Reshape six braces to accomodate alternate layout.

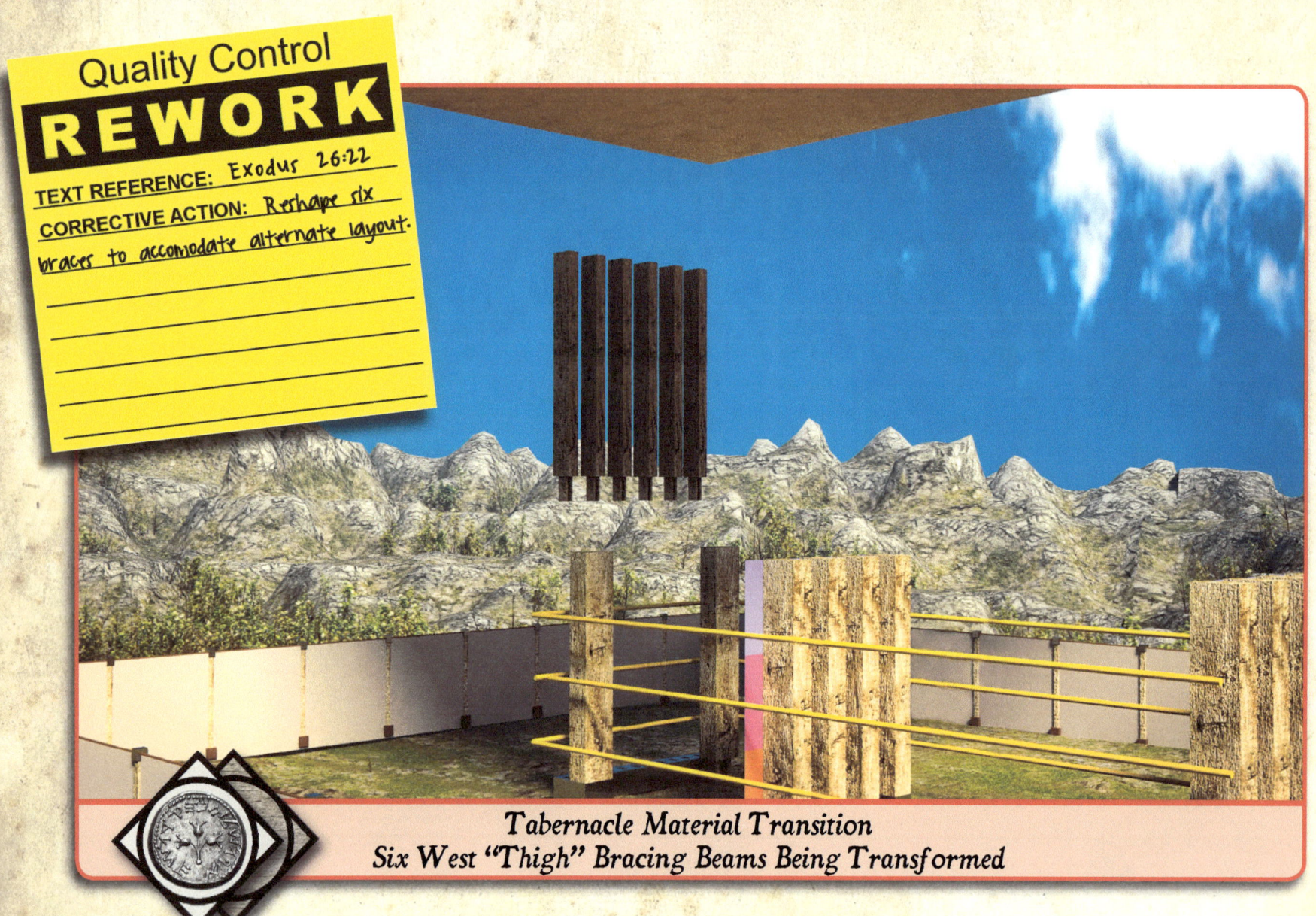

Tabernacle Material Transition
Six West "Thigh" Bracing Beams Being Transformed

Western Wall Beam Arrangement Assumptions

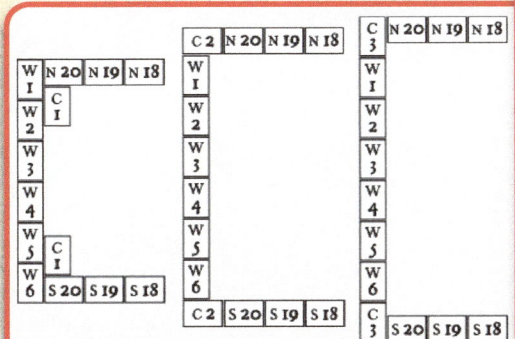

Typical Rectangular Wall Arrangements

Because the overall dimensions of the Tabernacle structure are not included in Moses' writings or other Bible texts, traditional rectangular tent model frames have been depicted a number of different ways. Most models are created assuming that west beams are 1.5 cubits wide, and that the west wall is placed west of the ends of south and north walls. This approach maximizes the overall size of the dwelling place and creates a structure measuring 12 cubits wide in the north-south direction.

"western wall" location, one thing is clear: Terms such as "westward" demand not only a point of origin, but also additional hints, references, or qualification to further define a final location.

Thigh Beams

As for the westward "sides" or "boards", the Hebrew terminology once again better speaks to the configuration, purpose, and location of the six beams. In particular, the Hebrew word translated generically as "side" more specifically refers to a "thigh", which functions as a brace or strong compression member. As the Hebrew term is used in its feminine form, it might also be used to refer to extreme parts or recesses—comparable to the stern section of a wooden ship below deck. While both rectangular and round Tabernacle arrangements might be seen as having recesses or extremities, it seems obvious that beams placed in the upper portion of the round Tabernacle best fit the "thigh" description.

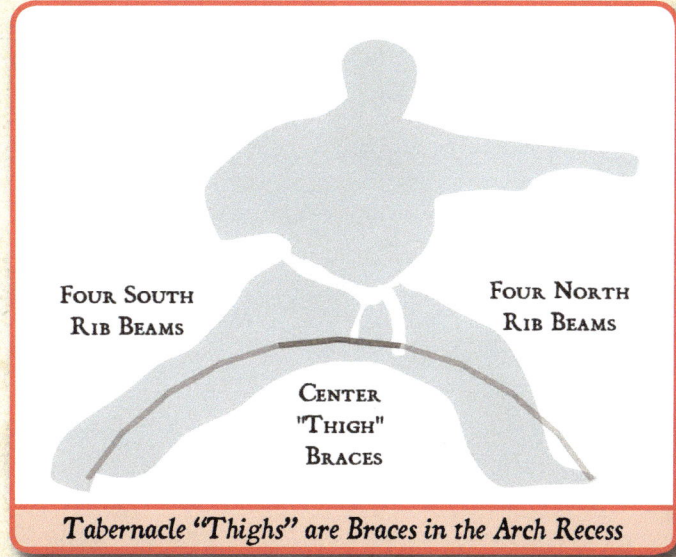

Tabernacle "Thighs" are Braces in the Arch Recess

Not only would the "thigh" term best correspond with the round model in shape and appearance, but also in utility as a "thigh" inherently performs bracing functions. Given that Exodus speaks of two rib sections—one set to the north and one set to the south—the large wood beams would be positioned such that they lean inward. Thus, the six beams that are located "toward the west" would be installed in the center, which is a location that is "westward" relative to the structure's eastern origin. Installed at the structure's center, the "thigh" beams would bear compressive loads as induced by opposing rib assemblies. Conversely, if used to form a west wall in a rectangular frame arrangement, the beams standing in a vertical plane wouldn't be subject to compressive loads or otherwise resemble "thighs".

The House of El Shaddai

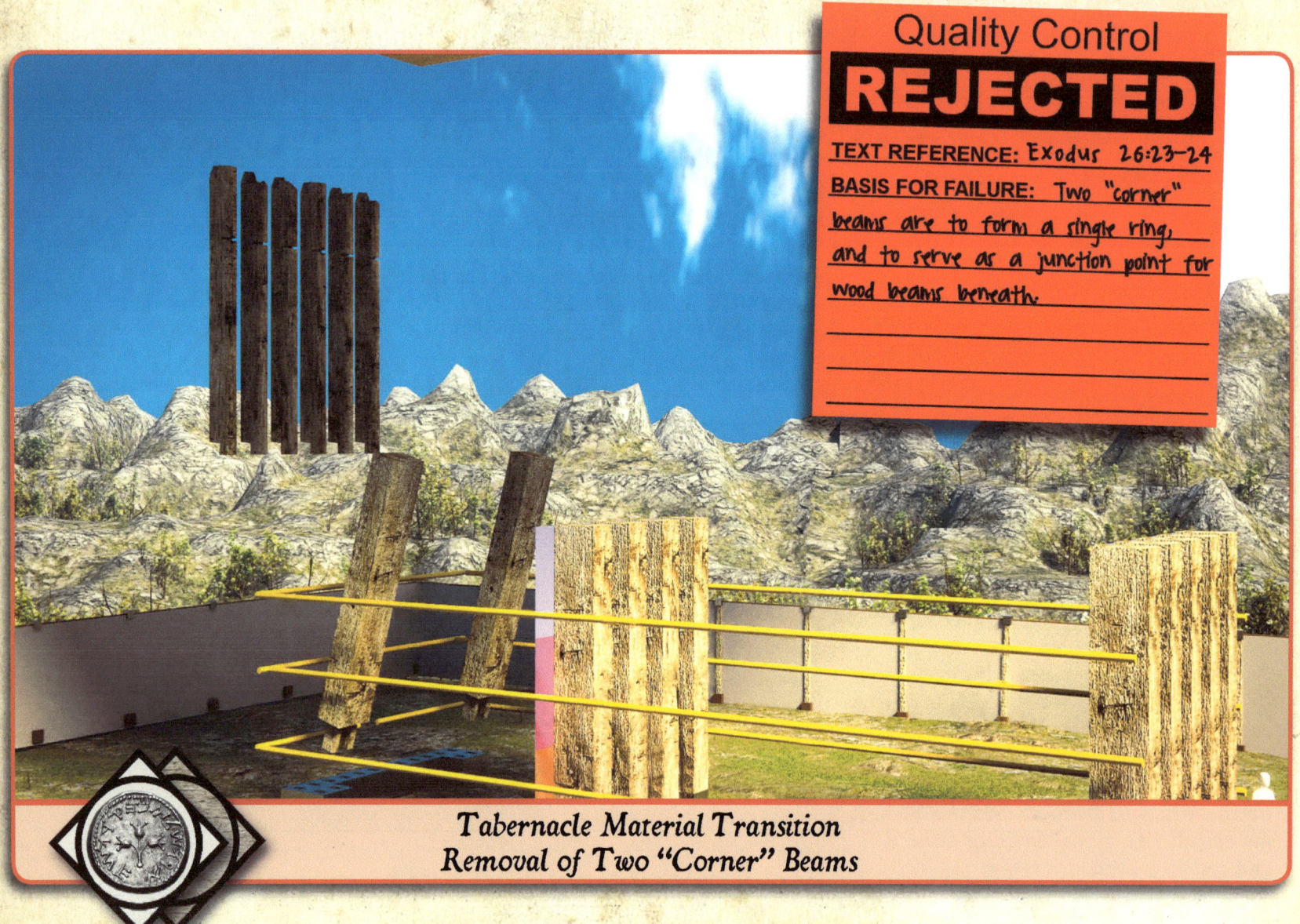

Quality Control
REJECTED

TEXT REFERENCE: Exodus 26:23-24
BASIS FOR FAILURE: Two "corner" beams are to form a single ring, and to serve as a junction point for wood beams beneath.

Tabernacle Material Transition
Removal of Two "Corner" Beams

God's Dwelling Place Reconsidered

Round Corners or Square Ring?

"And two boards shalt thou make for the corners of the tabernacle in the two sides. And they shall be coupled together beneath, and they shall be coupled together above the head of it unto one ring: thus shall it be for them both; they shall be for the two corners."

~ Exodus 26:23-24, KJV ~

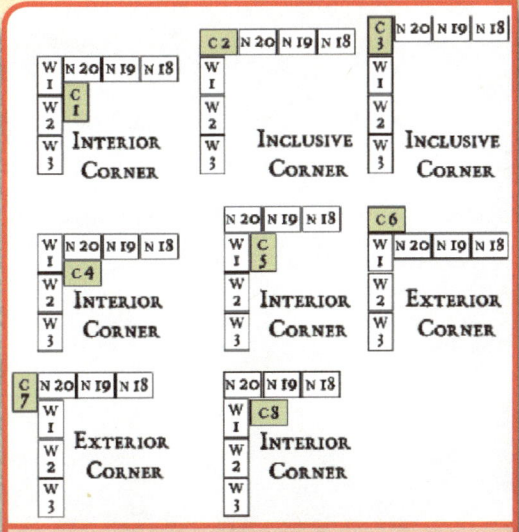

Rectangular Corner Beam Location Options

Wall and corner configurations of traditional models vary, but none of them provide good reinforcement.

While the westward beams in the round model seem to correspond well with the Hebrew "thigh" description, the six wood beams don't seem to correlate with other previously mentioned hardware quantities. How can this be explained, given that there are five linen curtain sets and five ribs on each side, as there are only six thigh braces specified?

Coupling Ribs and Thighs

Given the numerical disconnect between "westward" center braces and the inward leaning rib subassemblies, it stands to reason that some sort of additional hardware is necessary to join the ten south and north ribs to the six inner thighs. Introducing two more wood beams, the Exodus text describes two "corners" used to join the Tabernacle beams together (Exodus 26:23-24). However, the text also describes these two "corners" as being joined "unto one ring", which is quite contrary to the shapes assumed for "corners" of traditional rectangular Tabernacle models.

Compounding the frame arrangement options, traditional tabernacle models generally depict these two corner beams as being installed one of three ways; either in line with the westward plank walls (i.e., adding two beams to the six west wall beams provided), within the structure's interior corner, or on the exterior corner. Regardless of the preferred approach, it is still hard to reconcile some of the English translation, as it still refers to "one ring", which inherently implies something round, or at the very least, something running in a complete circuit. Adding to the confusion, the English term "corner" is typically associated with a 90 degree angle—with polygons being a possible exception. On occasion, rectangular models depict these "ring-corner" beams as two long L-shaped pieces installed on top of the north, south, and west walls (and possibly as C-shaped pieces if spanned over east the side) in order to secure the tops of large vertical beams. But are any of these interpretations valid, given the contrasting square-ring language, as well as the lack of precedent of vertical corner beams within tent making traditions?

Round Ring Corners

While the word translated as "corner" is reinforced by a compounding string of mistranslations, the term is more literally rendered as "segmented circle" from the Hebrew. Assuming these boards are shaped as two half-circles, coupling such hardware together would not only form

The House of El Shaddai

Tabernacle Material Transition
Two "Corner" Beams Extended

Quality Control REWORK

TEXT REFERENCE: Exodus 26:23-24

CORRECTIVE ACTION: Lengthen the corner beams to enable complete interconnection of all ribs and braces.

God's Dwelling Place Reconsidered

Quality Control
REWORK
TEXT REFERENCE: Exodus 26:23-24
CORRECTIVE ACTION: Reshape the corner beams to form a ring shape.

Tabernacle Material Transition
Two "Corner" Beams Bending into Ring Sections

The House of El Shaddai

Tabernacle Material Transition
Six Thigh Braces and Two "Corner" Ring Beams Relocated

God's Dwelling Place Reconsidered

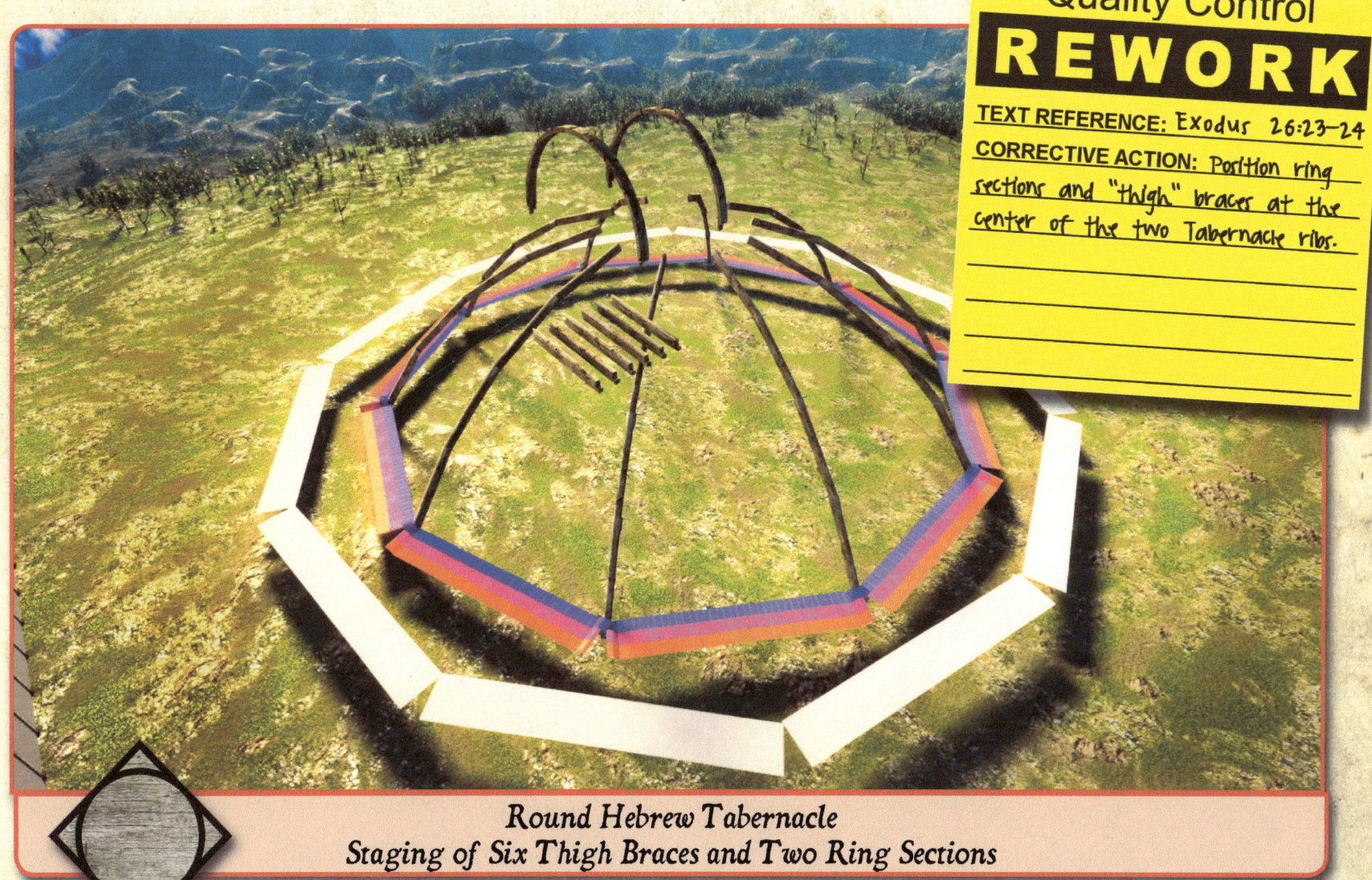

Quality Control REWORK
TEXT REFERENCE: Exodus 26:23-24
CORRECTIVE ACTION: Position ring sections and "thigh" braces at the center of the two Tabernacle ribs.

Round Hebrew Tabernacle
Staging of Six Thigh Braces and Two Ring Sections

The House of El Shaddai

Quality Control REWORK
TEXT REFERENCE: Exodus 26:23-24
CORRECTIVE ACTION: Position ring sections and "thigh" braces at the center of the two Tabernacle ribs.

Round Hebrew Tabernacle
Six Thigh Braces Placed at Apex / Westward of Eastern Origin

God's Dwelling Place Reconsidered

Quality Control APPROVED
TEXT REFERENCE: Exodus 26:23-24
VALIDATION BASIS: Two "corner" sections form a single ring which receives 10 rib assemblies and 6 interior "thigh" braces.

Round Hebrew Tabernacle
Two Ring Segments Installed around Six Thigh Braces

"one ring", but also come together as "the head" above the structure, just as verse 24 describes. Likewise, the two semicircle beam sections coupled together would be ideal for joining the set of ten rib sections to the six center "westward" braces inside the assembly. Not only would it be capable of joining two sides of the Tabernacle, but it would do so in a way whereby the rib plank assemblies would be balanced—and in effect coupled—to its mirror image counterpart, given the symmetry implied previously and as established by the Tabernacle's decagonal curtain set.

Silver Ring Controllers

As in the case of the north and south rib assemblies, Exodus also allocates two silver controllers per beam for the six westward thigh braces and two "ring-corner" sections. Once again, traditional Tabernacle models consistently depict these silver controllers as silver "sockets" or bases, with sizes and shapes that are inconsistent with the Exodus texts, much like hardware assumed for the vertically anchoring north and south beams. But as previously demonstrated, it is apparent that form, function, and vocabulary hardly permit such an impractical explanation.

Used in conjunction with eight wood beams total, including six westward braces and two "corner ring" sections, how are sixteen pins—or other silver controlling apparatus—positioned in a way to control and couple all of the wood beams together?

Pinventory

Given the numerous possibilities of overlapping hardware, pin inventory and appropriation might be compared to a logic puzzle or regarded to be a matter of semantics. For example, if two ring-halves are coupled together by two single pins on opposite sides, does that meet the "two pins under each beam" requirement as specified by Exodus, even though this would result in a configuration where only two pins were used for two boards? Or is it possible that the text is referring to the coupling of the six inner braces to the ring, as well as the ten outer beams to the ring, for a total of sixteen silver pin-joints? Furthermore, if the ring is divided into two halves, which way is it oriented relative to its divisions? And what about the six inner braces (spaced at 60 degree equiangular intervals) relative to the north and south rib-plank assemblies (spaced at 36 degree equiangular intervals)? Do inner thigh-brace pins overlap with outer rib joint pins?

Coupling Ring

Five south rib assemblies are coupled to five opposing north rib assemblies by a two-piece ring, which is reinforced by six inner thigh bracing beams. Silver pins are used to join wood beams.

Segmented Wood Coupling Ring

"And they shall be eight boards, and their sockets of silver, sixteen sockets; two sockets under one board, and two sockets under another board."

~ Exodus 26:25, KJV ~

God's Dwelling Place Reconsidered

Quality Control REJECTED
TEXT REFERENCE: Exodus 26:25
BASIS FOR FAILURE: Silver bases or sockets use more material than specified in Exodus 38:27.

Rectangular Tabernacle Model
Sixteen Oversized Silver Sockets on West End

The House of El Shaddai

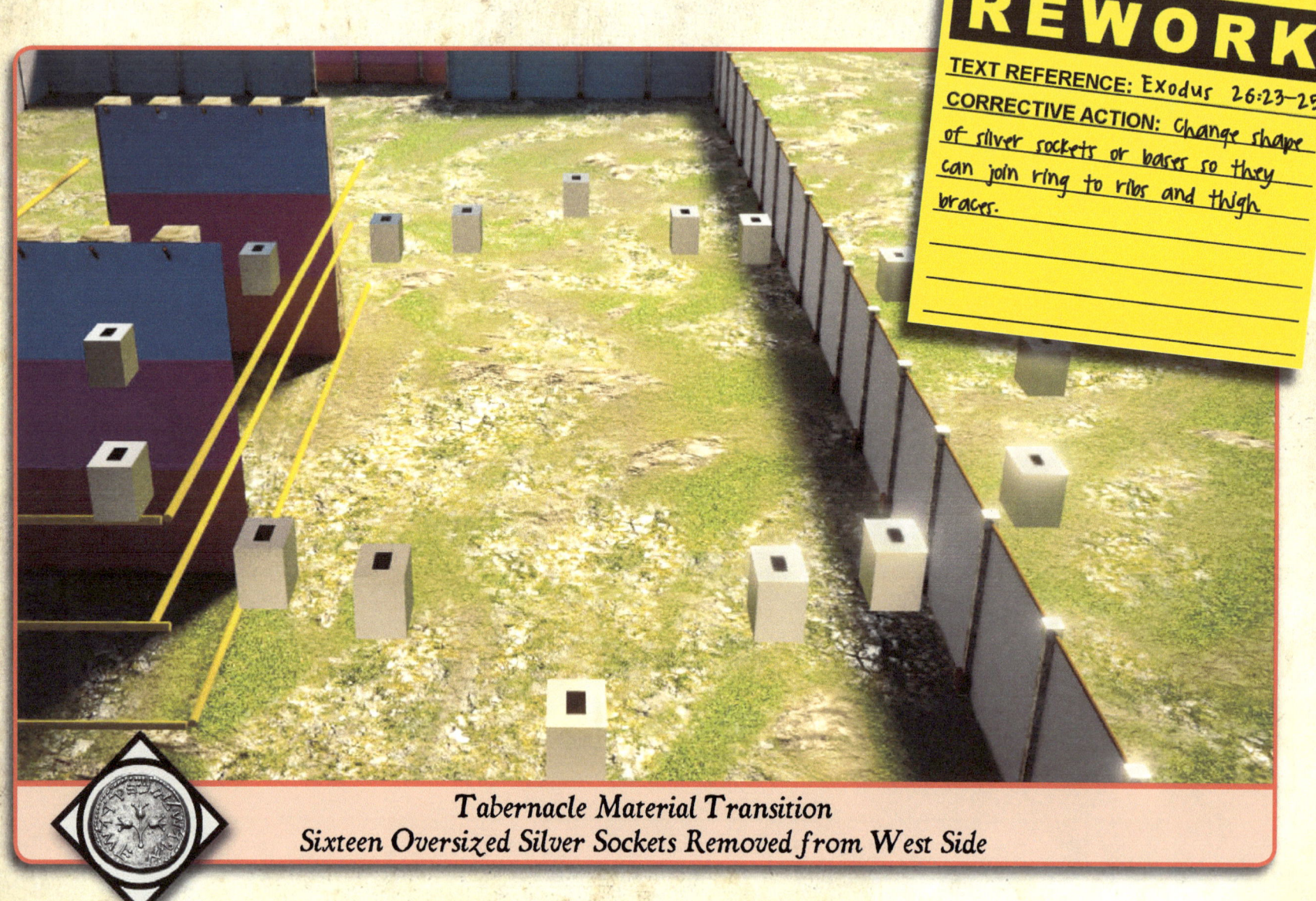

Quality Control REWORK

TEXT REFERENCE: Exodus 26:23-25
CORRECTIVE ACTION: Change shape of silver sockets or bases so they can join ring to ribs and thigh braces.

Tabernacle Material Transition
Sixteen Oversized Silver Sockets Removed from West Side

God's Dwelling Place Reconsidered

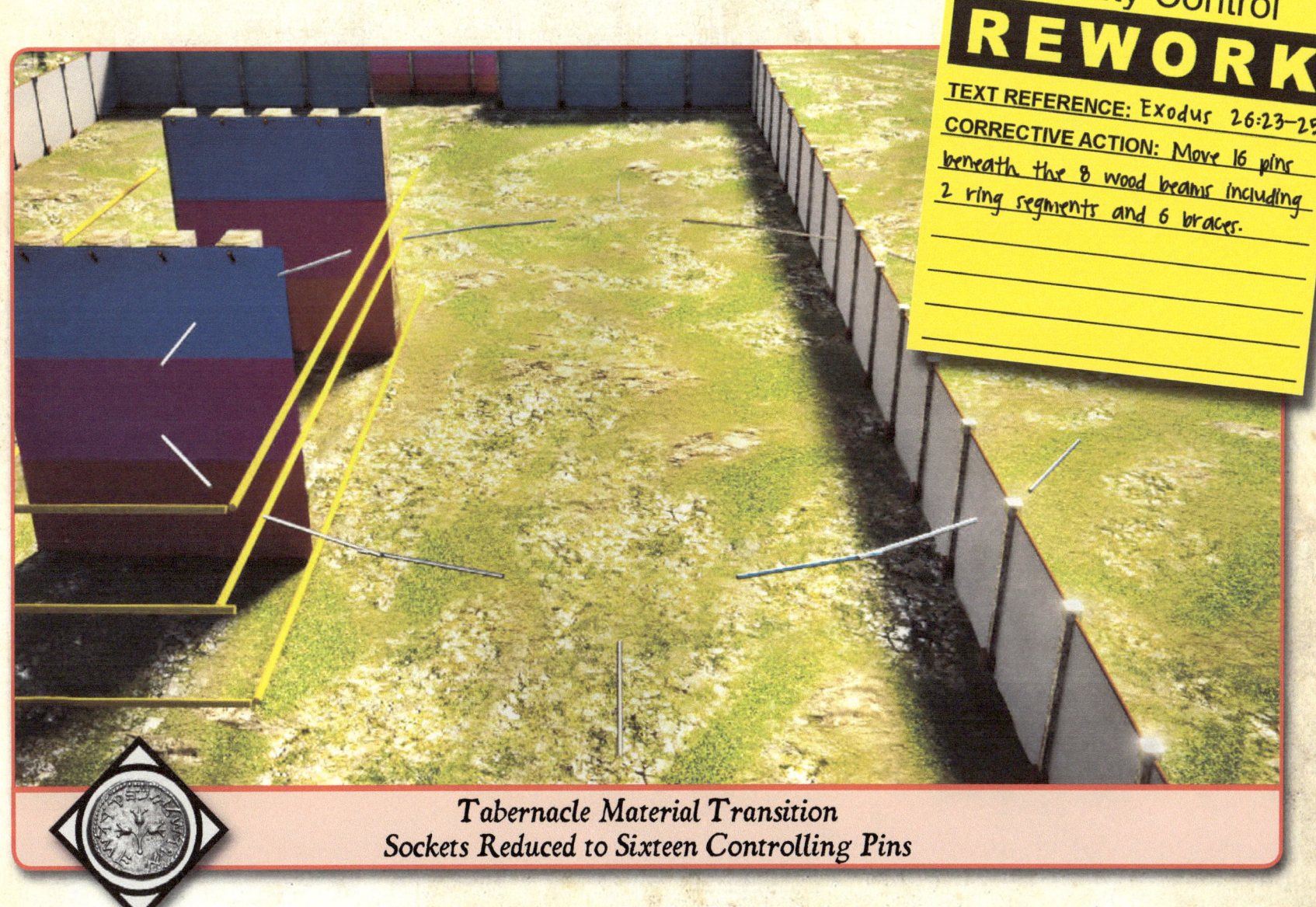

Quality Control REWORK

TEXT REFERENCE: Exodus 26:23-25
CORRECTIVE ACTION: Move 16 pins beneath the 8 wood beams including 2 ring segments and 6 braces.

Tabernacle Material Transition
Sockets Reduced to Sixteen Controlling Pins

The House of El Shaddai

Quality Control
APPROVED

TEXT REFERENCE: Exodus 26:23-25
VALIDATION BASIS: The 16 pins are to be installed beneath the 2 ring sections, 6 braces, and 10 ribs.

Round Hebrew Tabernacle
Sixteen Silver Controlling Pins Installed Beneath Ring Beams

Two Matching Wood Bar Sets

"And thou shalt make bars of shittim wood; five for the boards of the one side of the tabernacle. And five bars for the boards of the other side of the tabernacle..."

~ Exodus 26:26-27a, KJV ~

Middle Bar Piercing South Side Beams

Wood bars are specified in sets of five, starting with five for the first (south) rib and five for the second (north) rib. Bars are often assumed to run through the Tabernacle beams the entire length of the three walls (Exodus 26:28), while other bars are assumed to be installed externally. Other rectangular models assume that all five full length wood bars are all installed externally (right).

Assuming sixteen pins, the most logical way to appropriate them is to use two pins to join the ring halves together, ten pins to join the upper rib planks to the ring halves, followed by the remaining four pins to join four of the six center bracing-planks (with two remaining braces sharing pins with north and south rib planks). This solution accounts for the coupling of beams as described in verse 24, with the understanding that four remaining silver controllers (not introduced until Part 3) are used to ensure that at least two silver parts are placed beneath each individual beam.

~ Tabernacle Bars ~

Introduced without any dimensional specifications, Exodus adds another fifteen "bars"—as opposed to "boards" or "beams"—to the Tabernacle frame assembly, which are grouped in three sets of five and installed "in the midst of the wood board... from end to end" (Exodus 26:26-28).

Once again, being unable to interpret the intention behind these wood "bars", traditional rectangular models attempt to use long wood poles to reinforce Tabernacle walls. However, piercing slender wooden dowels through long holes bored through a solid wall of freestanding wooden beams, or through attached metal rings, is far from standard or prudent building practice, be it for temporary tents or permanent structures. However viable this may look on paper, such an approach would prove to be extremely difficult, impractical, and ineffective in real-life. After all, a "kabob-esque" bar and beam reinforcement arrangement through many tons of hewn lumber would prove to be challenging, if not impossible to align,

Five Horizontal North Bars - Medhurst No. 491

The House of El Shaddai

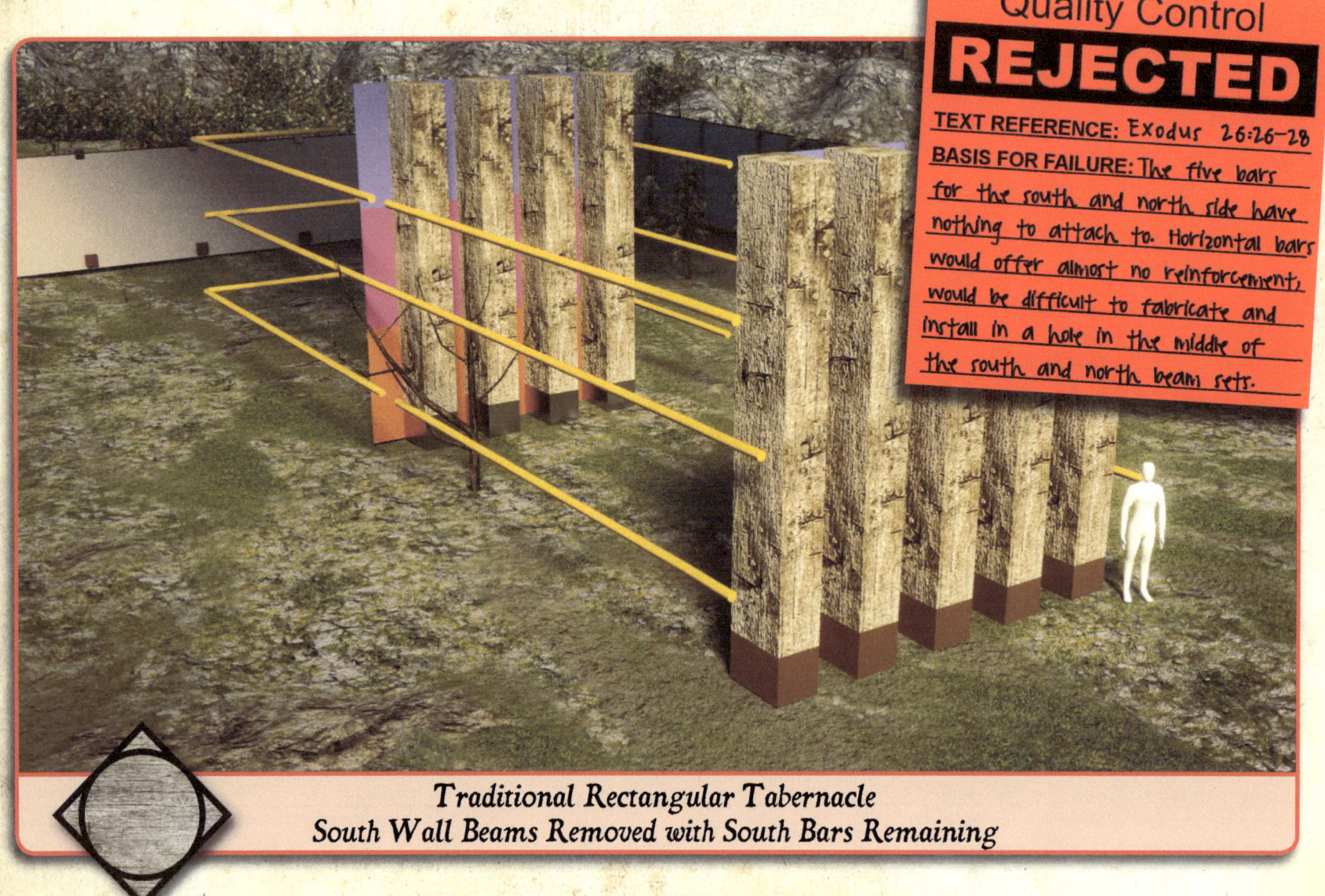

Quality Control
REJECTED

TEXT REFERENCE: Exodus 26:26-28
BASIS FOR FAILURE: The five bars for the south and north side have nothing to attach to. Horizontal bars would offer almost no reinforcement, would be difficult to fabricate and install in a hole in the middle of the south and north beam sets.

Traditional Rectangular Tabernacle
South Wall Beams Removed with South Bars Remaining

God's Dwelling Place Reconsidered

Tabernacle Material Transition
South Bar Transformation

Quality Control REWORK
TEXT REFERENCE: Exodus 26:26-28
CORRECTIVE ACTION: Increase the diameter of the south wood bars.

The House of El Shaddai

Quality Control REWORK

TEXT REFERENCE: Exodus 26:26-28

CORRECTIVE ACTION: Reduce the length of the bars so they are equal and so they correspond with the height of the linen curtains.

Tabernacle Material Transition
South Bars Resized and Reshaped

God's Dwelling Place Reconsidered

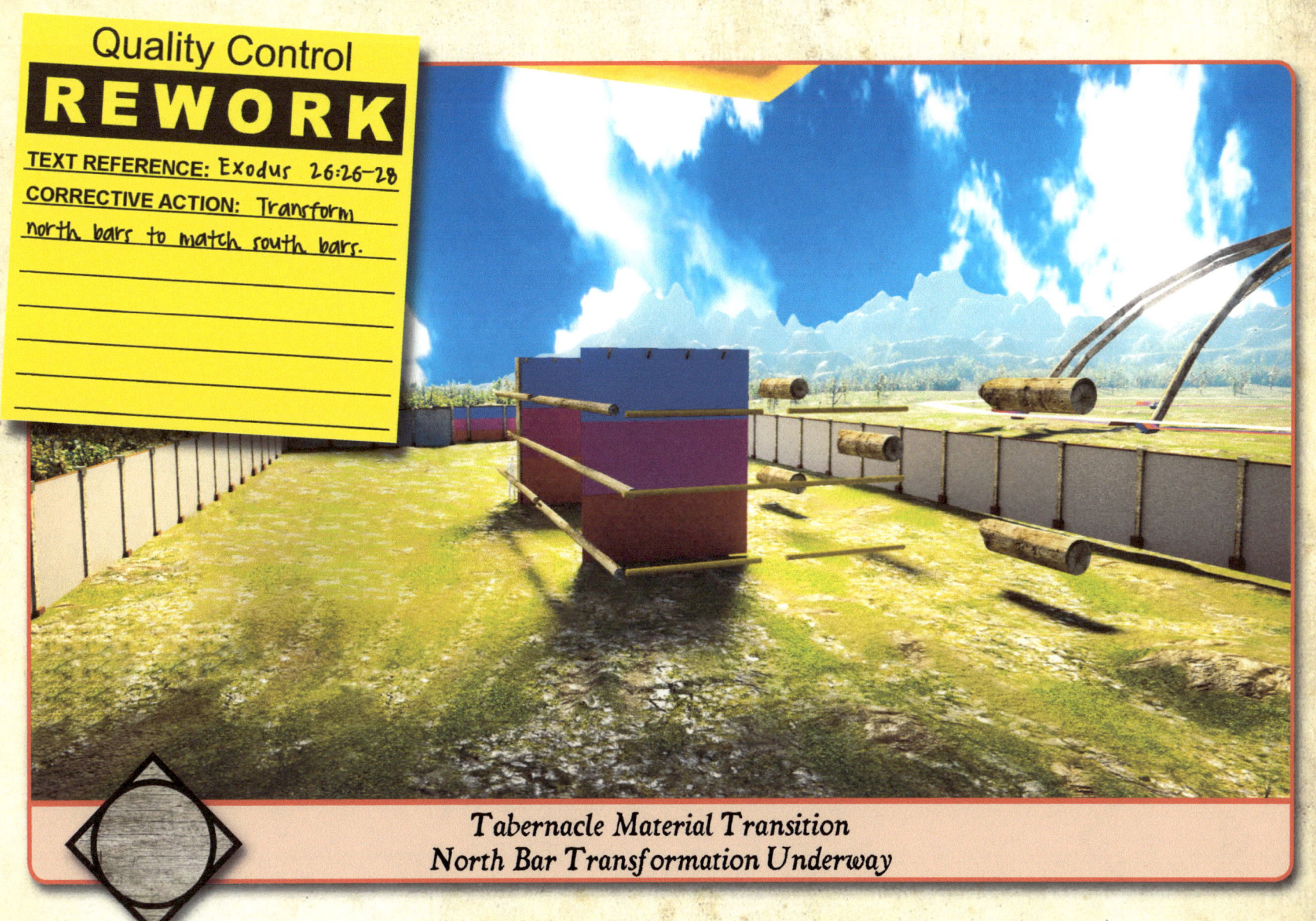

Quality Control
REWORK
TEXT REFERENCE: Exodus 26:26-28
CORRECTIVE ACTION: Transform north bars to match south bars.

Tabernacle Material Transition
North Bar Transformation Underway

The House of El Shaddai

Quality Control REWORK
TEXT REFERENCE: Exodus 26:26-28
CORRECTIVE ACTION: Orient ten bars in the vertical direction.

Tabernacle Material Transition
Five South Bars and Five North Bars Reoriented Vertically

Bars through Beams?

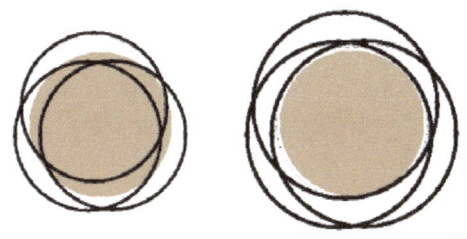

Tabernacle Bars through Beams or Rings

If the twenty beam holes or rings made for the bars are misaligned, bars would not fit through holes or rings. If holes or rings are oversized, bars would fit but would fail to rigidly secure wall panels made from beams.

Round Tabernacle Balanced & Divisible Hardware Quantities		
Object	Quantity / Side	
Curtains	5 South	5 North
Rib Beams	20 South	20 North
Silver Parts	40 South	40 North
Outer Bars	5 South	5 North
Ring Piece	1 South	1 North

especially as wood poles and beams inevitably warp. Likewise, the attached guide rings or holes in beams would be hard to align if the ground isn't level, thus requiring precision surveying, grading, or shimming. Furthermore, a long bar or pole would prove to be even more difficult to remove from the sleeve, as traditional designs offer no practical means by which to grab or extract such a pole. Finally, in the event that the holes in the beams were enlarged to reduce hole concentricity and pole removal problems, doing so would ultimately negate the purpose of the bars—which are inferred to be used for beam alignment or structural stability.

Vertical and Matching Bars

Given the specified quantities and a round or decagonal arrangement of the linen curtains and Tabernacle frame hardware, installing bars as vertical members makes perfect sense and would result in the hardware serving multiple purposes. Just as the curtains are assembled into two sets of five, and just as the rib plank assemblies are referred to as "the first" and "the second" set, two of the three sets of five bars seem to perfectly correlate both numerically and linguistically with the balance of previously described Tabernacle hardware. In fact, the first ten bars are not designated for the Tabernacle "sides", but more specifically, for the first and second

Vertical Bars - Allowing for Wind Passge

"ribs". Moreover, ten south and north bars would be ideal for securing the blue loop-joints that are fabricated on the ends of the ten linen curtains. Thus, the ten bars could be used to elevate not only the wood rib frame, but also the linen curtains so that they are suspended off the ground, as the items previously listed seem to offer no such utility. Naturally, these ten bars would be fabricated with sleeves or housings (Exodus 26:29) in order to interface with other hardware, like the silver controllers (i.e., pins) and the bottom ends of the rib beam assemblies. But how do the remaining five "west" bars (Exodus 26:27b) relate to the structure?

The House of El Shaddai

Quality Control APPROVED
TEXT REFERENCE: Exodus 26:26-28
VALIDATION BASIS: Position ten wood bars at ten corners of frame.

Round Hebrew Tabernacle
Five North Bars and Five South Bars Staged above Loops and Rib

God's Dwelling Place Reconsidered

Round Hebrew Tabernacle
Ten Bars Placed beneath Ten Rib Beam Assemblies

Quality Control APPROVED
TEXT REFERENCE: Exodus 26:26-28
VALIDATION BASIS: Ten bars are placed beneath ten rib assemblies.

The House of El Shaddai

One Set of Fifty Blue Loops are Required to Join Adjacent Linen Curtain Ends

First Loop | Second Loop

Quality Control APPROVED
TEXT REFERENCE: Exodus 26:26-28
VALIDATION BASIS: Ten bars to be placed through blue loops of ten linen curtains.

Round Hebrew Tabernacle
Ten Wood Bars Securing Blue Loop Joints on Linen Curtains

God's Dwelling Place Reconsidered

Middle Bar Run

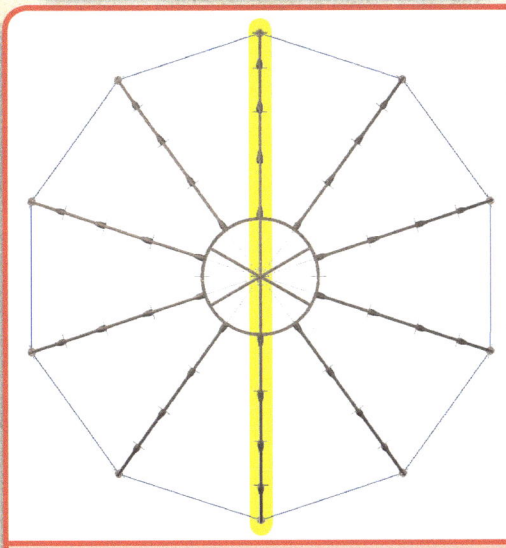

Contiguous Bar Running South to North

"... and five bars for the boards of the side of the tabernacle, for the two sides westward. And the middle bar in the midst of the boards shall reach from end to end. And thou shalt overlay the boards with gold, and make their rings of gold for places for the bars: and thou shalt overlay the bars with gold. And thou shalt rear up the tabernacle according to the fashion thereof which was shewed thee in the mount."

~ Exodus 26:26-30, KJV ~

West Bars

As for the last five bars listed in verse 27, the Hebrew text specifies them to be used both for the "rib" and "westward thighs". Given this clarification, the English "two sides westward" translation makes little sense, and it is particularly difficult to reconcile this description to rectangular models, which are depicted as having a single west wall. On the other hand, it is very logical to place these five remaining bars in the round Hebrew Tabernacle model, as it is necessary to provide some mechanism beneath the wood ring to support both the rib and the interior center "westward" thigh-beams. While at first glance this might be perceived as an asymmetrical arrangement, later texts offer additional detail with respect to other corresponding hardware.

Bars Passing Through Blue Loops

Middle Bar in the Midst

Finally, the mysterious and controversial "middle bar" text (Exodus 26:28) can be understood, but only if a radial and non-traditional arrangement of Tabernacle frame hardware is considered. The Exodus text specifies, "the middle bar in the midst of the boards shall reach from end to end", which is not calling for the fabrication of especially lengthy hardware or abnormal pole placement, but rather offers a description of a nearly completed frame assembly. While items such as beams, braces, and bars all seem to be arranged based upon a simple north-south division of hardware, several alternate hardware arrangement schemes could be conceived, given the latitude left by Exodus texts. However, with the reference to the "center bar" and the "end-to-end" reference, which might be more literally translated as "from cutting-to-cutting", it is apparent that a contiguous "bar" is formed along the middle (i.e., north-south axis of the structure) by butting together the middle-bars-to-beams-to-thigh-braces, that is, given that two of the six braces are aligned in the north-south direction. In turn, this thigh-brace arrangement seems to demand a ring orientation, whereby the divisions are at east and west ring extremities.

The House of El Shaddai

Quality Control
REJECTED

TEXT REFERENCE: Exodus 26:27
BASIS FOR FAILURE: Five bars are created for both thigh braces and rib members. Rectangular design only uses bars for west thigh beams.

Traditional Rectangular Tabernacle
Five West Wood Bars

God's Dwelling Place Reconsidered

Quality Control

REWORK

TEXT REFERENCE: Exodus 26:27
CORRECTIVE ACTION: Extend length of five bars so they are equal in length.

Tabernacle Material Transition
Five West Wood Bars Extended

The House of El Shaddai

Quality Control
REWORK

TEXT REFERENCE: Exodus 26:27
CORRECTIVE ACTION: Relocate five bars to support rib assemblies and thigh beams via center ring.

Round Hebrew Tabernacle
Relocation of Five West Bars

God's Dwelling Place Reconsidered

Round Hebrew Tabernacle
Five West Bars Beneath Rib and "Thigh" Braces

Quality Control APPROVED
TEXT REFERENCE: Exodus 26:27
VALIDATION BASIS: Five west bars support the rib as well as the six "thigh" bracing beams.

Part 3 – Tabernacle Internals

After defining the external coverings and the primary structural elements of the Tabernacle frame, the Exodus account continues with a variety of items which are employed in the capacity of internal partitioning and additional structural support. Comprised of a combination of wood, linen, gold, silver, and copper materials, the two internal Tabernacle assemblies that are listed within the Exodus texts are as follows:

a. Holy of Holies Partition (Exodus 26:31-35)
b. Tent Entrance Screen (Exodus 26:36-37)

Like the wooden bars used to support the Tabernacle frame, the collection of items used to create these two boundaries are likewise described without much detail or dimensional specification; as such, the size, arrangement, and purpose must be inferred by the item quantities, item descriptions, location of interconnecting hardware, and overall structural configuration.

Holy of Holies - Holman Bible, 1890

~ Holy of Holies ~

Regarded to be the most sacred of all spaces in the Tabernacle—and perhaps on the entire earth—the Holy of Holies was dedicated to housing the Ark of the Covenant, upon which the divine presence of God rested. According to Exodus, this partition used to create the Holy of Holies was comprised of a curtain, wood columns or "pillars", pegs or "hooks", and rods or "sockets" (Exodus 26:31-35). Without this section of the Exodus text articulating a clear location for the "Holy of Holies" or a

Holy Parts

"And thou shalt make a vail of blue, and purple, and scarlet, and fine twined linen of cunning work: with cherubims shall it be made: And thou shalt hang it upon four pillars of shittim wood overlaid with gold: their hooks shall be of gold, upon the four sockets of silver. And thou shalt hang up the vail under the taches, that thou mayest bring in thither within the vail the ark of the testimony: and the vail shall divide unto you between the holy place and the most holy. And thou shalt put the mercy seat upon the ark of the testimony in the most holy place."

~ Exodus 26:31-34, KJV ~

If corner beams are aligned with the six west wall beams, and the south and north sides are made with beams that measure 10 x 1.5 x 1, the rectangular exterior would measure 12 cubits wide, with the interior measuring 10 cubits wide, making the Holy of Holies measure 10 cubits in two directions. However, there is no definitive means of determining the H1-H4 column locations relative to the curtain barrier or the south, north, or west walls.

point of reference for the placement of its partition curtain, a number of different configurations have been proposed.

When it comes to rectangular Tabernacle models, the most prevalent Holy of Holies arrangement is based on the assumption that this inner veil is placed ten cubits to the east of the interior side of the west wall. Assuming six west wall-planks measuring 1½ cubits wide are placed side-by-side, along with two corner-boards also measuring 1½ cubits (i.e., edges of corner beams aligned flush with the north and south walls), the interior section of the Holy of Holies would take the shape of a perfect cube, measuring 10 cubits x 10 cubits x 10 cubits.

While this proposed 10 x 10 x 10 cubicle arrangement may have special appeal to mystics and those with a strong affinity to numerology, various structural problems and Bible text conflicts remain unresolved. For example, in the case of the four Holy of Holies columns, the pillar support configuration and function cannot be explained. For example, if pillars for the Holy of Holies are presumed to measure 10 cubits in height, and there is only a single small silver "socket" base (one talent or 75 pounds) furnished to support each pillar assumed to stand 10 cubits high, how is it

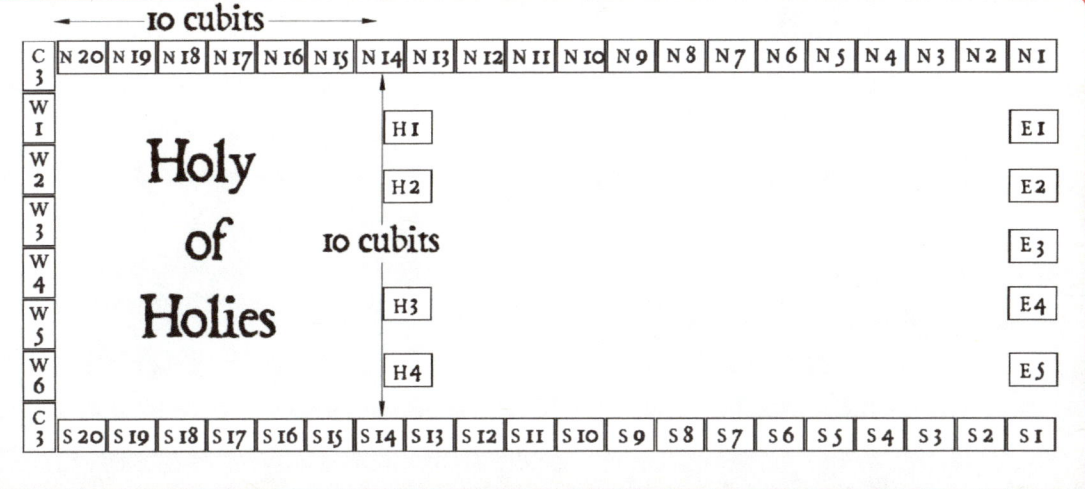

Holy of Holies Dimension Assumed for Many Rectangular Tabernacle Models

The House of El Shaddai

Quality Control
REJECTED

TEXT REFERENCE: Exodus 26:31-34

BASIS FOR FAILURE: Four silver sockets could not support tall wood beams. Also, the rectangular design needs curtain rods and more than four gold hooks to properly hold fabric veil.

Traditional Rectangular Tabernacle
Four Columns for the Holy of Holies

God's Dwelling Place Reconsidered

Quality Control REWORK

TEXT REFERENCE: Exodus 26:32
CORRECTIVE ACTION: Remove and reshape beams so they can stand, integrating them with other structural hardware.

Tabernacle Material Transition
Four Columns Removed from Oversized Silver Bases

THE HOUSE OF EL SHADDAI

Quality Control
REWORK
TEXT REFERENCE: Exodus 26:32
CORRECTIVE ACTION: Remove and reshape curtains, gold hooks/pegs, and silver "bases" or "sockets" to provide a means of hanging the Holy of Holies curtain barrier.

Tabernacle Material Transition
Holy Veil, Four Silver Rods/Bases, and Gold Hooks

Which Taches?

"And thou shalt make fifty taches of gold, and couple the curtains together with the taches: and it shall be one tabernacle.

And thou shalt make fifty taches of brass, and put the taches into the loops, and couple the tent together, that it may be one."

~ Exodus 26:6 & 11, KJV ~

Moses and Joshua - James Tissot, 1902

If the Holy of Holies curtain is hung from gold hooks that are attached to four columns (Exodus 26:32), the gold taches used to join linen curtain sets would not be required to hang the Holy of Holies curtain.

reasonable to assume that the pillars will remain freestanding in the middle of the structure with little to no lateral support offered at the top of the pillar, when the south, north, and west wall beams all required two bases or sockets? Worse yet, Exodus describes no apparatus to secure the four pillar-tops, and even if the silver or gold hardware was assumed to do so, the listed hardware description and quantities (i.e., four gold "hooks") do not coincide with the required function. There are only four silver parts listed, which are normally assumed to serve as column bases; and bracing the four pillars with the nearby walls would require five parts, as there are five spaces between the walls and four columns.

Traditionally, the cubical 10 x 10 x 10 Holy of Holies box paradigm is further justified by gold "taches" as listed in Exodus 26:6, which are used to join five linen curtains into two assemblies of five. However, in the event that the fifty taches of the linen curtains were

Taches and Curtains Assumed at East Holy of Holies Partition

coincidentally intended for the purpose of hanging the Holy of Holies curtain, only a fraction of them might be used. Taches used to hang the Holy of Holies curtain would be limited to an interior location only, but this does not explain why there are far more gold taches on the outside of the Tabernacle than there are on the inside. Likewise, this proposed use for the gold taches fails to explain the unique purpose of the fifty copper taches, which are assumed to be located immediately above and are used to join the wool curtains together (verse 11). Thus, it is ambitious to assume that the taches of Exodus 26:33 are the same as those in Exodus 26:6.

The House of El Shaddai

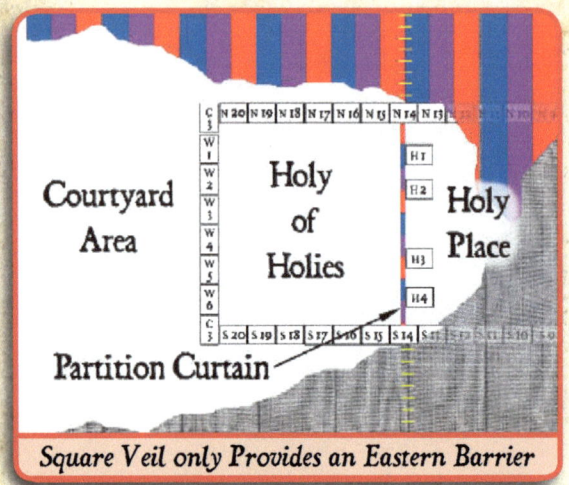

Square Veil only Provides an Eastern Barrier

Finally, if the curtain "taches" of verse 6 are used for hanging the Holy of Holies partition curtain, it begs the question as to what the gold "hooks" of verse 32 are used for, if not for hanging the curtain or positioning the beams.

Still another approach to determining the Holy of Holies veil placement is based on the location of the "staves", which are used to lift the Ark of the Covenant (Exodus 25:15). However, "staves" cannot be used to determine chamber size, particularly as the poles are introduced without physical dimension specification.

Partitioning Function

"And thou shalt hang up the vail under the taches, that thou mayest bring in thither within the vail the ark of the testimony: and the vail shall divide unto you between the holy place and the most holy."

~ Exodus 26:33, KJV ~

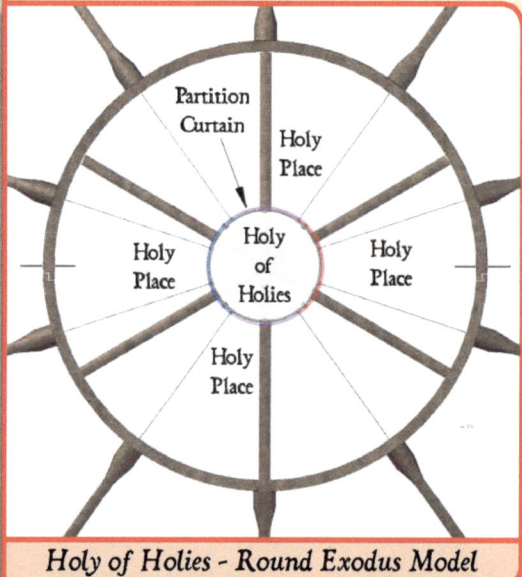

Holy of Holies - Round Exodus Model

A veil can separate people from Holy of Holies in all directions if the fabric used for partitioning is suspended from above in a cylindrical arrangement.

The Holy Partition

Before committing to a perfect cube, proposing an exotic platonic solid, or making any other assumptions about the shape of the Holy of Holies, the first question that should be asked should probably be, "What is used to separate the Holy of Holies from the rest of everything else?" It seems that as a simple and obvious answer is given literally according to the Exodus account, which reads, "the vail shall divide unto you between the holy place and the most holy." Contrary to traditional models, there is no indication that a south, north, or west wall is used as a boundary. Likewise, there is nothing in Exodus describing the Holy of Holies as being found on the west side of the Tabernacle building. In taking the text literally, it would seem that the entire Holy of Holies is defined and surrounded by a single piece of colored linen fabric.

The Holy Curtain Rod

While the Exodus description of the Holy of Holies seems to be devoid of any mention of shapes like squares, rectangles, or circles, it seems reasonable to conclude that the Holy of Holies partition must assume the shape of a vertical column. After all, the Hebrew text in verses 32 and 33 indicate that the curtain is hung on four wood columns, and that four gold pegs were put upon

Round Hebrew Model
Four Columns, Silver Ring Sections, and Gold Pegs

The House of El Shaddai

Quality Control APPROVED

TEXT REFERENCE: Exodus 26:32-33

VALIDATION BASIS: Holy of Holies tri-colored curtain hangs around the Most Holy Place, on a four piece silver ring forming a barrier in all directions. Ring is secured to four wood posts by four gold pegs.

Round Hebrew Tabernacle
Holy Veil Installation Underway

A Holy Ring and Cylinder?

four silver "controllers", which were equipped with protruding features (i.e., taches) for hanging the fabric. Assuming the hardware is symmetrical, equidistantly spaced, or both, logic would dictate that the horizontal rods on top of the columns would be either curved to form a circle, or left straight to assume a square perimeter, with four posts at four corners.

Placing the Most Holy Place

Given that the ten linen curtains defining the dwelling place (Exodus 26:1-6) is also regarded to be "the Holy Place", it follows that the structure's center is the most logical location for the "Holy of Holies" or "Most Holy Place". After all, in a structure formed by angled walls or slanting "rib" sections, a center location would best allow for a symmetrical column arrangement. However, this location would require that the columns were of the height and proportion necessary to be laterally secured by members above, which is the most logical conclusion, given the size, possible utility, and shape of silver "controllers".

Upon further review, it becomes clear that a central Holy of Holies location is not based upon mere speculation or preference—it is rather based upon of necessity. According to the Exodus texts, silver "controllers" are used in construction of south and north rib assemblies, and in order to balance, secure, and stiffen the tent frame, rib assemblies need to be individually tethered from beneath to a termination point, ideally in a central location. As four silver pieces are employed in a Holy of Holies "curtain rod" capacity, it becomes clear that it is not practical to arrange them in a square shape or perched them high upon four posts. Instead, the four silver pieces would logically be arranged in a circular pattern, as a ring would be extremely useful in a central tethering and load-bearing capacity—balancing forces from the ribs' silver tension-members as they are transferred from any one of the ten directions.

Rectangular Model with Holy of Holies Partition Removed - Giles, 1890

Traditional Tabernacle artwork often depicts enormous pillars being used to support wood ceiling panels or braces, although Exodus only specifies leather and fabric for the roof and partitions.

~ Tent Entrance ~

Using language similar to the description of the Holy of Holies partition hardware, chapter 26 of Exodus concludes by describing hardware used for the tent's "door" (Exodus 26:35-37).

Hoping to offer a simple explanation for this text, traditional rectangular models incorporate a simple curtain at the east side to protect the Tabernacle from the elements. But given this interpretation, several things still don't add up. For example, the Tabernacle's east entrance is traditionally believed to employ five wood columns, whereas the west side is depicted as having six or eight wood beams. Not only does the odd column count of the east entrance seem to contradict the precedent set with the west side hardware, but the five columns used for the east gate are also inconsistent with the four pillars provided for the Holy of Holies column. Why would a curtain of essentially the same size and orientation need to be supported or secured with five pillars at the east gate, whereas four pillars would suffice for supporting the Holy of Holies partition, which would be subjected to more overhead load from fabrics and leather roof coverings?

Perhaps more importantly, the Exodus text fails to provide the traditional rectangular Tabernacle design with a means of lateral column support. Whether the front entrance columns are assumed to be round, rectangular, thick, or thin, the columns and curtains would require some form of bracing at the top, as the east tent door "hanging" and pillars are exposed to the wind and other elements. Even the draping of the ends of the linen and wool curtains over eastern columns would impose either an inward or outward load, demanding some sort of simple load bearing apparatus to be installed (e.g., braces between the five columns and north and south walls) to hold columns in place. While Exodus describes no such column stabilization hardware, many traditional models take a measure of artistic latitude. Recognizing the need for support, they add a horizontal wood plank above to secure the east columns, whereas others will be so bold as to add multiple wood planks or paneling over the top of the entire structure, contrary to Bible texts. Like in the case of the silver "sockets" assumed for Tabernacle wall bases, the Israelites did not have enough copper (per Exodus 38:29, they were allotted 30 percent less copper than silver). Usually preferring to allocate copper to bases below as opposed to curtain rods or stabilizers above,

East Screen

"And thou shalt set the table without the vail, and the candlestick over against the table on the side of the tabernacle toward the south: and thou shalt put the table on the north side. And thou shalt make an hanging for the door of the tent, of blue, and purple, and scarlet, and fine twined linen, wrought with needlework. And thou shalt make for the hanging five pillars of shittim wood, and overlay them with gold, and their hooks shall be of gold: and thou shalt cast five sockets of brass for them."

~ Exodus 26:35-37, KJV ~

Tabernacle Interior - Holman Bible, 1890

Hanging door and partition curtains were one piece and three colors, not two pieces and one color. Likewise, the cloth used to cover the Ark of the Covenant was blue (Numbers 4:6).

God's Dwelling Place Reconsidered

Quality Control REJECTED

TEXT REFERENCE: Exodus 26:36-37

BASIS FOR FAILURE: Tent entrance posts have no means of lateral restraint and would tip over without support. Bases use too much copper and curtain has no means of hanging uniformly.

Traditional Rectangular Tabernacle
Five "Pillars" with Oversized Copper Bases

The House of El Shaddai

Quality Control
REWORK

TEXT REFERENCE: Exodus 26:36-37
CORRECTIVE ACTION: Transform wood post shape and length, and change shape of and size of copper bases or sockets.

Tabernacle Material Transition
Holy Veil, Five Gold Hooks, & Copper Bases or Rods

~ 125 ~

A-Frame Tabernacle - Holman Bible, 1890

To balance loads, an equal number of beams and columns or "pillars" are needed on both east and west sides, especially assuming an A-Frame roof.

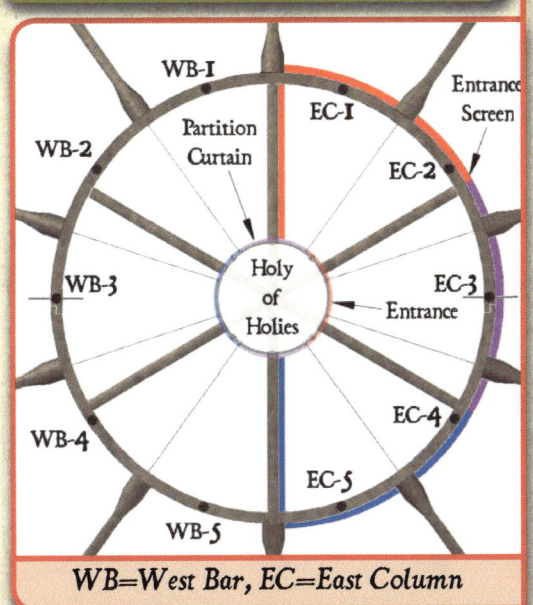

Which Tent Opening?

WB=West Bar, EC=East Column

traditional arrangements lack a consistent or realistic means of hanging the curtain from above. In the case of the Holy of Holies curtains, some propose that some of the 50 taches overhead would be used for supporting the partition, but in the case of the east entrance curtain(s), neither loops nor taches are mentioned as a means of hanging the entrance curtain.

Why Five Tent Screen "Pillars"?

To put the tent entrance materials in context, item quantities and functional descriptions must be carefully considered. So far, curtain sets, wood rib-beams, silver controllers, thigh-braces, and ring sections have been proven to demonstrate patterns of greater purpose and symmetry as they have been incorporated into a round model. In the case of bars, however, a total of fifteen were specified (Exodus 26:26-28); ten of which are literally ascribed to the two symmetrical rib sections, while the remaining five bars are dedicated to the west ribs and "thigh" braces. Given this list of hardware, there remains an asymmetrical and open gap on the east side of the structure, opposite of the five west "bars" which perform a mission-critical load bearing function.

Placing five wood "door hanging pillars" beneath the wood ring on the east side may offer a structural solution and provide west rib/thigh bar symmetry; however, this arrangement is not intuitive if an east "tent door hanging" is expected per tradition and translation. Nevertheless, it makes sense given a big picture perspective and Hebrew Tabernacle description. Per the Exodus Hebrew text, this final "hanging" is better described as a mesh or sackcloth-like "screen", being designed to ventilate, filter, and diffuse wind. Likewise, the English "door" is more literally translated as "opening"; and the Hebrew word for "tent" applies to vertical fabric barriers—not being limited to roofed shelters. While the cylindrical Holy of Holies partition may not be traditionally regarded as a "tent" with a "door", logic dictates for the veil barrier to have an eastern opening or access point. Thus, this "tent door hanging" of Exodus 26:35-37 is better understood to be a "screen for a barrier opening". When other "tents" or barriers are open for human entry (e.g., linen/wool curtains of Exodus 26:1-13), the final Holy of Holies barrier and entrance could be subjected to wind and not separated from exterior line-of-sight viewing—hence the need for the east entrance screen! Finally, the "bars" are uncovered and subjected to light breezes, with the Hebrew term alluding to cutting of small wind, whereas the standing "pillars" are sheltered from the wind by the screen as outer tent curtains are opened, and thus not referred to as "bars".

The House of El Shaddai

Quality Control APPROVED

TEXT REFERENCE: Exodus 26:36-37

VALIDATION BASIS: Five wood columns are placed beneath wood corner ring mirroring five west bars, corresponding with five gold pegs and five copper curtain rods.

Round Hebrew Tabernacle
Five Wood Pillars, Copper Rods, and Gold Pegs

God's Dwelling Place Reconsidered

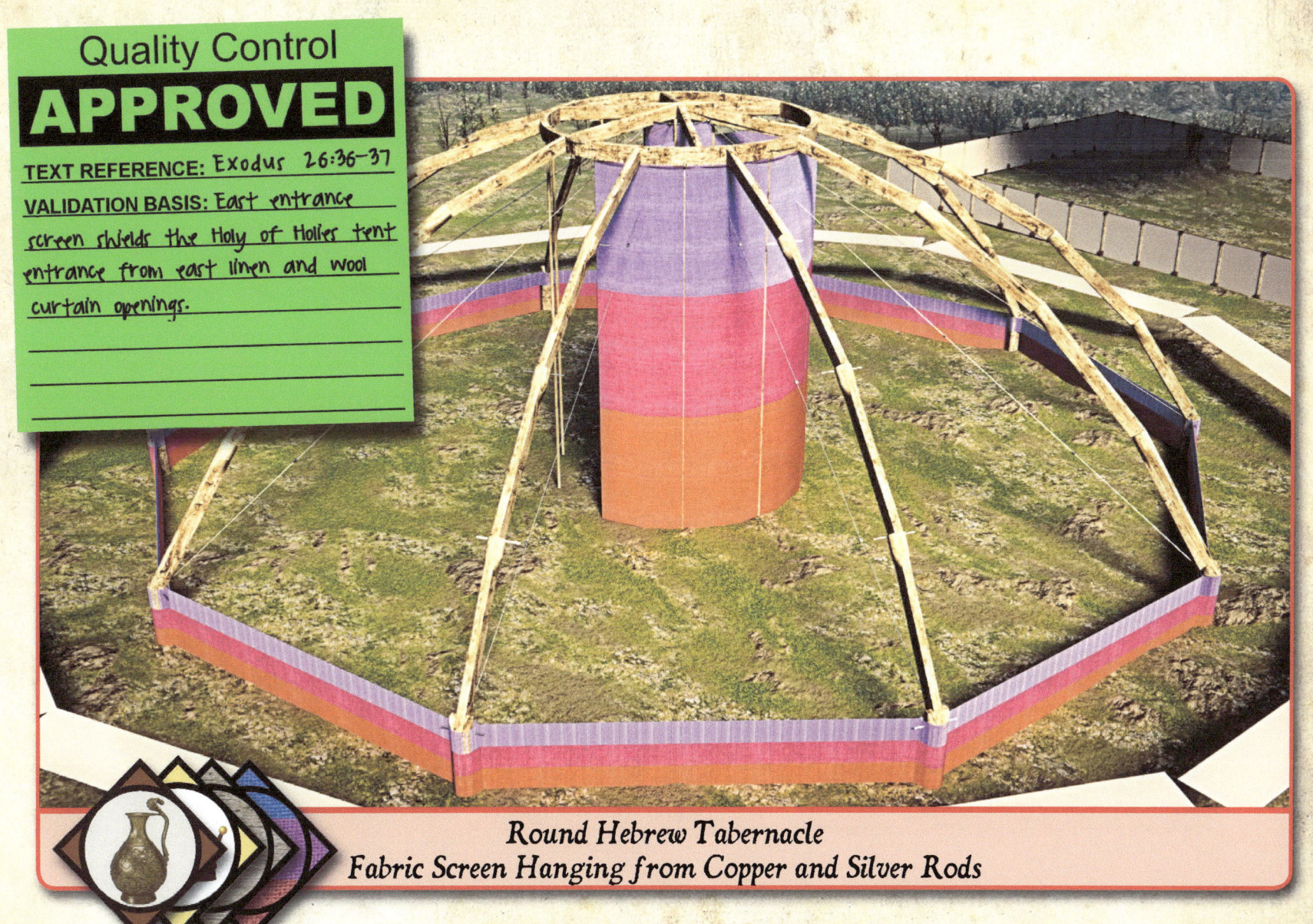

Quality Control APPROVED

TEXT REFERENCE: Exodus 26:36-37

VALIDATION BASIS: East entrance screen shields the Holy of Holies tent entrance from east linen and wool curtain openings.

Round Hebrew Tabernacle
Fabric Screen Hanging from Copper and Silver Rods

Part 4 – Roof & Courtyard Items

Roof & Courtyard Hardware Materials

Linen Silver
Wool Copper
Leather Wood

As the Exodus 26 Tabernacle account is examined using a literal step-by-step method that defers to the Hebrew texts over English scriptures, it becomes evident that the Tabernacle plans have always been hidden in plain sight—although the image of the dwelling place has been obscured by bad translation and antique Bible artwork. From the totality of the rich Bible narrative, it is made clear that the end result of the meticulous instructions is anything but a crude or unsophisticated rectangular shack in desperate need of additional reinforcement. To the contrary, the single chapter of Exodus not only demonstrates the succinct nature and precision of God's word, but it reveals a formidable free-standing tent, which is made in the Creator's image.

While most of the Exodus 26 Tabernacle instructions allow for interpretation of the text using a progressive verse-by-verse approach, there are a few exceptions where its revelation isn't perfectly sequential. As previously indicated, without a fully defined frame, the final configuration of the leather coverings (Exodus 26:14) could not have been addressed. Likewise, even though Exodus texts give a fair amount of layout and configuration information for eleven wool curtains (Exodus 26:7-13) critical framework detail has yet to be defined. Finally, details of courtyard furnishings are briefly outlined in Exodus 27 and 30. Thus, in order to conclude the Tabernacle structure and facility study, the following items will be addressed:

   a. Tabernacle Roof (Exodus 26:14)
   b. Courtyard Edge/Frame (Exodus 27:9-15)
   c. Courtyard Gating (Exodus 27:16-19)
   d. Copper Alter (Exodus 27:1)
   e. Copper Basin (Exodus 30:18)

As these final pieces are introduced, the Tabernacle facility puzzle will be made complete.

God's Dwelling Place Reconsidered

Traditional Rectangular Tabernacle
Four Layer Roof with Two Layers of Leather

Quality Control: REJECTED

TEXT REFERENCE: Exodus 26:14

BASIS FOR FAILURE: Leather layers stacked would be conducive to trapped moisture. Also, if layered, colored leather adds no aesthetic value.

~ Tabernacle Roof ~

As previously proposed, the Exodus 26 text goes to great lengths to describe Tabernacle curtains, but by way of comparison, it barely mentions any detail when it comes to the leather sections. Two leather layers are described in one verse immediately following the description of two fabric curtain sets over the course of 13 verses. Is this leather roof instruction just exceedingly vague, or does it represent a careless oversight by Moses after meticulously recording the Tabernacle's divinely described details?

In surveying traditional Tabernacle models, the approach to sizing leather coverings seems relatively consistent, namely, "make the leather slightly bigger than whatever is beneath it." With most models being depictred with a flat single-level roof, the two leather layers (sometimes comprised of skins with hair) are illustrated as one lying over the other. However, if this approach is to be seriously considered, practical reasons for the distinctions of leather treatment between the two layers should be evident. Assuming it is sandwiched in between a leather layer above and a wool layer beneath, it is impractical to assume that the skin is dyed red as a form of weather treatment, as the leather would not be exposed to the elements. Likewise, to propose a symbolic or aesthetic explanation isn't practical, as it would not be visible for the majority of its service. Furthermore, the prudence of using a double layer of leather as a tent roof is subject to debate, as unventilated space in between the two layers would be conducive to trapping moisture. Since the leather roof layers are likely to leak at some point, they would be especially susceptible to mold or mildew, which the Bible describes as a risk to human health—potentially leading to building demolition in some situations (Leviticus 14:34-57).

Top Coverings

"And thou shalt make a covering for the tent of rams' skins dyed red, and a covering above of badgers' skins."

~ Exodus 26:14, KJV ~

Moses' Exodus descriptions include no mention of horizontal panels for the roof or beams for roof bracing.

Extra Wooden Ceiling Beams Added to Span and Strengthen Ceiling
John Kitto - Illustrated History of the Bible.

Tabernacle Material Transition
Two Leather Layers above Rectangular Courtyard

The House of El Shaddai

Quality Control
REWORK

TEXT REFERENCE: Exodus 26:14
CORRECTIVE ACTION: Install lower leather layer over lower section of frame (where Tabernacle ribs are).

Round Hebrew Tabernacle
Lower Reddened Leather Layer over Domed Frame

~ 133 ~

God's Dwelling Place Reconsidered

Leather Math

Surface Area = $2\pi Rh$

The leather roof sections are fabricated from hundreds of irregular leather skins. Although Moses encoded the π constant in the Exodus text, it makes little sense to labor in mathematics or language to define the size of various leather roof sections when the frame inherently defines the final roof shape and leather could be just "cut to fit".

Leather Shapes and Treatment

Assuming the alternate radial arrangement of tent frame hardware, use of a two-tone leather roof is practical as well as aesthetic. After all, the two wooden beams serving as "ring-corners" form a center circle on top, which is an area distinct from the domed area beneath. Given that the leather for the lower section was to be thicker and tanned or reddened, the leather might offer greater strength and improved weather-resistant characteristics, making it better for wider spans, larger slope, and higher wind loads. In contrast, the upper leather was to be treated differently, and is thought to be made from a different animal skin—presumably one that is thinner (perhaps deerskin over ram skin) and of a higher opacity. In the event that the center leather section allowed more light to pass through it, the entire structure would benefit from a muted skylight and might also be able to be used as a sort of sundial. This might be yet another hint as to why the structure was erected in the spring, possibly coinciding with the equinox—when the sunrise and sunset are due east and west.

Typical Cowhide Shape - Kürschner, 2011

Given that the Tabernacle frame formed a domed shape, this would easily explain why there is no dimensional information given to describe the leather. After all, the tent frame structure would feature some 46 facets which the leather would have been spanned and stretched over, demanding that the leather sections resemble irregular trapezoidal, triangular, or conical shapes that could not be quickly expressed in terms of simple planar geometry. Of course, in the event that the leather was to be fabricated in two large rectangular swatches, overall dimensions could have been expected. Contrarily, the enormous domed leather roof needed to be custom tailored by a small army or a large tribe of leather workers, who came out of Egypt with flocks and herds.

THE HOUSE OF EL SHADDAI

Quality Control APPROVED
TEXT REFERENCE: Exodus 26:14
VALIDATION BASIS: Lower leather layer is installed over lower section of Tabernacle frame.

Round Hebrew Tabernacle
Lower Reddened Leather Layer Complete

God's Dwelling Place Reconsidered

Round Hebrew Tabernacle
Upper Leather Layer Complete

Quality Control APPROVED

TEXT REFERENCE: Exodus 26:14

VALIDATION BASIS: Upper leather layer is installed over upper section of Tabernacle frame.

~ Courtyard Edge and Frame ~

As the hardware to complete the Tabernacle is identified in Exodus 26, it follows that a boundary would also be established around the perimeter of God's dwelling place in order to protect it from man, animals, and weather once it is erected. However, as thousands of men would need ample space to set up the massive Tabernacle structure, installation of a courtyard barrier in close proximity to the Tabernacle could not commence until the structure erection was completed. For this reason, the circular perimeter implied by the wool curtains introduced in Exodus 26:7-13 would not be physically established without the provision of its corresponding metal frame, which is finally introduced in Exodus 27:9-15, after the manpower-intensive activities are completed.

Given this Exodus excerpt, traditional courtyard models consistently depict a perimeter measuring 100 cubits in the east-west direction and 50 cubits in the north-south direction. While some believe truth to be a product of consensus, history has shown repeatedly that fact is not a byproduct of popular opinion. To the contrary, in the case of the rectangular courtyard model, idiosyncrasies and Exodus-text contradictions seem to testify as a witness against the scores of rectangular interpretations—standing as an irrefutable proof that not a single one is correct.

After comparing Exodus texts to traditional Tabernacle and courtyard models, it seems fitting that the models or illustrations have been recreated from scratch hundreds, if not thousands of times. While the motives for creating new Tabernacle and courtyard depictions may vary from person to person, on many occasions, new models or illustrations are proposed with the hopes of resolving some of the problems encountered in reconciling text to an image or physical model. Why? Because in committing to a rectangular paradigm, the Exodus texts inevitably yield a number of logical contradictions which simply cannot be overcome—regardless of translation. In particular, things contributing to the rectangular courtyard model confusion include:

    1) assumed "pillar" or post material type,
    2) assumed copper "base" / "socket" or "controller" application,
    3) assumed post count overlaps, and
    4) post-to-post spacing assumptions.

Court Frame Text

"And thou shalt make the court of the tabernacle: for the south side southward there shall be hangings for the court of fine twined linen of an hundred cubits long for one side: And the twenty pillars thereof and their twenty sockets shall be of brass; the hooks of the pillars and their fillets shall be of silver. And likewise for the north side in length there shall be hangings of an hundred cubits long, and his twenty pillars and their twenty sockets of brass; the hooks of the pillars and their fillets of silver. And for the breadth of the court on the west side shall be hangings of fifty cubits: their pillars ten, and their sockets ten. And the breadth of the court on the east side eastward shall be fifty cubits. The hangings of one side of the gate shall be fifteen cubits: their pillars three, and their sockets three. And on the other side shall be hangings fifteen cubits: their pillars three, and their sockets three."

~ Exodus 27:9-15, KJV ~

No wood is used in courtyard frame construction; only metal (brass/copper and silver) and fabrics are specified.

God's Dwelling Place Reconsidered

Dishonest Art

"How can you say, 'We are wise, And the law of the Lord is with us'? Look, the false pen of the scribe certainly works falsehood."

~ Jeremiah 8:8, NKJV ~

Enormous Tabernacle Courtyard Frame Depicted - Holman Bible, 1890

Artists qualify as "scribes" as they also use pens as tools for storytelling. Compare courtyard post, base, and rail sizes in the Holman Bible illustration to Exodus descriptions.

Material Misappropriation

Although the courtyard post material type may not sound like it should have much bearing on courtyard viability, it nevertheless speaks directly to the problem at hand—which has to do with commitment to the Bible record. As a case in point, if the Exodus Tabernacle is depicted contrary to how Exodus actually describes the Tabernacle, then the entire exercise of depicting the Tabernacle – ultimately becomes an act of sacrilege or blasphemy. In many traditional courtyard depictions, it is obvious that large wood posts are assumed. In examining the Exodus record, it becomes apparent that the use of the wrong post material is not even a translation problem. Irrespective of translation preferences, no wood whatsoever can be found in the entire Exodus 27 courtyard description. This material substitution is a matter of illiteracy or outright carelessness, especially as copper/brass is the post material of record, according to verses 10 and 11.

As material types are not literally identified in most illustrations, it is probably only fair to give the designer or artist the benefit of the doubt with respect to the selection of material. However, this does not negate questions pertaining to assumed post sizes. In scaling artists' renderings, courtyard posts typically appear to measure somewhere between approximately 4 and 16 inches wide. If made to these dimensions, solid copper courtyard posts would weigh in between 450 and 10,000 pounds. Assuming at least 60 courtyard posts are employed (20 south, 20 north, 10 west, and 10 east), the courtyard posts alone would require somewhere between 30,000 and 600,000 pounds of copper—which is between 6 and 120 times more than the 70 talents dedicated for the entire Tabernacle facility (Exodus 38:29). While a fraction of traditional rectangular courtyard models seem to take Exodus copper quantities into account, the balance of courtyard models are predicated upon the assumption that the enormous copper posts were somehow made hollow

The House of El Shaddai

Quality Control
REJECTED

TEXT REFERENCE: Exodus 27:9-15

BASIS FOR FAILURE: Post quantities and post spacing fails to meet Exodus text requirements. Also, design uses incorrect material (wood) and more metal (copper and silver) than allotted.

Traditional Rectangular Tabernacle
Rectangular Courtyard Arrangement

God's Dwelling Place Reconsidered

Post Design Prudence

Poor Material Use & Support (2-Piece Base and Post)

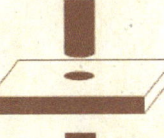
Poor Post Restraint (2-Piece Base and Post)

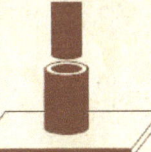
Improved Post Restraint (2-Piece Base and Post)

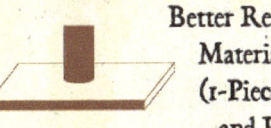
Better Restraint & Material Use (1-Piece Base and Post)

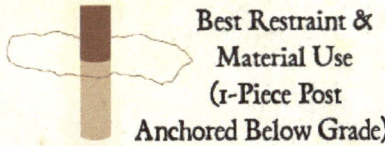
Best Restraint & Material Use (1-Piece Post Anchored Below Grade)

Vertical posts can be secured many different ways, but designs with the deepest shaft engagement and the widest bases provide the most stability. Hence, underground embedment of post ends would offer the best support.

and formed into rectangular or round cross sections, inherently complicating the fabrication processes assumed to be performed by the displaced nomadic Israelites.

Copper Post Shape and "Base" Design

Provided that the courtyard posts are indeed relatively narrow copper rods, the question of the copper "sockets" comes into question as it did in the case of the tent frame (Exodus 26:19, 21, 25, 32, and 37). First of all, if the posts and the anchoring socket-bases are both made of copper, the question arises, "Why fabricate two separate parts to perform a single function?" In other words, given the workability of copper, why not just make a one-part post if the same material was specified for both the post and base items?

If the courtyard used copper posts anchored in copper bases, integrating the two parts together would negate the need for "socket" hardware, which would not only complicate the fabrication and setup, but would limit the effectiveness of the material's use as a base. After all, a "socket" used as a stand would need to be tall enough in order to ensure the post inserted into it is vertically restrained. In contrast, it is best for a platform "base"

Oversized Courtyard Beams Gerhard Schott - 1723-1729

to be as wide and low to the ground as possible to maximize stability. Thus, given the matching courtyard post and base material type, it is reasonable to conclude, once again, that the Hebrew term traditionally translated as "sockets" or "bases", is in fact neither.

Finally, most rectangular models presume the outer courtyard posts are secured by ropes and tent pegs, in which case, the copper posts' bases would be structurally redundant—perhaps akin to wearing a belt with suspenders. Why make copper "bases" to secure posts if ropes and stakes are added to keep the posts upright? Rather than making copper "bases", prudence dictates that the copper be used to make curtain rods instead, since curtains, hanging unsupported from post to post, would be subject to high stress and prone to sagging and tearing. Although many

The House of El Shaddai

Quality Control
REJECTED

TEXT REFERENCE: Exodus 27:9-11
BASIS FOR FAILURE: Courtyard post material is incorrect. Only copper is allocated for post material. No wood is specified.

Traditional Rectangular Tabernacle
Improper Post Material and Improper "Socket" Design

God's Dwelling Place Reconsidered

Quality Control REWORK

TEXT REFERENCE: Exodus 27:9-11
CORRECTIVE ACTION: Change post material from wood to copper. Resize post in accordance with Exodus material quantities.

Tabernacle Material Transition
Socket & Wood Post Based Replaced with Copper Pole

rectangular courtyard designs do depict curtain rods, they typically do not do so in exchange for the copper bases, which is required to comply with Exodus descriptions and copper inventories.

Counting Court Hardware

Even after resolving courtyard material misappropriation and sizing problems—which are prevalent in traditional rectangular courtyard models and translations—remaining courtyard post quantification and placement problems have proven to be even more problematic. For example, if there are 20 posts and 20 curtains or curtain rods placed on the south and north sides and aligned to form a barrier as Exodus suggests, how can this be accomplished? After all, two posts are required to span a single horizontal rod; therefore, the number of posts used to span a set of horizontal rods must always exceed the number of rods by a quantity of one. In other words, with 20 posts, there can only be 19 curtains or rods hanging in between them; or conversely, if there are 20 curtains or curtain rods, there must be 21 posts altogether. Befuddled by this riddle, some traditional models propose that the corner posts on the west courtyard wall act in the capacity of the 21st post, so each of the 20 curtain hanging intervals along the 100 cubit wall measure 5 cubits. But if the finished courtyard is to have 20 posts on the south and on the north walls, how is it possible to add a west wall of 10 posts, two of which would reside on the south and north corners, while pretending that there are not 21 posts on the north and south walls? Also, adding a 21st post on the west side results in overall length changes, as the 20 posts were to be spanned at a distance of 100 cubits. Obviously, this quantity and corner post classification problem is bad enough given the west wall possibilities, and is ultimately magnified when the east wall and gate posts are also considered.

Post Spacing and Measurement Complications

As suggested above, the post count and taxonomy problems haunting traditional rectangular courtyards introduce a host of unresolved post spacing measurement and consistency problems. In cases where the south and north courtyard walls are comprised of 20 posts, they would have 19 "hangings" between them. Given that the south and north courtyard walls measure 100 cubits,

Post Confusion

Differences in interpretation result in different courtyard post arrangements, quantities, and post distance intervals if a rectangular courtyard is assumed.

Court Section	Posts Inferred	Posts Created	Posts Counted	Sling Spans	Sling Interval
South Side	20	20	21	20	5
North Side	20	20	21	20	5
West Side	10	10	10	9	5.556
East Flank	6	4	4 (or 6)	6	5
East Gate	4	4	4	3	6.667
TOTAL	60	58	n/a	58	n/a
⚠	South and North walls have too many posts.				

A Wall of 10 West Posts is Added to the End of 20 South and North Posts

"For the south side southward there shall be hangings for the court... of an hundred cubits long for one side... And the twenty pillars thereof... And likewise for the north side in length there shall be hangings of an hundred cubits long, and his twenty pillars... And for the breadth of the court on the west side shall be hangings of fifty cubits: their pillars ten..."

~ Exodus 27:9-12, KJV (Abbreviated) ~

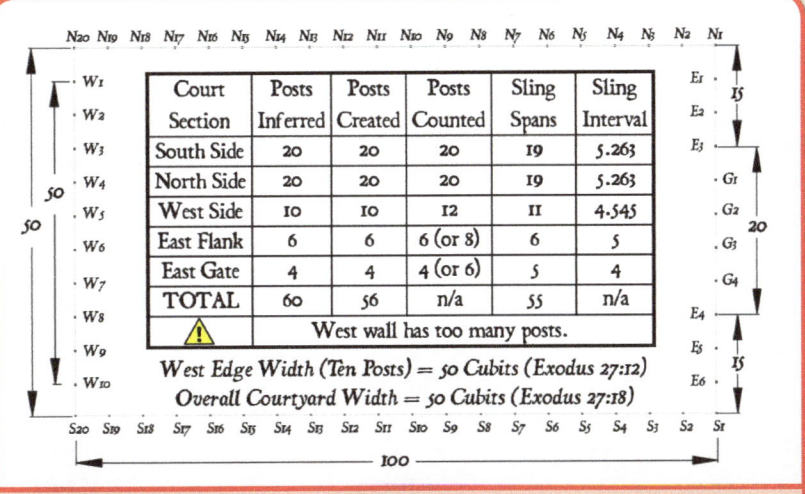

A Wall of 10 West Posts Added between 20 South and North Posts

Every possible rectangular courtyard configuration results in some form of logical or Exodus text conflict.

All Four Walls Share Corner Posts

this would mean that the posts would be spaced at 100/19 cubits; in other words, spaced with the post centerlines at $5\ ^5/_{19}$ cubits apart. The use of an odd and large prime number like 19 in a denominator is terrifying to almost anyone who has completed grade school level mathematics or used fractions in making real-life measurements; and the decimal equivalent of approximately 5.263 is equally impractical and unappealing. Assuming only ten posts on the west wall produces a similar—but not equal—problem. Spaced at 50 cubits, the distance between the posts would not be a tidy 5 cubits, but rather 50/9 cubits apart, or $5\ ^5/_9$ or 5.555.... cubits. Of course, if the 10 west posts of Exodus 27:12 are assumed to be in line with posts at the west end of the south and north walls, then there would be 11 curtain spans between 12 posts, yielding a west wall span distance of 50/11 or $4\ ^5/_{11}$, which is 4.545 cubits apart. Needless to say, odd and imperfect measurements create numerous fabrication and setup complications.

Logically, in making curtains and curtain rods, it would be easiest to position and fabricate as many things as possible to be the same measurement, and to use whole number measurements while doing so—as opposed to obscure fractions and decimals. After rounding to 3 digits, even tent making specialists like Aholiab would hardly appreciate working to measurements like 5.263, 5.555, or 4.545 cubits. However, without a need to physically fabricate hardware using cubits as units of measure, it's unlikely that this inexact measurement problem that is implicit to rectangular courtyard layouts will be brought to attention, or for that matter, accurately depicted. Some may go as far as taking a stand on this debate that has been lingering for centuries, and others may be inclined to spiritualize the anomaly, relegating it to enigmatic symbolism and esoteric numerology. Still others might blame the text, at which point the resolution of the post count and spacing dilemma boils down into two options—either cheat some of the language to fix some of the math or cheat some of the math to fix some

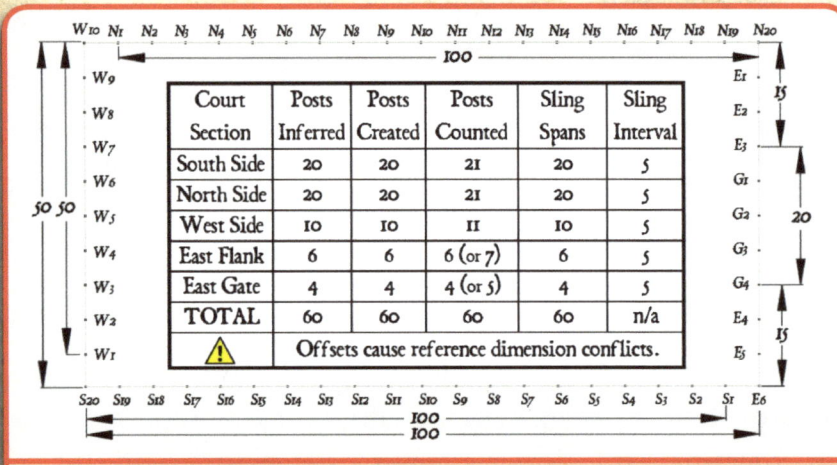

Each Wall of Posts are Offset from Adjacent Corner

of the language. Thus, every post location scheme is inherently suspect; each can be rejected based upon bad semantics, and each test the limits of academic integrity. Of course, tradition need not concern itself with actual numbers or specific language, as a picture is worth a thousand words, and for every voice raising questions about the status quo, there are probably a thousand images offering a "big picture view". Are there 20, 21, or 22 posts on the south and north walls? Are there 10, 11, or 12 posts on the west wall? According to tradition, it doesn't really matter—nor could it ever matter.

Courtyard Considerations

Exodus 27:9-15 texts briefly describe the courtyard, and the interpretation of the text is highly contingent upon simple assumptions. Given Moses' description,
- *Should all posts be spaced equally?*
- *Do all post spans measure 5 cubits?*
- *Are any posts counted twice?*
- *Does the Bible list any posts twice?*
- *Can measurements exceed post spans?*
- *Is courtyard post layout symmetrical?*
- *Which fabric is used for the court?*
- *Are the courtyard walls aligned with four cardinal compass points?*

Eastern Post Spacing

Perhaps in recognition of the various post interval idiosyncrasies and associated fabrication challenges, translators have apparently quarantined specifications as it pertaining to post spacing intervals. In particular, Exodus 27:14-15 is translated, "The hangings of one side of the gate shall be fifteen cubits: their pillars three, and their sockets three. And on the other side shall be hangings fifteen cubits: their pillars three, and their sockets three." According to this text, it would seem that the only posts subject to the five cubit interval (presumed by the 15 cubit spacing of 3 posts) are those adjacent to the gate. However, it seems the Hebrew term for "shoulder" or "flank" is translated as, "of one side of the 'gate'" with agenda and addenda,

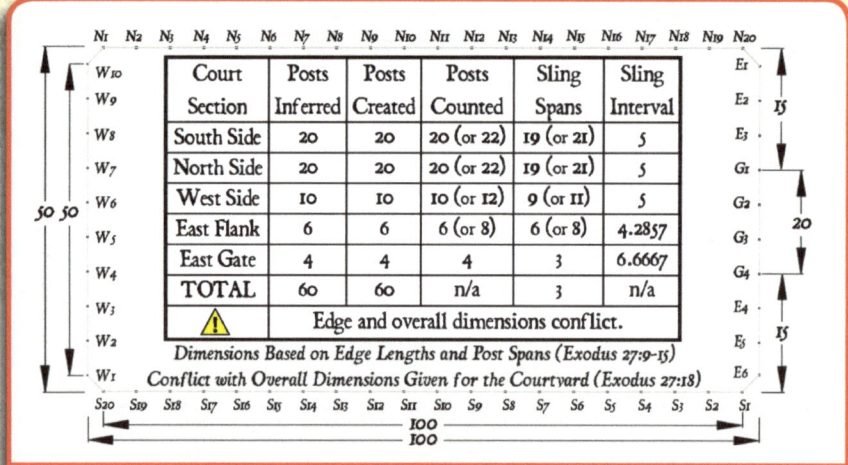

Octagonal Courtyard with Angled Corners

Post Spacing Math and Measurements

"The hangings of one side of the gate shall be fifteen cubits: their pillars three, and their sockets three. And on the other side shall be hangings fifteen cubits: their pillars three, and their sockets three."

~ Exodus 27:14-15, KJV ~

Traditional
5 Cubit
Post Spacing

Literal
7.5 Cubit
Post Spacing

As 15 cubit "hangings" span three posts (represented by black squares) on each flank, it is more reasonable to perceive two sections of 7.5 cubit spans rather than three sections of 5 cubit spans, as three spans require four posts.

even though the Hebrew text does not refer to a "gate" in either verse. Thus, it seems the translation has been crafted to influence the reader into believing that these verses refer to the east side of the Tabernacle courtyard, perhaps such that the south, north, and west sides of the courtyard need not conform to the implied and exacting post spacing interval.

However, a diligent review of Exodus 27:14-15 shows how a bad rectangular paradigm and

Courtyard with 20 N/S Posts & 10 W/E Posts - Needham, 1874

post spacing tradition can result in confusion just as easy as a twisted translation. Although tradition interprets a five cubit post spacing interval, logic dictates that only two "hangings" would be spanned between three posts at a 15 cubit measure. Consequentially, the post spacing would be calculated to be a span of 15/2 or 7½ cubits apart, not 15/3 or 5 cubits apart.

South Courtyard Edge

Even though the Tabernacle described in Exodus 26 has been demonstrated to transform from a crude and impractical structure resembling a shoe box into a majestic tent and ancient engineering marvel, the rectangular courtyard paradigm—in spite of all of its dysfunction—is likely to remain an obstacle to perceiving a round configuration. This is to be expected, as Exodus 27:9-13 describes a courtyard measuring 100 x 50 cubits with south, north, and west sides.

Before citing courtyard mistranslation specifics, it is important to understand that a number of different words can be used in a wide number of capacities, but that they also might find special limits in certain contexts. To give an English example, a sheet can be used generically to describe anything from fabric on a bed, a page of paper, or a piece of plywood. While a curtain might also be regarded to be a sheet, this is not to say that sheets of plywood are regularly used as curtains, or for that matter, referred to as "curtains of plywood". Equal exchange between nouns is not unconditionally permissible. Likewise, it is possible to confuse nouns and verbs, especially by introducing different prepositions or definite and indefinite articles, which may or may not have basis in the original text. An English example where nouns and verbs can be confused might be illustrated by saying, "I want to run", "I want to go for a run", and "I want to go to a run." Mistranslations pertaining to the Tabernacle courtyard description might be compared to a failure to relay such subtle differences.

Hangers vs Hangings

"And thou shalt make the court of the tabernacle: for the south side southward there shall be hangings for the court of fine twined linen of an hundred cubits long for one side:"

~ Exodus 27:9, KJV ~

In the courtyard narrative, the first translation mishap pertaining to the south courtyard edge is found in Exodus 27:9, which uses the familiar "south side southward" phrase found in the Exodus 26:18 wood beam layout description. In the case of wood beams for the frame assembly, the "south side southward" phrase was demonstrated by means of language and layout to be understood as "toward the south and toward the right". In the case of the Exodus 27 courtyard hardware, the same principle applies, albeit the Hebrew offers a slightly different nuance. Conveying the same clockwise layout direction, the literal Exodus 27 Hebrew instructs, "make the tabernacle court to edge south, toward the right...". While both the English and the Hebrew texts begin with the imperative "make" verb, the English translation substitutes the infinitive Hebrew "*to edge*" verb for a definite article, a preposition, and a noun, rendering "*for the* south *side* southward", whereas the original Hebrew mandate was "*to edge* south (and) towards the right".

Hangers are hanging on a rod; fabrics are hanging on hangers.

In the case of the courtyard, verse 9 goes on to say, "there shall be hangings for the court of fine twined linen". The term "hangings" (literally "slings" in Hebrew) is traditionally thought to refer to the fabric curtains which are hanging as opposed to copper rods that are doing the hanging. Given that nouns are regularly constructed from verbs, switching the subject and object roles in

As Old English Exodus courtyard texts refer to "hangings", modern readers presume new fabrics are being specified. The metal rods created to court or to edge the Tabernacle are understood to be "hangers" as opposed to "hangings".

Courting Bleached Wool

The Hebrew word translated as "linen" in Exodus 27:9 can also mean "six", suggesting the six-stranded weave was named from the letters and numbers.

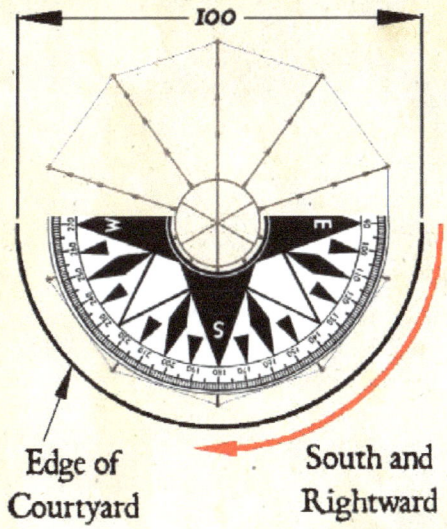

Much like the wood beams span the linen fabric in a clockwise direction, the metal courtyard frame spans the wool fabric in a clockwise direction.

this case is perhaps linguistically equivalent to confusing a shirt with a wire frame hanger. In addition, the word "court" is another word that can be used as either verb or noun. With the Hebrew preposition "to" preceding it (as opposed to using a definite article like "the"in the term), the "court" reference here seems to better correlate with verb usage as opposed to being listed as a noun, where the definite article is added in the translation as a matter of inference. Thus, it would be more fitting if the English read, "slings (are) to court twisted fabric", meaning that the slings would form a physical barrier with the fabric as they "courted" it. Finally, it is of note that the possessive "of" in the prepositional phrase "of fine twisted linen" is also inferred by translators, who seemed convinced that the "hangings" were made of fabric and "for the court". Contrary to this, the Hebrew indicates that the slings are doing the courting, and that courting is what is happening to the fabric. This begs the question, "courting is happening to which fabric?" Interestingly, this Exodus excerpt does not instruct for fabric to be made at this point, but rather seems to refer to the fabric as if it is already preexisting, which would seem to correlate well with the eleven curtains fabricated per Exodus 26:7-13. As for the fabric and fiber type, the Hebrew term that is translated as "linen" is being translated more narrowly than the language will allow. The Hebrew word is not necessarily referring to an exact fiber type, but rather may be referring to that which is bleached, or possibly that which is woven into a six-stranded braid. In the case of the courtyard curtains, they could be both braided and bleached, but they need not necessarily be linen—as tradition might dogmatically insist.

South Courtyard Edge Length

When describing the measurement of the south edge "hangings", verse 9 specifies, "of an hundred cubits long for one side". However, as is the case for orientation, measurement demands a context and a point of reference. Considering this principle and the original language, it might be more literal and fitting to say, "a hundred in cubit length to the first edge". Supposing that this edge, comprised of slings, began in the east and swept toward the right (i.e., clockwise along the entire south edge), it would have two reference points for measurement. To measure this southern 180 degree arc of "slings" was to measure 100 cubits reaching from the first end to the final end—which is to say the from the far east edge back to the far west edge. Given that the π constant (approximated at 3.14) describes the ratio between a circle's circumference and a circle's diameter, the 100 cubit south edge dimension described in Exodus 27:9 seems to correlate quite well with a 100 cubit diameter given that the wool curtain set (Exodus 26:7-13) that was specified, quantified, and sized in such a way to require a perimeter measuring a total of 314 cubits. Granted, assembled lengths and quantities of curtains must ultimately be reconciled to the balance of courtyard hardware and descriptions, but at first glance it seems like this implied ratio of a 314 cubit circumference to a 100 cubit span could hardly be by mistake.

Exodus 27:10 goes on to qualify the metal hardware used to support the court's south edge "slings", including twenty copper posts, twenty copper "controllers", and "fillets" of silver. With the vast majority of the 70 talents of copper being dedicated to the courtyard frame to make "slings" for the curtains, simple calculations demonstrate the viability of making a large set of copper rods to be used for courtyard posts and curtain rods. While the courtyard curtain rod frame accounted for the bulk of the copper, trace amounts of silver were also used, amounting to less than 1% of that which was allocated to the ribs and the ring assemblies. To be more specific, Exodus 38:28 allots only 1775 shekels, or about 55 pounds for these silver "fillets", which amounts to a little more than one pound of silver per post (occupying under 4 cubic inches). This is in stark contrast to that which is depicted in the rectangular courtyard models, which often presume that large silver items are mounted upon the top of courtyard posts, or possibly an array of items, including rings, hooks, blocks, and even enormous decorative spheres. Regardless of traditional indifference to hardware weights and measures, the amount of silver allocated for these joints would allow for the hardware to perform the function of a hook or tee joint.

Approximate 40 Shekel / Single Tee Volume

While the material inventory, item quantities, item weights, and overall dimensions seem viable, how does this interpretation correspond to the irregular eleven curtain set of Exodus 26:7-13?

What is a Shekel?

A shekel is a silver coin and also a unit of weight used in ancient times. In today's units, a shekel weighs about 11 grams (close to a modern half dollar).

How Big are Silver Hooks or "Fillets"?

"And the twenty pillars thereof and their twenty sockets shall be of brass; the hooks of the pillars and their fillets shall be of silver.

And of the thousand seven hundred seventy and five shekels he made hooks for the pillars, and overlaid their chapiters, and filleted them."

~ Exodus 27:10 & 38:28, KJV ~

With only 1775 shekels allocated towards courtyard hardware, only 30 or 40 shekels of silver (about 1 pound—occupying the same volume as a mobile phone) could be allotted for each part.

God's Dwelling Place Reconsidered

Quality Control
REWORK

TEXT REFERENCE: Exodus 27:9-11
CORRECTIVE ACTION: Remove copper posts and rods and silver joints so they may be spaced and sized in accordance with Exodus instructions.

Tabernacle Material Transition
Copper Courtyard Posts and Rods Joined by Silver Tee

The House of El Shaddai

Quality Control REWORK
TEXT REFERENCE: Exodus 27:9-19
CORRECTIVE ACTION: Eliminate wood posts as there are no provisions for wood courtyard posts in the Exodus instructions.

Traditional Rectangular Model
South Courtyard Curtain and Metal Frame Removed

God's Dwelling Place Reconsidered

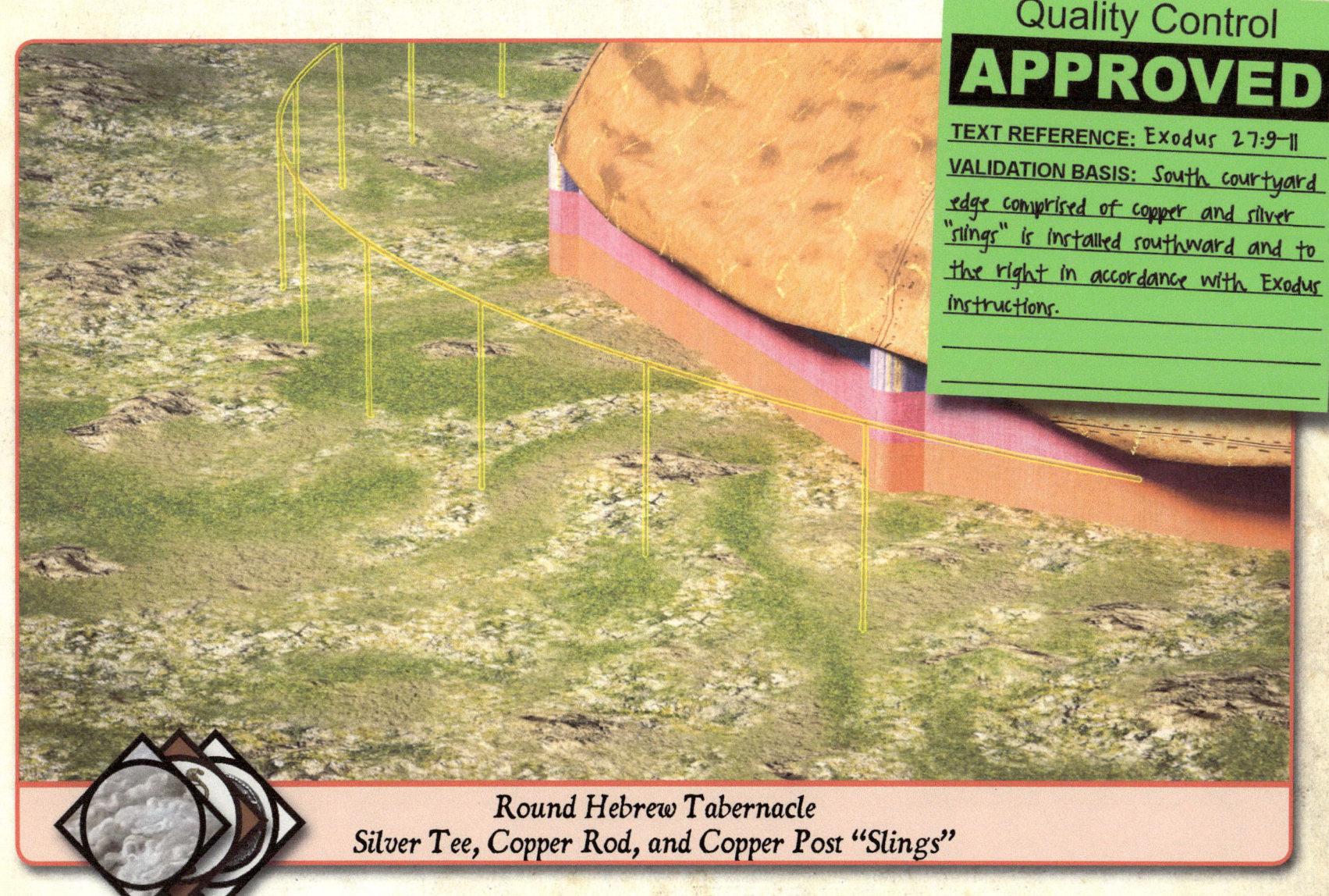

Round Hebrew Tabernacle
Silver Tee, Copper Rod, and Copper Post "Slings"

Quality Control APPROVED
TEXT REFERENCE: Exodus 27:9-11
VALIDATION BASIS: South courtyard edge comprised of copper and silver "slings" is installed southward and to the right in accordance with Exodus instructions.

The House of El Shaddai

Quality Control APPROVED

TEXT REFERENCE: Exodus 27:9-11

VALIDATION BASIS: Single wool curtain measuring 30 cubits (Exodus 26:7-13) is installed on copper and silver frame or "slings".

Round Hebrew Tabernacle
Single 30 Cubit Wool Curtain Installed

God's Dwelling Place Reconsidered

Round Hebrew Tabernacle
Courtyard "Slings" and Curtain - Interior View

Quality Control APPROVED
TEXT REFERENCE: Exodus 27:9-11
VALIDATION BASIS: Silver joint used to connect rods and ports is made with silver quantity as described in Exodus 38:28.

The House of El Shaddai

Quality Control APPROVED

TEXT REFERENCE: Exodus 27:9-11

VALIDATION BASIS: South courtyard hangings complete; wool curtains are installed on 20 copper posts, 20 copper rods, and with 20 silver joints.

Round Hebrew Tabernacle
Southern Courtyard Barrier Complete

Mirror Image

"And likewise for the north side in length there shall be hangings of an hundred cubits long, and his twenty pillars and their twenty sockets of brass; the hooks of the pillars and their fillets of silver."

~ Exodus 27:11, KJV ~

The north edge is described exactly as the south edge—with 20 posts, 20 rods, and 20 tees.

Exodus Text Reorientation

"And for the breadth of the court on the west side shall be hangings of fifty cubits: their pillars ten, and their sockets ten. And the breadth of the court on the east side eastward shall be fifty cubits."

~ Exodus 27:12-13, KJV ~

From the translated Exodus texts, a rectangle with a 2:1 aspect ratio is traditionally envisioned. However, given two courtyard ring halves or archs measuring 100 long x 50 wide, a rectangle need not be assumed.

North Courtyard Edge

With many of the same points of translation clarification, the north edge, as summarized into Exodus 27:11, seems to be described as a mirror image of the southern counterpart. This description of the courtyard in two halves seems reasonable, especially as the Tabernacle frame is described in the same way in Exodus 26—with a south half followed by a north half. But what about other edges or sides of the Tabernacle, as mentioned after Exodus 27:11?

West and East Courtyard Edges

Perhaps mimicking some of the unusual precedent established by the Tabernacle's westward "thigh" description of Exodus 26:22, it would appear that the courtyard's western edge is described in a pattern similar to that of Exodus 27:12. However, the western courtyard edge description in verse 12 is unusual, in that it does not instruct the reader to "make" anything—either in translation or in the Hebrew text. In fact, the only commandment to "make" anything for the courtyard is first issued in Exodus 27:9, which is where the overarching commandment to "make" the courtyard is given—which is followed by qualifying language that focuses on the *how* instead of the *what*.

Following this primary courtyard fabrication mandate, the Exodus 27 text continues with a multi-verse description of the courtyard's configuration. This approach is unique, in that it doesn't command the reader to "make" each thing on a per-item basis, as did Exodus 26; but rather it describes the courtyard in terms of features, where the "courtyard" was the only item that was specified to be "made". Thus, when pondering how the courtyard's western edge is configured, it is important to consider that mere mention of a west courtyard edge isn't exactly equal to

Both Halves Measure 100 Cubits in Length

The House of El Shaddai

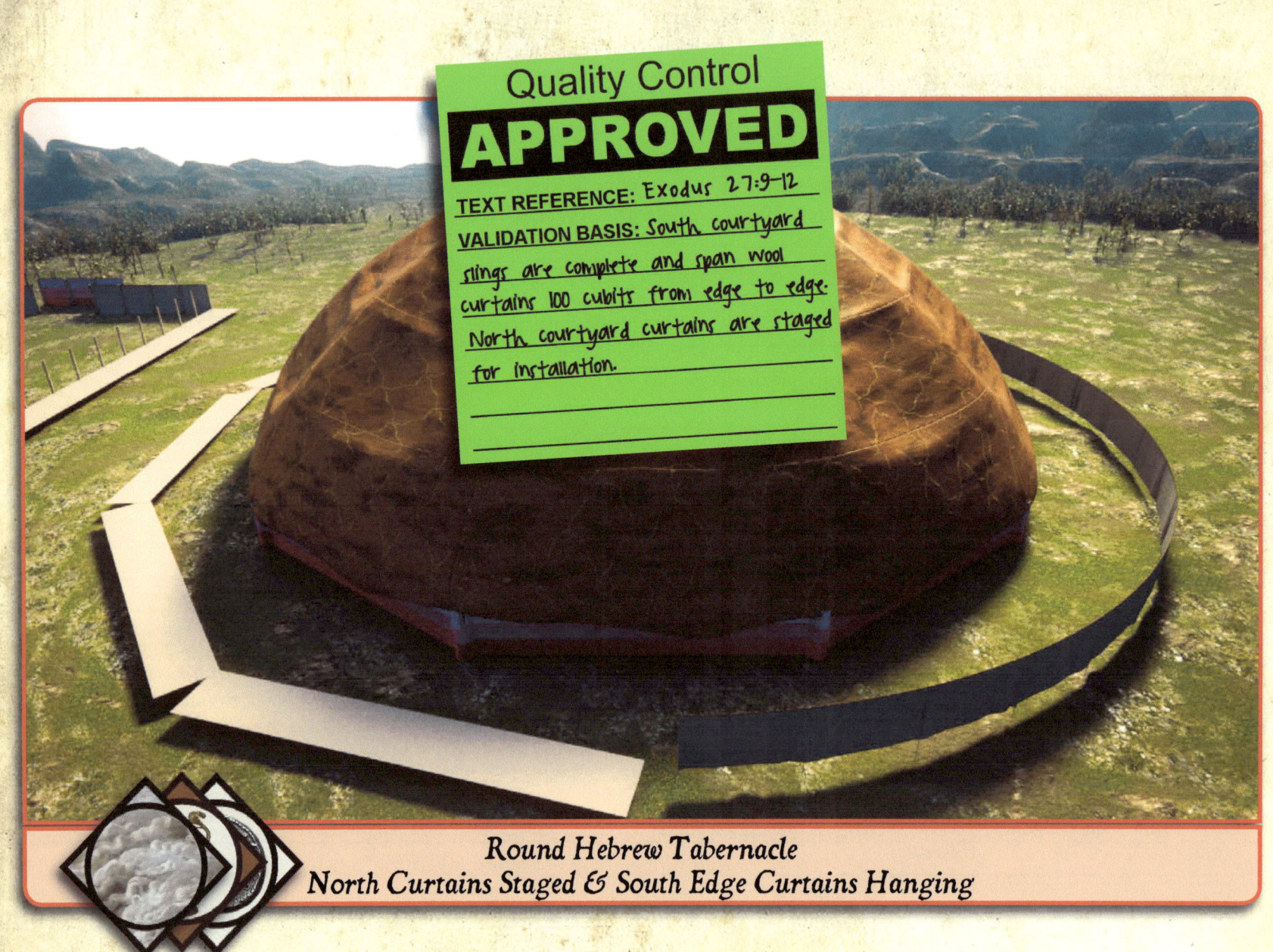

Quality Control APPROVED

TEXT REFERENCE: Exodus 27:9-12

VALIDATION BASIS: South courtyard slings are complete and span wool curtains 100 cubits from edge to edge. North courtyard curtains are staged for installation.

Round Hebrew Tabernacle
North Curtains Staged & South Edge Curtains Hanging

God's Dwelling Place Reconsidered

Quality Control APPROVED

TEXT REFERENCE: Exodus 27:9-11

VALIDATION BASIS: North courtyard curtains are hanging on courtyard frame (south courtyard is moved to the south temporarily to distinguish between north and south sections).

Round Hebrew Tabernacle
North Curtains Hung & Courtyard Split for Illustration

instructions to go and make a new or independent west courtyard edge. In fact, as verse 12 mentions the dimensions of west edge "hangings", it merely adds to the description, "their pillars ten, and their sockets ten"; but it does not issue a verbal command and say "make ten pillars and make ten sockets for them". While this may be an untraditional way to interpret verse 12, it is not a baseless proposition, as two courtyard halves were already introduced, each of which possess a western half given that the two sections—north and south—were created as two half-circles. But what purpose could there be in describing preexisting south and north courtyard hardware a second time, and from a second—and specifically western—vantage point?

Post Counting

Exodus 27:9-13 describes two courtyard halves spanning a length of 100 cubits with 20 posts in the south and 20 posts in the north. Of these halves, it also describes 10 west posts, and west and east edges measuring 50 cubits wide.

Courtyard Orientation

From a careful survey of the Exodus Tabernacle texts, it would seem that Exodus 27:12 is written to provide hardware orientation clarification, as did Exodus 26:28. Exodus 26:28 did not direct the reader to "make" anything, but rather described the tent frame as having a contiguous spine in the north-south direction, which ultimately prescribed a particular "westward" brace and ring orientation. In a similar way, exact courtyard post locations have yet to be defined for the north or south edges. As such, verse 12 could just as easily be understood to be a means of clarifying courtyard post placement—along with north and south courtyard orientation, whereby the north edge is to be oriented such that half of the 20 posts on the north edge reside on the west side. Granted that the posts are spaced equidistantly on a semicircle, this would suggest that the north edge is orientated in a way whereby the southernmost posts would be aligned perfectly parallel to an east-west axis. Likewise, the north most extremity of the north courtyard half could not be offset from cardinal compass axes, lest the posts along the west arc of the north courtyard become less than ten in number.

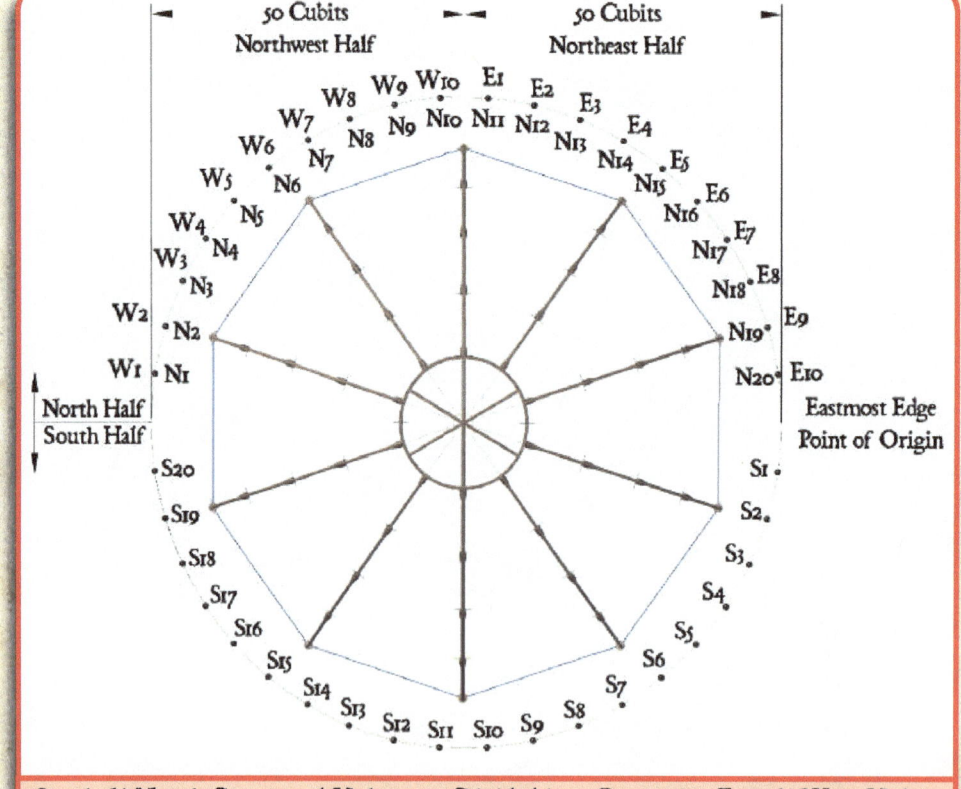

South & North Courtyard Halves are Divided into Respective East & West Halves

Mirror Image

As the courtyard is created in two halves—south and north, two west court sections would be created, as well as two east sections, also split down an east-west axis.

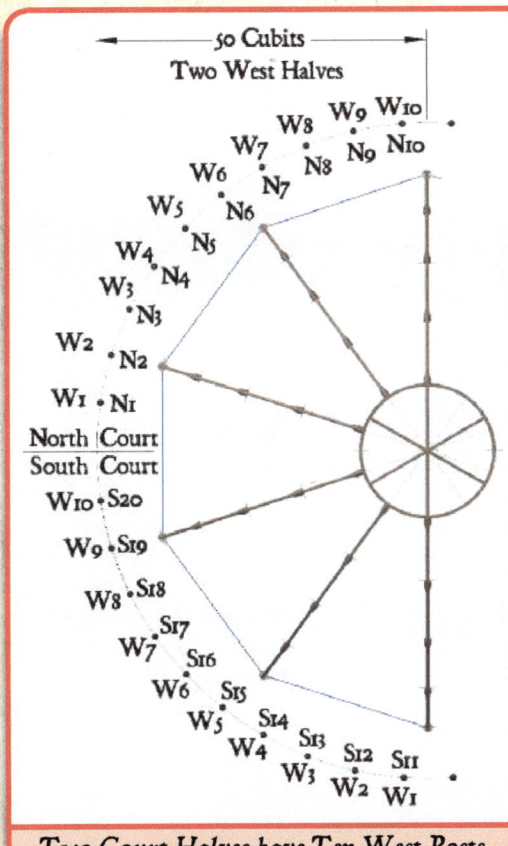

Two Court Halves have Ten West Posts

While post quantity descriptions speak to courtyard orientation, the same can be said of the west edge "width" measurement as introduced in Exodus 27:12. Given that the north court half is a semicircle spanning 100 cubits, it stands to reason that its radius would measure 50 cubits, the western side being no exception. This alignment objective coincides with verse 12, "And for the breadth of the court on the west side shall be hangings of fifty cubits," as the perfectly aligned northern semicircle section would need to span exactly 50 cubits to the west. Of course, if not perfectly aligned, the western portion of the courtyard would not measure 50 cubits from the center to the west edge. This begs the question, "Does the 'breadth of the court on the west side' refer to a measurement of the overall courtyard spanning in the north-south direction, or is it a measurement of the western half of the court, taken in the east-west direction?" What is the scope of the "court" that is referred to in verse 12 (i.e., half or full circle), and from where are "breadth" measurements taken? In order to understand the courtyard's shape and size, measurement terminology and points of reference need to be considered in context.

Hebrew Width

Exodus 27 seems to make a distinction between court "length" and "breadth" or "width" as it uses two different terms; but from where are these measurements to be taken? In English, a so-called "length" measurement is typically the longest edge or side of an object, and likewise, "width" or "breadth" is typically associated with the full edge length that is normal to either the long edge or to the axis of the viewer's vantage point on a horizontal plane. But is this consistent with Hebrew terminology and reasoning? The ancient Hebrew word for breadth or width used in verse 12 is comprised of three pictorial letters that signify three simple things; a "head", a "wall", and a "tent". Could it be a matter of coincidence that the ancient Hebrew spelling seems to directly speak to

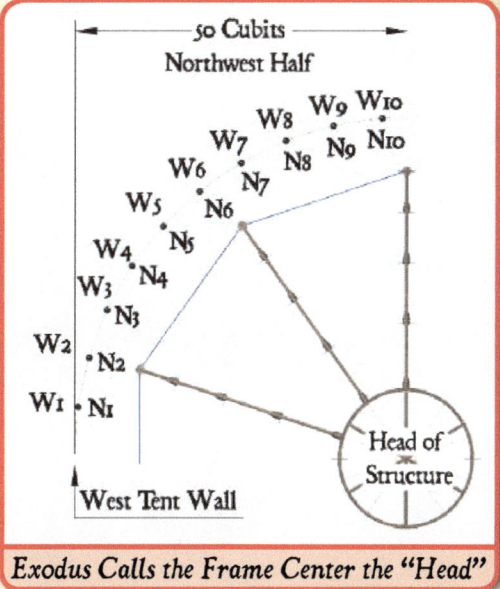

Exodus Calls the Frame Center the "Head"

The House of El Shaddai

Quality Control APPROVED

TEXT REFERENCE: Exodus 27:9-12

VALIDATION BASIS: North courtyard curtains are oriented so they have a west edge (10 copper posts and rods are placed on the west).

Round Hebrew Tabernacle
North Curtains Staged & South Edge Curtains Hanging

God's Dwelling Place Reconsidered

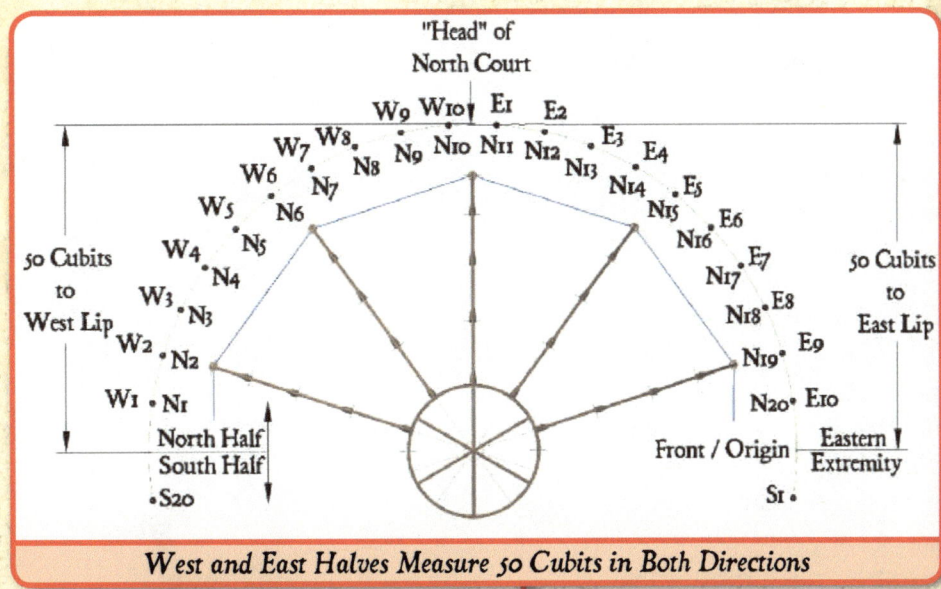

West and East Halves Measure 50 Cubits in Both Directions

the subject matter in question? What if the point of origin for this "breadth" measurement is the "head" or center of the tent, whereas the end point of the measurement was the tent wall—in this case, the west edge? This reasoning is consistent with Exodus 26:24, which clearly refers to the tent-frame's top and center as the "head". As proposed above, it would seem that the "head" and starting point of measurement, in the case of a northern courtyard edge, is the middle and northmost part or leading edge of the northern arc—being a center reference point that is neither western nor eastern. Given that the north edge of the courtyard is made from sweeping an arc clockwise and from west to east, it is logical to think that the arc is referred to as being divided two halves. After all, a circle has a west half and an east half, and that the "width" of the west half would logically be equal to one half of the entire circle.

East Side Eastward

"And the breadth of the court on the east side eastward shall be fifty cubits."

~ Exodus 27:13, KJV ~

Similar to the "south side southward" language in frame and courtyard descriptions, the "east side eastward" is redundant language in the English, but the Hebrew is making reference to the beginning (of the structure) and toward the direction of the sunrise.

As for the limit or scope of measurement, the language in Exodus 27:13 describing the eastern courtyard edge includes additional hints. Much like the case of the south rib beams and the south courtyard edge, the oversimplified English text describing the direction or location of the eastern edge demands further explanation. In the case of the "east side eastward" description, there are two distinct Hebrew words being used—one alluding to the direction of the sunrise, and the other alluding to the front or the beginning. Thus, the measurement which is normally considered to be merely the "eastern edge" should really be considered to be "toward the sunrise and toward the front" (rotating clockwise/southeast). This seems to negate the possibility that the entire eastern edge is the subject of measurement in the north-south direction. Obviously, given two half circles measuring 100 cubits in diameter, the radius is always equal to half of the diameter, whereby the radius is always measured from a circle's center (or head) to its edge or wall.

Courtyard Post Spacing

As proposed above, perceiving proper courtyard and post layout seems to be predicated upon understanding the π constant and how it dimensionally relates the wool curtain assembly as derived from Exodus 26:7-13 to the courtyard length as described throughout Exodus 27. While it is possible to achieve the same results without understanding how 314 mathematically relates to 100 by adherence to every detail revealed in the Hebrew texts, harmonizing the math and Bible language remains a prerequisite to completing the courtyard design. This becomes especially apparent when inferring a rectangular shape from the Exodus 27 text, as it yields disastrous results from the standpoint of symmetry, layout, and hardware allotment.

Although a round courtyard solution seems to suggest that courtyard hardware is arranged symmetrically, it would be perhaps premature to insist that the posts were placed around the courtyard in an equidistant arrangement at this point. After all, the Exodus 27:9-13 texts only speak of total post quantities and total distance spans—not defining the space between individual posts. However, Exodus does offer comprehensive instructions for courtyard post spacing, even though they have been perverted by translators. As previously proposed, many English Bibles are penned with translation bias with the objective of helping the end user better perceive a rectangular Tabernacle. This intention is apparent in Exodus 27:14-15, which seem to describe courtyard post spacing for only the posts immediately adjacent to the gate, which is understood to be in the east. Describing the post spacing, it is translated as, "The hangings of one side of the gate shall be fifteen cubits: their pillars three, and their sockets three. And on the other side shall be hangings fifteen cubits: their pillars three, and their sockets three."

As discussed previously, given the Exodus 27:14-15 description, three equidistant sections are traditionally inferred, with rectangular courtyard models assuming east courtyard wall posts are to be spaced at 15/3 or a 5 cubit spacing, even though three posts would more logically correspond with two equidistant sections spaced at 15/2 or at 7 ½ cubits apart. Recalling that Exodus 26:7-13 specifies eleven curtains measuring 30 cubits in length, it is only logical to see Exodus 27:14-15 as referring to two "flanks" of the same curtain—one to the left and the other to the right, with the center post being a point of reference for each "flank". In other words, the left half of a 30 cubit long wool curtain measures 15 cubits, and the right flank measures 15 cubits, all of which would be supported by a total of five posts that equidistantly space the curtain into four divisions, measuring 7 ½ cubits each. Assuming there are ten curtains at the full 30 cubit length and one

Post Intervals

"The hangings of one side of the gate shall be fifteen cubits: their pillars three, and their sockets three. And on the other side shall be hangings fifteen cubits: their pillars three, and their sockets three."

~ Exodus 27:14-15, KJV ~

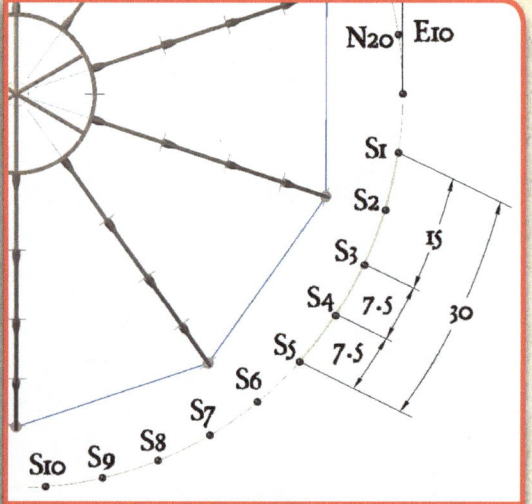

Courtyard Post Spacing for Single Curtain

If divided by a shared center post, a single wool curtain measuring 30 cubits (Exodus 26:7-13) would form two 15 cubit "flanks". Each 15 cubit flank would be spanned by three posts measuring 7.5 cubits apart.

God's Dwelling Place Reconsidered

Quality Control APPROVED

TEXT REFERENCE: Exodus 27:14-15

VALIDATION BASIS: Posts are spaced at an interval of three posts over 15 cubits. The 30 cubit curtain is spanned by 5 posts, with one "flank" being left of the center post and the other "flank" being right of the center post.

Round Hebrew Tabernacle
Single Wool Curtain - Two Sides or "Flanks"

reduced to 15 cubits when folded in half, the metal courtyard "slings" would "court" the wool fabric in a complete circle. Knowing that nominal courtyard circumference is reduced from 315 to 314 by mandated curtain loop overlap (Exodus 26:13), it follows that the measurement between posts is not center-to-center, but rather post-edge-to-post-edge (i.e., taking pole diameter into account) along the courtyard's circumference. Thus, the difference between the 314 cubit fabric dimensions can be reconciled to the specified courtyard post spans, which are at 15 cubit intervals for a total sum amounting to less than 315 cubits (minus post diameters, which relate to loop overlap).

While this proposed 7 ½ cubit post-interval solution seems to work with the eleven wool curtains of Exodus 26:7-13 measuring 30 cubits each, how does it work given the specified quantities of 40 courtyard posts, as Exodus 27:9-10 specifies? Logically, a circle with a circumference measuring nearly 315 cubits that is supported by posts spaced at a 7 ½ cubit span would require a post quantity that is defined as 315 cubits / 7 ½ cubits per post, or 42 posts. Again, Exodus specified only 20 posts for the south edge, along with another 20 posts for the north—which amounts of a sum of only 40 posts. So what's missing?

~ Courtyard Gating and Closure ~

In finishing the description of the courtyard bounding the Tabernacle facility, the Exodus account makes a single verse reference to what is presumed to be remaining hardware required for a single gate, and concludes by expounding on the purpose or arrangement of previously introduced hardware (Exodus 27:16-19).

Given rectangular courtyard assumptions and the English Exodus translation above, courtyard gates are depicted in a variety of different ways. Of course, the curtain's color scheme is assumed to be a matter of the artist's discretion. Furthermore, because of the standing confusion surrounding the courtyard post descriptions and arrangement, traditional models are not consistent in how the courtyard gate is depicted. Sometimes the four gate posts are assumed to have no commonality with adjacent posts that form the east wall of the courtyard, whereas other times the two exterior posts of the courtyard are assumed to be shared with the courtyard. Still

Gate Confusion

"And for the gate of the court shall be an hanging of twenty cubits, of blue, and purple, and scarlet, and fine twined linen, wrought with needlework: and their pillars shall be four, and their sockets four."

~ Exodus 27:16, KJV ~

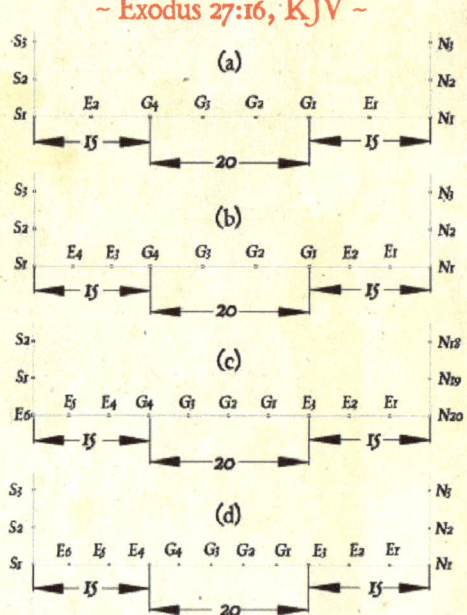

Different assumptions yield different east wall and gate post spacing. Wall and gate post intervals created in typical models might be (a) 7.5/6.66, (b) 5/6.66, (c) 5/5, or (d) 5/4 cubits, respectively.

Court Size & Shape

"All the pillars round about the court shall be filleted with silver; their hooks shall be of silver, and their sockets of brass. The length of the court shall be an hundred cubits, and the breadth fifty everywhere, and the height five cubits of fine twined linen, and their sockets of brass."

~ Exodus 27:17-18, KJV ~

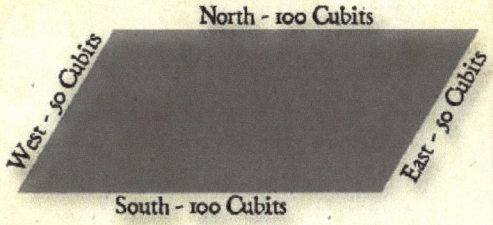

Could a four-sided shape be anything but a rectangle? A polygon with four walls of defined lengths may not necessarily form a rectangle or have right angle corners. Furthermore, the Exodus texts never use the term "rectangle" to describe the Tabernacle or the courtyard. To the contrary, Exodus 27:17 describes posts that are "round about the court". A circle has an in-"side" and out-"side", and a compass, even though it is round, is often regarded to have four "sides".

other times the courtyard barrier proposed for the gate is thought to be altogether separate from the courtyard's east wall—spaced at some undefined dimension. Regardless of the gate location or post allocation approach, traditional models seem to consistently assume that the courtyard entrance area measures 20 cubits in width, thus creating three curtain and post intervals at the Tabernacle's gate, measuring 6.66 cubits between posts!

Apart from the new courtyard gate detail, there is the matter of explaining remaining courtyard dimensions. From verse 18, traditional models almost universally presume a courtyard barrier height measuring 5 cubits. Ignoring logistical liabilities and disregarding Exodus 27 post material specifications with a sense of impunity, a small fraction of courtyard models (e.g., the Holman Bible illustration) seem to depict extremely tall courtyard posts, reaching 5 cubits above the overall height of the Tabernacle itself, which is presumed to be approximately 10 cubits in height. While proposing the extra tall 15 cubit posts seems to be attached to some form of reasoning, such as obscuring the entire Tabernacle from exterior line-of-sight viewing, the use of 5 cubit posts otherwise seems to be requested without basis or correlation to other hardware dimensions.

Furthermore, the reiteration of overall courtyard dimensions at this point seems to be even more bizarre. If the courtyard is to be arranged as a rectangle measuring 100 x 50 cubits along the cardinal points of the compass, why make it a point to detail the overall length of each side? If the Tabernacle courtyard is rectangular, why indicate that it has a south wall measuring 100 cubits, a north wall measuring 100 cubits, a west wall measuring 50 cubits, and an east wall measuring 15+20+15 cubits, only to say again at the conclusion of the description, that it measures 100 x 50 cubits? If not for the concluding dimension, should the Exodus reader be otherwise inclined to assume a courtyard in the shape of a parallelogram or a trapezoid as opposed to a rectangle with perpendicular walls and 90 degree corners?

Finally, there is the matter of pins or pegs as described in Exodus 27:19. Without any instructions listed in Exodus to tether the courtyard posts to the ground, traditional models typically depict two pegs being used to keep each post upright (requiring ~128 pegs for the courtyard alone). Needless to say, such pegs would need to be fabricated long enough to allow for sufficient embed depth and thick enough to provide ample resistance against bending induced by wind loading on

The House of El Shaddai

Quality Control
REJECTED

TEXT REFERENCE: Exodus 27:16-17
BASIS FOR FAILURE: Courtyard posts are to be made of metal, not wood. Also, insufficient material exists to create large copper socket bases or silver post caps. If posts are secured with tie downs, ropes and pegs create a tripping hazard at the entrance.

Traditional Rectangular Tabernacle
East Gate Curtain, Posts, Sockets, Rods, and Connectors

Anchor Pins?

"All the vessels of the tabernacle in all the service thereof, and all the pins thereof, and all the pins of the court, shall be of brass."

~ Exodus 27:19, KJV ~

If copper pegs are made for tie-down stakes to tether courtyard walls and the rectangular Tabernacle roof to the ground out of necessity, insufficient copper would be available for courtyard posts and rods.

the curtains, especially if the courtyard wall was 15 cubits high instead of 5 cubits high. Either way, given this proposed duty, the relatively small amount of copper already committed to other uses according to Exodus, including courtyard and gate posts and rods, presumed courtyard post "sockets" or "bases", and the altar, would be further reduced, resulting in smaller parts. To propose that pins, mentioned here at the conclusion of the courtyard description, are also to be employed to help keep the rectangular tent upright only adds further insult to injury when it comes to copper material allotment. It becomes all the more absurd given the absence of prior mention, instruction, or corresponding hardware features incorporated to perform a substantial load bearing task. After all, the Tabernacle structure is traditionally thought to be twice as tall as the courtyard posts, and use of the copper pegs in a wind resistance capacity on the Tabernacle would be a mission-critical design consideration. Ironically, life-sized models resemble billboards and require lateral anchoring to prevent them from toppling in the wind; yet the Exodus text does not seem to expound on this design requirement in any meaningful way.

Round Courtyard and Gate Posts

As discussed above, Exodus 27 describes four gate posts and another gate screen measuring 20 cubits in length. Moreover, it was noted previously that a round courtyard arrangement seems to have a deficiency when it comes to gate posts, as it would take 42 posts at a 7½ cubit span to court a circumference measuring 315 cubits. In contrast, Exodus 27 describes 20 south posts and 20 north posts—half of which are on the west edge, and half of which are on the east edge. From this description, is it reasonable to consider the possibility that some of the gate posts are required to do "double duty", acting as a courtyard perimeter post as well as a post for the gate? How would a 20 cubit screen for the gate be required to interface with a circle, featuring gate posts spaced at 7½ cubit intervals, on a courtyard with a circumference of 314 cubits?

Timna Park Tabernacle Model with Steel Braces & Anchors - © 2016 Andrew Hoy

To put the courtyard gate into proper perspective, Exodus

The House of El Shaddai

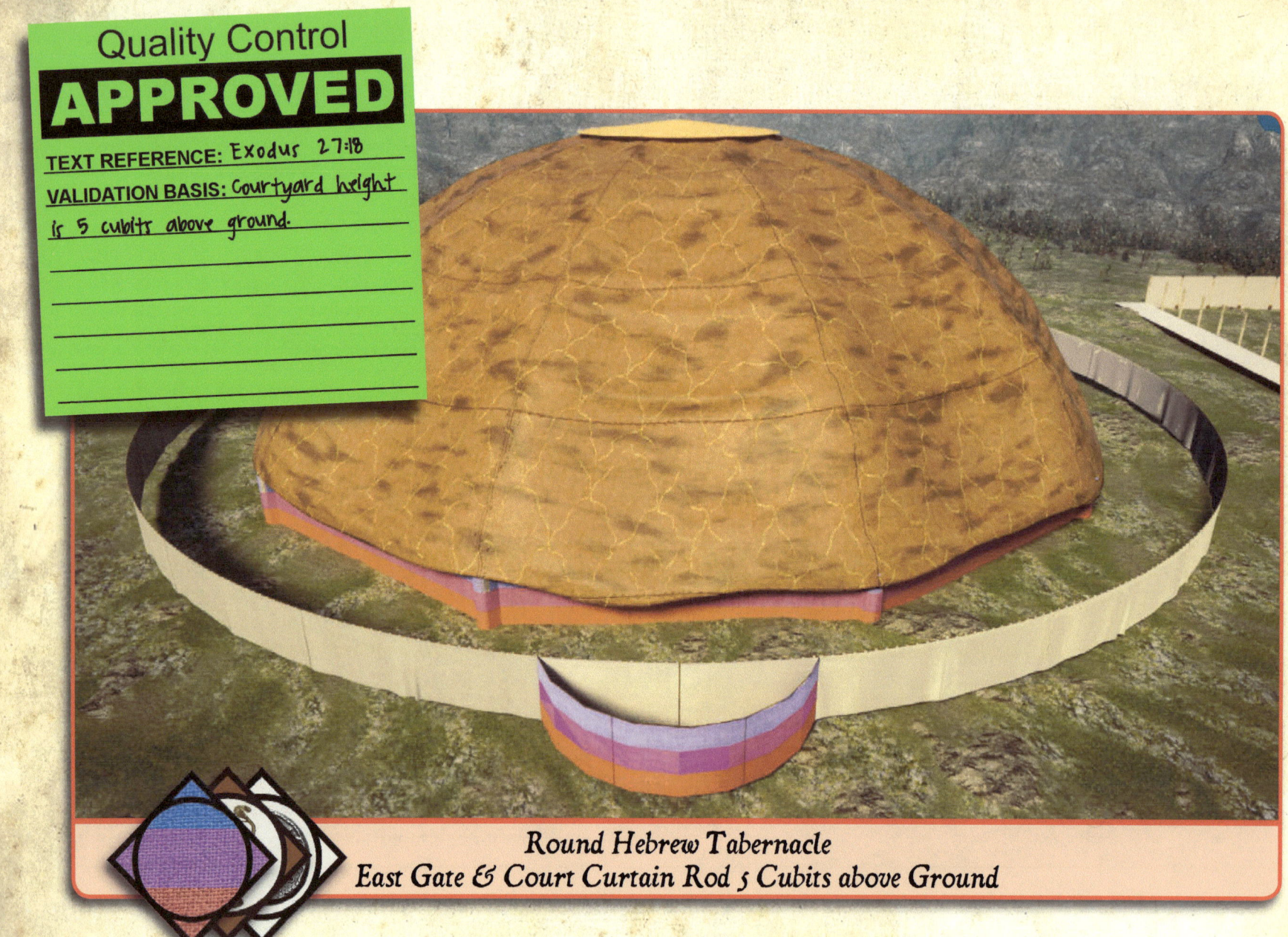

Quality Control APPROVED
TEXT REFERENCE: Exodus 27:18
VALIDATION BASIS: Courtyard height is 5 cubits above ground.

Round Hebrew Tabernacle
East Gate & Court Curtain Rod 5 Cubits above Ground

Gate Posts

A west post (which is neither south nor north) is included "to gate" two halves, which have 20 posts installed only on north and south sides. The remaining 3 gate posts are used to hang both the 15 cubit (eleventh folded C11) wool sheet and 20 cubit (outer east gate) fabrics.

English texts must again be compared to the literal Hebrew text. In English, Exodus 27:16 reads, "And for *the* gate of the court shall be an hanging of twenty cubits". However, the Hebrew translation more literally reads, "and *to* gate the court screen twenty cubits". On numerous occasions, verbs have been confused or substituted with prepositions and nouns (e.g., "edge" and "court"), and it seems the Tabernacle courtyard "gate" narrative contains yet another occurrence. While this subtle grammar distinction may sound trivial, adding just one definite article misleads the reader into thinking there is only one gate.

With four posts being provided as hardware "to gate the courtyard", it is first necessary to consider what "to gate the courtyard" might mean. Traditional models, of course, begin with the assumption that the four posts are required for *the* courtyard gate, that is, a single and particular gate. However, these models don't always fully consider the possibility of single objects being employed for multiple uses, or for that matter, as things having multiple descriptions. Neither do they consider the importance of verbs in the scheme of discerning hardware. Assuming "gate" to be a verb as opposed to a noun, any hardware that is provided "to gate" might simply perform an open-and-close function.

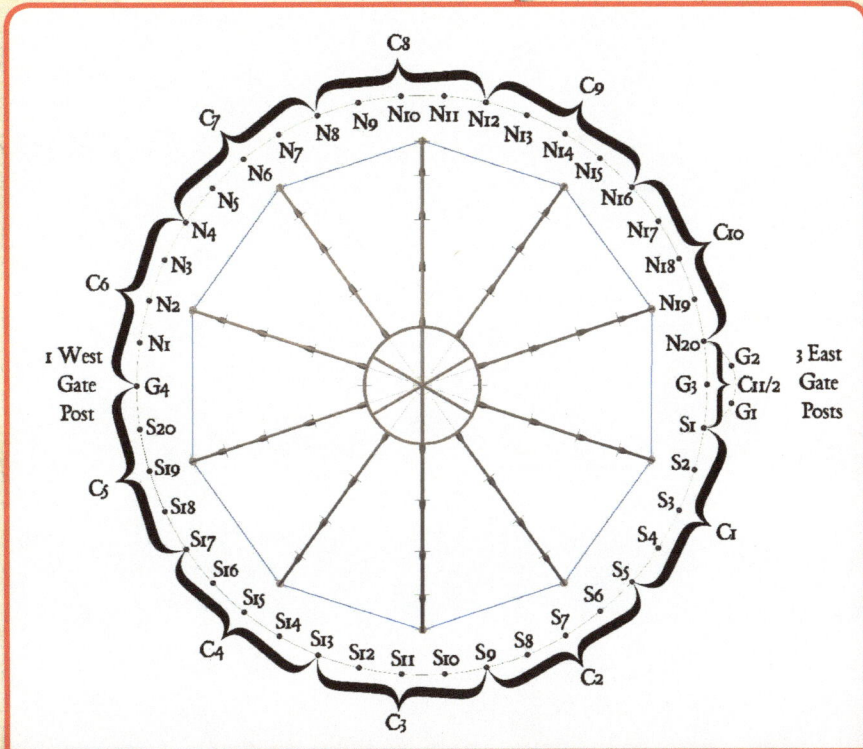

Four Posts Installed at West and East Gate Connections

Of the four gate posts of Exodus 27:16, two of the four are provided to "close" or "gate" the two halves of the courtyard circle (see G3 and G4 on adjacent diagram). As first illustrated in Part 1, the eleven wool curtains were divided into two sets—a set of five (designated by C1-C5) and a set of six (designated by C6-C11/2). While Exodus 26:11 indicated that the two sets were to become joined together, it didn't exactly say *how*. Likewise, as illustrated in Part 4, the courtyard "hangings" or frame was to be made in two sections—a south half and a north half. With both south and north halves comprised of 20 posts each, for a total of 40, it would seem that a nominal circumference could not be attained in the event that post interval spacing was defined as 7½ cubits between each post, since 40 x 7½ would yield a total of 300 cubits, not a nominal circumference of 315. However, if two "gate" posts are added, one on the far east side and the other on the far west side, closing the circle, the courtyard begins to resemble a mathematical symphony. Furthermore, with the two posts being due east and due west, it explains why they could not be listed among posts of the south edge or the north edge, as they are neither.

Regarding the final two copper posts (designated by G1 and G2) that are provided "to gate" the courtyard, they would logically be used in conjunction with the two courtyard end posts (designated by S1 and N20) in order "to gate" the fabric screen. To provide a special entrance area protruding from the eastern side of the courtyard circle, copper curtain rods would be spanned between the four gate posts (designated by N20, G2, G1, and S1). With these four posts, a gate screen spanning 20 cubits in length would be easily accommodated. Moreover, sharing a common courtyard gate post (designated by S1) where three curtain sets meet would lend itself as an extremely practical place to install fifty brass clasps or buttons (Exodus 26:11), such that the gate entry point might be both accessible and capable of being secured.

Admittedly, the observed overlap between these four posts might be described as bizarre, especially as the four posts can be perceived so differently. For example, in a literal sense, the addition of four posts (designated by G1, G2, G3, and G4) is required to complete both the gate and the courtyard. However, performing a gating function on the primary courtyard circle itself, there are but four posts (designated by G4, as well as G3, N20, and S1, to close the doubled 15 cubit curtain). Finally, the primary east entrance can also be seen as a four piece set (designated by N20, G2, G1, and S1). While Exodus does not make hints about the potential parallel meaning and versatility of the model, all of them are without dispute the logical outworkings of the literal Hebrew language.

Fifty in Fifty

"The length of the court (is) a hundred by the cubit, and the breadth fifty by fifty, and the height five cubits, of twined linen, and their sockets (are) brass..."

~ Exodus 27:18, YLT ~

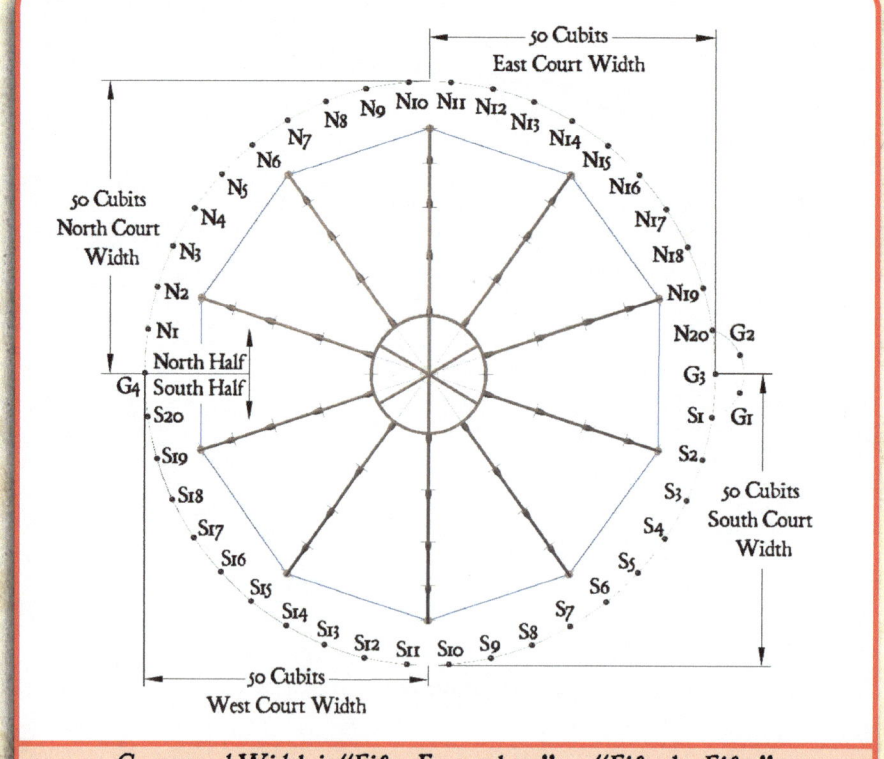

Courtyard Width is "Fifty Everywhere" or "Fifty by Fifty"

God's Dwelling Place Reconsidered

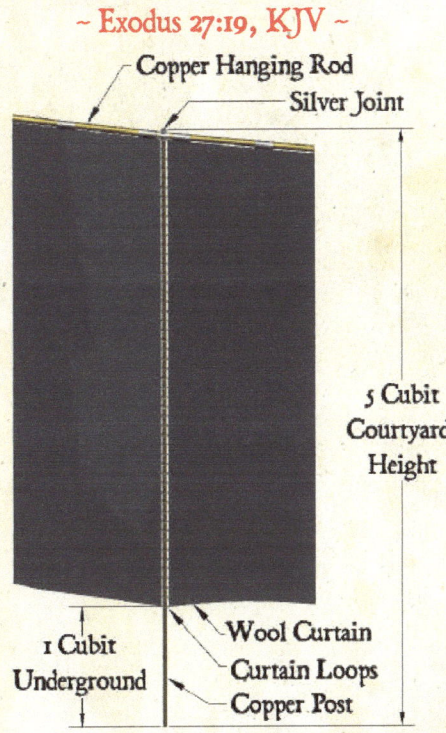

Posts = Pins

"All the vessels of the tabernacle in all the service thereof, and all the pins thereof, and all the pins of the court, shall be of brass."

~ Exodus 27:19, KJV ~

Exodus 27:19 refers to the courtyard's copper posts as pins. With an embed depth of 1 cubit, 5 cubit posts raise court curtains 4 cubits above ground.

Pillars and Pins around the Courtyard

Understanding that the dimensions of two courtyard frame halves are given in Exodus 27:9-13, it seems somewhat strange that overall size of the courtyard is provided. Expressing what appears to be the overall measurement of a three-dimensional courtyard, King James' English Exodus reads, "The length of the court shall be an hundred cubits, and the breadth fifty *everywhere* and the height five cubits of fine twined linen." While this text is traditionally assumed to envelope the space occupied by the rectangular courtyard, the language is rather unusual—both in English and in Hebrew. What does it mean when it says, "the breadth fifty *everywhere*"? Why doesn't the text say, "the length of the court shall be an hundred cubits *everywhere*", or "the height five cubits *everywhere*", as it does for the width or breadth measurement?

When examining the Exodus 27:18 text in Hebrew, a number of nuances become apparent. First of all, when describing the length and width dimensions, it offers no orientation reference, as if the length (i.e., the maximum distance measurement) could be measured from any point across the span of the courtyard. As for the courtyard width or breadth, the Hebrew does not actually say, "the breadth fifty everywhere"; instead it says that the breadth is "fifty in fifty". Understanding that the Hebrew preposition for "in" is represented by a pictograph of a tent, it might also be understood as "fifty tenting fifty". As for the redundant "fifty" not usually translated into English (Young's Literal Translation being one exception), bear in mind that Exodus 27:9-12 conveys this very idea, as it described two courtyard sections with a length of 100 cubits but a width of 50 cubits. Combined, these two fifty cubit halves connected together might be expressed as "fifty in fifty" or perhaps "fifty tenting fifty". Of course, this round courtyard configuration would be consistent with Exodus 27:17, which described the courtyard's pillars as being arranged "round about the court". Thus, the description and dimensions are exactly what might be expected, given a circular courtyard arrangement. Each half is fifty cubits wide, and each quadrant measures fifty cubits in cardinal and radial directions relative to the center location.

Finally, the courtyard's five cubit courtyard height must be somehow reconciled to the round courtyard model. In particular, use of four cubit curtains would seem to contradict the English Exodus text which states, "the height five cubits of fine twined linen". So how could the courtyard

The House of El Shaddai

Quality Control APPROVED

TEXT REFERENCE: Exodus 27:18-19

VALIDATION BASIS: Courtyard height is still 5 cubits, but courtyard posts are pinned or embedded 1 cubit into the ground.

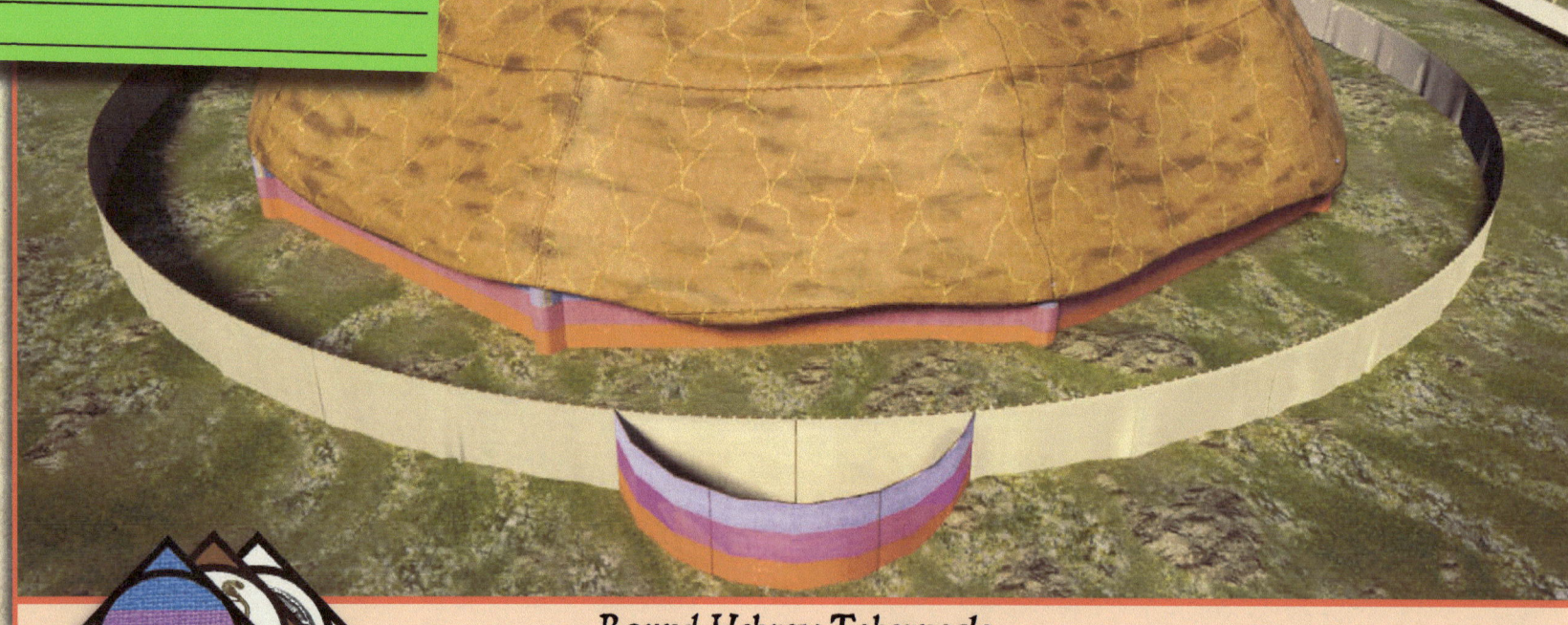

Round Hebrew Tabernacle
Courtyard is 4 Cubits above Ground (1 Cubit Post Depth)

God's Dwelling Place Reconsidered

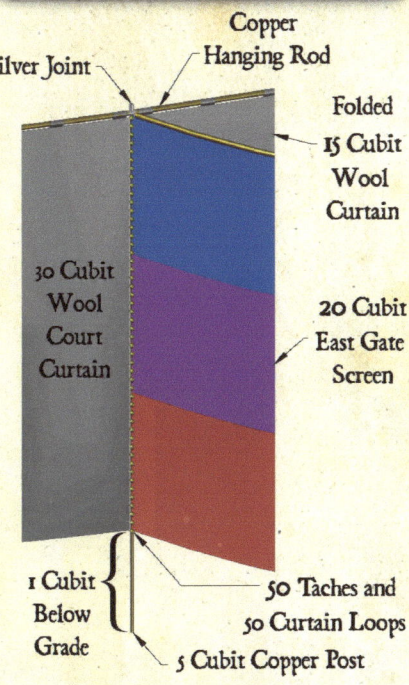

Putting it All Together

At the east gate and point of origin for Tabernacle construction, hardware including copper posts, copper rods, copper taches, silver joints, and curtain fabrics described in Exodus 26:7-13 and Exodus 27:9-19 converge—provided that the Hebrew texts are considered to be accurate and superior to traditions and translations.

reach four cubits high as the English Exodus indicates, if the rods from which the wool curtains hung only measured four cubits wide? Once again, there is a measurement reference problem at hand, as well as a translation problem. The text might be better translated as "and rise five cubits corded fabric". This begs the question, "from where is the rise to be measured?" Assuming that the courtyard post is a length (or height) of five cubits, how is it practical to use curtains that are one cubit shorter than the maximum post height? The answer is simple: by inserting the courtyard post a.k.a. "pillar" into the ground a total of one cubit below grade. Unfortunately, the English translations are not conducive to this conclusion – in part based on ambiguity of the English language.

In the simplest terms, the Hebrew word used for the courtyard post (Exodus 27:9-17) might be described as a "standing thing". However, perceptions of what Tabernacle courtyard "posts" or "pillars" are sized and shaped like and how they function is obfuscated based on modern English connotations and inference. Depending upon the situation, a "pillar" might possibly be equated to a post, pole, peg, shaft, bar, column, rod, stake, pile, or pin; although in everyday English, "pillars" are most likely associated with massive round columns bearing large vertical loads. In contrast, "posts" are more often associated with smaller vertical members like those used for signs, lights, or fencing—which is unlikely to be thought of as "pinned" into the ground, since pins are typically used in the context of fabrics, machinery, and dainty things. Nevertheless, contrary to what translations convey and traditional artwork depicts, the courtyard post is a copper bar or rod with a relatively small cross sectional area (dimensions being deduced from curtain loop overlap, hardware quantities, and total copper material allotment), which allows it to act as a stake or peg which can be "pinned" into the ground. Thus, as the courtyard frame is completed, it is "pinned" into the ground per the Exodus 27:19 instructions, allowing thin copper posts to elevate copper rods, which together are used to sling a wool courtyard barrier.

~ Copper Altar ~

Although the large brazen or copper altar is not required to make the Tabernacle stand, its size, shape, and location all become relevant parameters as it relates to the Tabernacle—and more particularly to the courtyard and the courtyard gate.

Similar to the four-layered roof installed over the Tabernacle and the 100 x 50 cubit courtyard, the large "brazen altar" outside of the Tabernacle seems to be yet another right-angled item that is incorporated into traditional Tabernacle models without question or dispute. While altars may be depicted as being adorned or ornamented differently in artwork, it is generally assumed to have a square footprint, measuring 5 cubits in length and width, but only 3 in height. As a shape seldom found in nature, a "foursquare" fire pit does not lend itself to even heat distribution and complete combustion. For this simple reason, people have made round fire rings since antiquity. Furthermore, traditional models might also raise the unusual square altar to abnormally high elevations—well above 3 cubits, and likewise they will create a long ramp that is used to better access the top of the altar. As for the altar's location, it seems that traditional models also depict a location with relative consistency, placing the altar in the center of the open courtyard area—almost equidistant between the courtyard gate and the main Tabernacle structure.

Built for Burning

"And thou shalt make an altar of shittim wood, five cubits long, and five cubits broad; the altar shall be foursquare: and the height thereof shall be three cubits."

~ Exodus 27:1, KJV ~

A square altar would create poor airflow and uneven heat distribution. Furthermore, the copper/brass altar was not intended for burning whole animals (Ex. 29:14-28, Lev. 1-7).

Built to Fit

In the sequence of the overall Tabernacle complex narrative, the first mention of the altar for burnt offerings appears to be deliberately interjected between the texts describing the Tabernacle tent fabrication and erection and the completion of the courtyard. Why is the altar described before the courtyard? Although Exodus 27 makes no mention of the altar's installed location, later Exodus texts seem to designate a very specific location for the burnt offerings. Even though the Exodus 27 texts seem to offer some burnt offering altar placement latitude, it is nevertheless clear that the Hebrew text does not afford such ambiguity in altar placement. In fact, the Hebrew Scripture does not include the phrase, "near the entrance to the tabernacle", but rather it is either at or in the Tabernacle entrance. This idea is further reinforced as the people were told that they were to bring their offerings *to the entrance of the Tent of Meeting*, as they inspected, slaughtered, bled, and to some extent burned them in close proximity (e.g., Leviticus 1). To the contrary, Israelites who were not part of the priestly caste were not given open invitation to wander aimlessly into the Tabernacle complex past the courtyard boundary.

Traditional Square Tabernacle Altar - Holman Bible, 1890

God's Dwelling Place Reconsidered

Quality Control APPROVED
TEXT REFERENCE: Exodus 27:1 & 38:18
VALIDATION BASIS: Courtyard copper and wood altar is placed at tent opening. Altar is quartered and measures 5 cubits by 5 cubits by 3 cubits high and surrounded by a 20 cubit gate curtain and a 15 cubit courtyard curtain.

Round Hebrew Tabernacle
Quartered Copper and Wood Altar - 5 x 5 x 3 Cubit Cylinder

With the altar placed directly in the Tabernacle entrance, and having a footprint measuring 5 cubits by 5 cubits, how does this relate to the decagonal Tabernacle structure and its circular courtyard? Could the copper altar fit in the doorway? If it would fit in the doorway, how and where might it fit? With an opening spanning approximately 15 cubits wide in the north-south direction at the courtyard entrance as bound by the 15 cubit wool curtain of Exodus 26:12, it seems like it would be no problem to fit the altar somewhere within the Tabernacle entrance breezeway. However, there are points of interference in the east-west direction that require some consideration. For example, placing the altar too far to the west would not only result in fire damage to the Tabernacle coverings, but it would also be impossible based on interference with the copper laver or water basin. Placing it in the midst of the altar at the 50 cubit courtyard radius seems to be contrary to logic, as the people were not invited past the courtyard barrier, and it would have been too close to the cleansing water basin. Thus, the only viable location for the burnt offering altar would seem to be immediately outside of the Tabernacle's courtyard but within its outer 20 cubit gate. But could the altar with a "foursquare" 5 x 5 cubit footprint fit in between the outer and inner tabernacle courtyard gates?

While the space created between the eastern 50 cubit radius courtyard extremity and 20 cubit long arc spanning 15 cubits would not accommodate a 5 cubit square altar footprint, it is most interesting that the east-west distance between the courtyard curtain rod edge and the outer gate courtyard rod is capable of accommodating a round altar measuring exactly 5 cubits in diameter! This also coincides with Exodus 38:18 courtyard gate texts, which reads, "The height in the breadth was five cubits, answerable to the hangings of the court." This mathematical specificity, being coupled to the textual anomalies, begs the question – is the altar really square in shape, or is it also round—as is the Tabernacle? Simple logic dictates that fire pits are fabricated in a circular configuration; lest the corner areas of the fire pit become subject to extremely uneven heat distribution and result in bad combustion. While it is uncustomary for ancient nomads to build rectangular dwellings, it is perhaps along the lines of absurd to envision anyone deliberately creating a square or rectangular fire pit. This perfect geometric correlation of a five cubit round altar relative to the round courtyard and five cubit gate puts the translation in question—given that the "foursquare" altar was merely "quartered" instead of being "square". If built in four sections, it would be easier to transport and easy to assemble four pie shaped sections.

Entrance Altar

"And thou shalt set the altar of the burnt offering before the door of the tabernacle of the tent of the congregation. And thou shalt set the laver between the tent of the congregation and the altar, and shalt put water therein."

~ Exodus 40:6-7, KJV ~

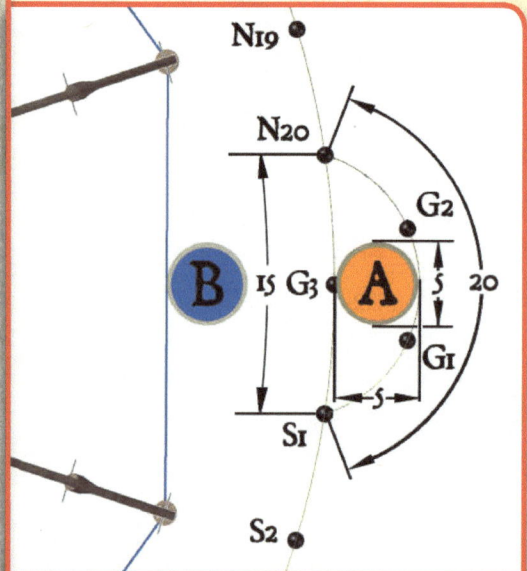

Altar (A) and Basin (B) at Courtyard Gate

With the altar placed at the courtyard gate, the outer 20 cubit outer gate arc and the interior 15 cubit arc together create a perfect space to surround the round copper alter measuring 5 cubits.

Blood, Fire & Water

"Thou shalt also make a laver of brass, and his foot also of brass, to wash withal: and thou shalt put it between the tabernacle of the congregation and the altar, and thou shalt put water therein."

~ Exodus 30:18, KJV ~

The copper basin or laver would need to be large enough to deal with any number of animals that might be offered over the course of a given day. A large diameter basin that is thin-walled, lightweight, and high in capacity would be preferred by nomadic Hebrews over one that is thick rimmed and ornate.

A Clean Place

"And he set the laver between the tent of the congregation and the altar, and put water there, to wash withal."

~ Exodus 40:29, KJV ~

The basin or laver would need to be placed close to the tent if the tent was to be kept clean, but also close to the altar and entrance locations for reasons of practicality.

~ Copper Basin ~

In addition to a copper fire pit for burnt offerings, the Tabernacle complex was also furnished with a basin for storing wash water.

With no apparent dimensional specification given throughout the pages of Bible texts, the copper laver was not limited by the amount of copper that the Israelites had collected for the Tabernacle items (Exodus 38:29), but rather was limited in size by the contributions made by the women (Exodus 38:8), who gave up their copper mirrors for the sake of fabricating the copper laver. Even though there is no mention of basin decoration, Tabernacle article artwork often depicts the basins as being vessels that are either formed to elaborate shapes or endowed with elaborate decoration, without giving much thought to necessary form and function. There is perhaps no greater irony, as women sacrificed tools of vanity only so the men might make objects of vanity. Nevertheless, most traditional models seem to depict a relatively small, yet heavy elevated dish for washing—resembling a shallow bird bath or goblet rather than a deep tank. Furthermore, the small basins tend to be depicted as being located in the midst of the altar and front of the Tabernacle, which is far from the tent entrance.

Tabernacle Copper Laver / Basin - H. Bill, 1871

Reshaping Traditions

Because copper is highly malleable and antimicrobial, it is an excellent material for basin construction and water storage. Being easy to work and shape, it stands to reason that Betzalel, Aholiab, and their Israelite craftsmen would have made the basin as large as possible and in

The House of El Shaddai

Quality Control APPROVED

TEXT REFERENCE: Exodus 30:18
VALIDATION BASIS: The copper laver or basin is to be placed between the altar and the tent of meeting. If the altar is placed next to the tent it could be used to catch rainwater.

Round Hebrew Tabernacle
Copper Basin / Laver Placed Between Altar and Tabernacle

God's Dwelling Place Reconsidered

Treasure in the Desert

The value of water in the desert cannot be overstated. Not only would wasting water be described as foolish, but the same could be said about dedicating labor to unnecessary transportation of something as heavy as water. Even an inch of rain falling on a tenth of the round roof would provide hundreds of gallons of water for cleansing.

proportion to the amount of copper that was dedicated toward the application. After all, the priests and Levites would be working in a hot climate near a large fire, at times assisting in the slaughter of dozens, if not hundreds, of animals. Ideally, they would have placed the basin immediately adjacent to the east Tabernacle wall, with hopes of catching rainwater runoff or gathering any dew that collected on the Tabernacle roof.

Open Field Stone Cistern - Borot Lotz, Israel - Udi Steinwell, 2011

Even though there is no mention of rainwater capture made in the Exodus text, catching rain in something analogous to an oversized rain barrel from a roof or sloped surface is hardly a novel idea, especially as the Exodus text already drops hints toward this practice given the prescribed copper basin location. In fact, permanent desert habitats demanded such resourcefulness from residents. For example, hidden in the rock walls of Masada, a two-thousand-year-old desert fortress built by Herod, contained large cisterns carved into the hillside, which collected acres of rainwater redirected from nearby mountain slopes. Obviously, it would be unlikely that the great tent was pitched in close proximity to water supplies, lest the Tabernacle be vulnerable to flooding or wastewater runoff, since the desert rains rush downhill in wadis or channels cut through soil comprised of tight sand and gravel. While the Tabernacle was not supposed to be set up on the "high places", logic would also dictate that the Tabernacle would not be erected in the lowlands, lest the walls of the divine dwelling place become immersed by flash floodwaters, and the continual flames be extinguished.

Masada Water Collection Cistern - Shlomi Chetrit, 2007

Part 5 – Transforming Ideas

In the four preceding parts of this book, the fabric, wood, metal, and leather used to construct the Exodus wilderness Tabernacle was transformed from a crude, dysfunctional, and traditional rectangular assembly, and rearranged into to a sophisticated, practical, and familiar round or decagonal shape. While scholars and artists have struggled for centuries, if not for thousands of years, trying to offer a legitimate representation of or explanation for Moses' Tabernacle, all have fallen short as they have embraced traditions and translations above the literal Hebrew revelation. In perhaps all cases, they have been subconsciously biased by images created by predecessors, and they have overlooked the various fabrication details and linguistic nuances necessary to solve the Tabernacle puzzle. Without beginning with a proper understanding of the curtain arrangements and curtain joints, most any serious Tabernacle study becomes an exercise in futility.

"What Difference Does it Make?"

Nevertheless, in response to this Tabernacle discovery and research, people might ask, "What difference does it make?"; or perhaps more frankly, "Who cares what shape the Tabernacle is or was?" However innocently or earnestly such questions may be presented, these questions are inherently immature and have serious ramifications. Playing the "devil's advocate", imagine if God would say, "What difference does it make if you forever remain working as slaves in Egypt?" Fortunately, when Moses was told to "make everything according to the pattern shown on the mountain", Moses and the Israelites didn't respond with objection or indifference at the foot of Mount Sinai, saying, "We'll make your house however it suits us!" This is a logical absurdity, and would be akin to openly proclaiming that God's word does not—and never did—matter.

Without divine revelation in recorded or written form, religion becomes a very arbitrary and subjective thing. With man being the measure of all things, and people thinking for themselves and so very differently than one another, religion would ultimately become a form of self-worship and self-deification—where there is no absolute truth, no absolute right and wrong, and no absolute good and evil. Without divine revelation, God is but an absentee landlord, whereby his tenants have no rules and his property is destined to degrade to a total state of disrepair. As an absentee

Thinking Ouside the Box

God's Dwelling Place Reconsidered

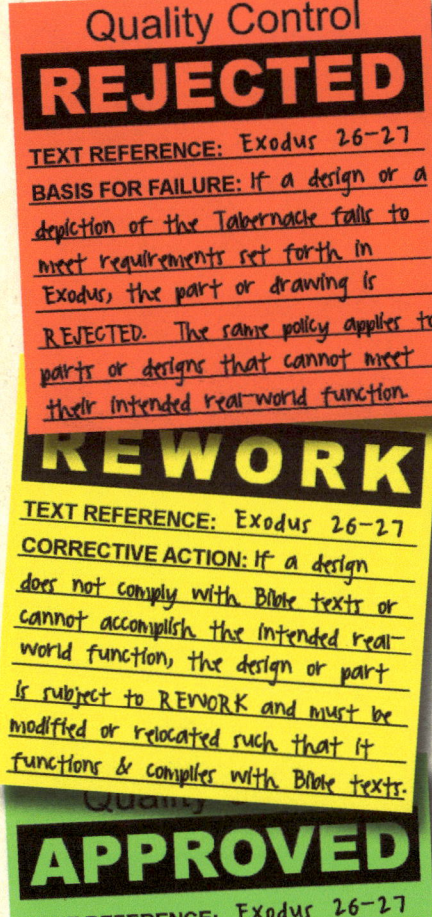

landlord, God is indifferent—loveless and not caring about or for his creation. But if God makes a set of plans for his house—whereby he might come to dwell among his people—and man has no interest in or outright rejects these plans, this would not be a case of God being an absentee landlord, but rather more comparable to a case of the tenants trying to deny their landlord access to the property, or perhaps equal to trying to evict their landlord from the building.

Conversely, if God did reveal himself to his creation, and more particularly, to the Israelites and Moses after the Exodus at Mount Sinai, the substance of this revelation should continue to be something of interest to people to this day. To consider this revelation in terms of generalities should not suffice; instead, every detail should be preserved and assumed to be something of merit, transcending thousands of years for countless generations. Within his revelation through Moses, God offered instructions for mankind, whereby we do either right or wrong—passing or failing according to the divine standard set before us.

~ Quality Review and Assessment ~

With the validity of God's word hanging in the balance, getting the Tabernacle details correct becomes a matter of extreme importance. After all, God's reputation as an authority figure and a source of knowledge is at stake. Is God to be regarded as a competent builder, a capable creator, or as a source of knowledge? He is not any of these things if he can't count, can't give instructions, or describes a building that would collapse under its own weight. Obviously, God's messengers can compromise their own testimony with a false narrative. As people promote a multitude of incorrect ways to look at the Tabernacle, the credibility of the source is undermined.

Throughout the course of the first four sections, a variety of short "quality control" notes pertaining to both Tabernacle designs have been employed. Some of the brief remarks are based on linguistic compliance, and some of which are based on deductive reasoning and simple physics. Given the introductory content, most remarks were introduced on a verse-by-verse or part-by-part basis, seldom addressing the Tabernacle design as a completed whole. However, now that the plans for the entire Tabernacle structure and its courtyard have been made known and compared to the traditional models on a verse-by-verse basis, a more comprehensive approach to comparison is now possible, as well as prudent, given the large gap in construction and interpretation philosophy. Parameters presented for comparison include:

1) Overall Purpose and Utility (Biblical),
2) Environmental Design,
3) Ergonomics (Human Factors), and
4) Material Utilization.

Overall Purpose and Utility

At Mount Sinai, religion was not a spectator sport. Thus, Tabernacle construction purposes are multi-faceted, as was the tent's roof. While the Tabernacle was a place for sacrifice, it was also for revelation, communication, residence, judgment, justice, confession, fellowship, atonement, celebration, forgiveness, healing, and instruction. Although God cannot be confined to any physical three dimensional space, and a number of these activities could be conducted in any place and without a physical worship facility (or regardless of shape), a few of these activities could not take place given the traditional rectangular Tabernacle and courtyard model, and would require a space that is larger and less congested than is offered by most traditional models.

Although proposing a rectangular Tabernacle does not demand animal sacrifice within the courtyard, it does result in serious logistical problems. For example, if the animal is to

A Clean House

Animals are sacrificed near the altar at the entrance of the tent (Leviticus 17:5).

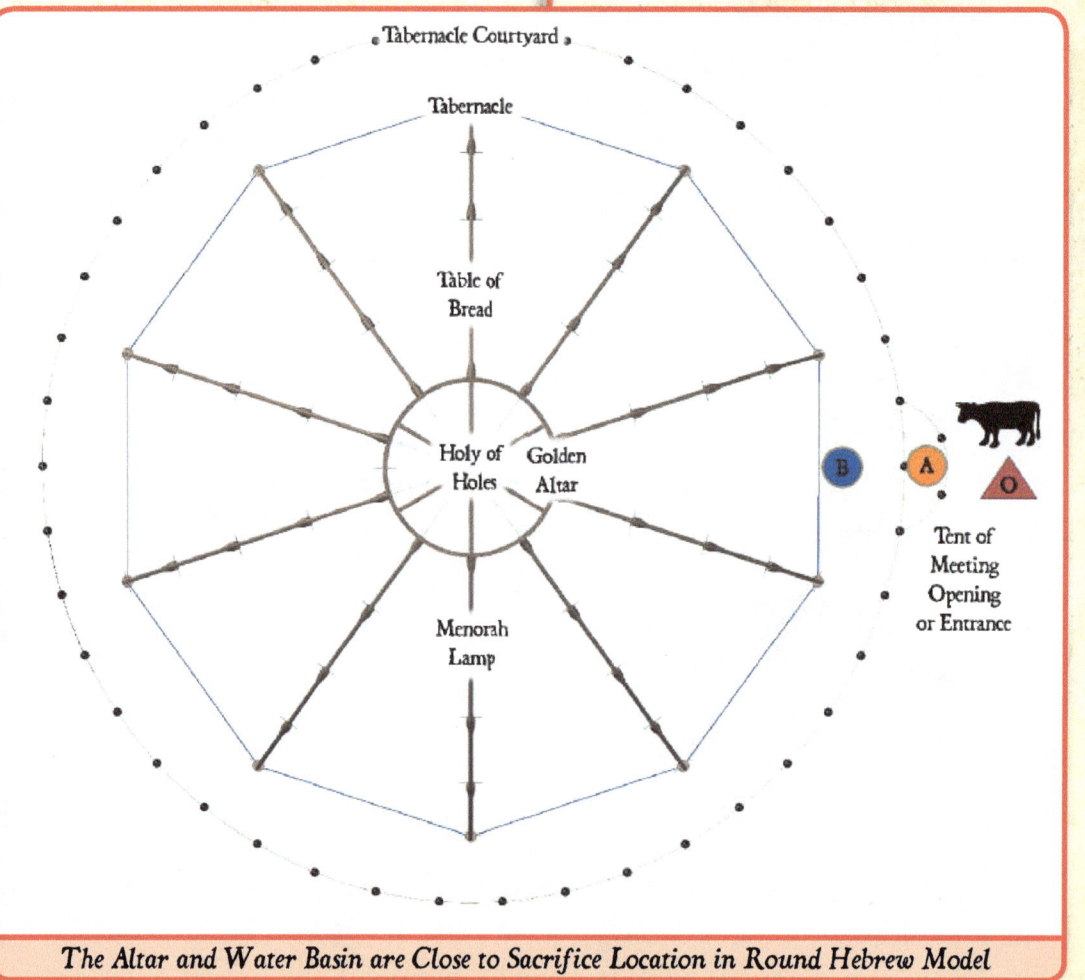

The Altar and Water Basin are Close to Sacrifice Location in Round Hebrew Model

Defiled Courtyard

"And thou shalt set the altar of the burnt offering before the door of the tabernacle of the tent of the congregation. He set the altar of burnt offering near the entrance to the tabernacle, the Tent of Meeting, and offered on it burnt offerings and grain offerings, as the LORD commanded him."

~ Exodus 40:29, KJV ~

Tabernacle Sacrifice Logistics Comparison

Design Parameter	Round Tabernacle	Rectangular Tabernacle
Sacrifice Location	Outside Gate/Court (O)	Outside Gate/Court (O1) or Tabernacle Entrance (O2)
Altar Location (A)	Outside Court, Inside Gate	Middle of Courtyard
Basin Location (B)	Between Tabernacle & Altar	Between Tabernacle & Altar
Clean Tent Entrance?	Yes	Yes (O1) / No (O2)
Animal Waste Problems?	No	Yes (O2)
Extra Walking Required?	No	Yes (O1)

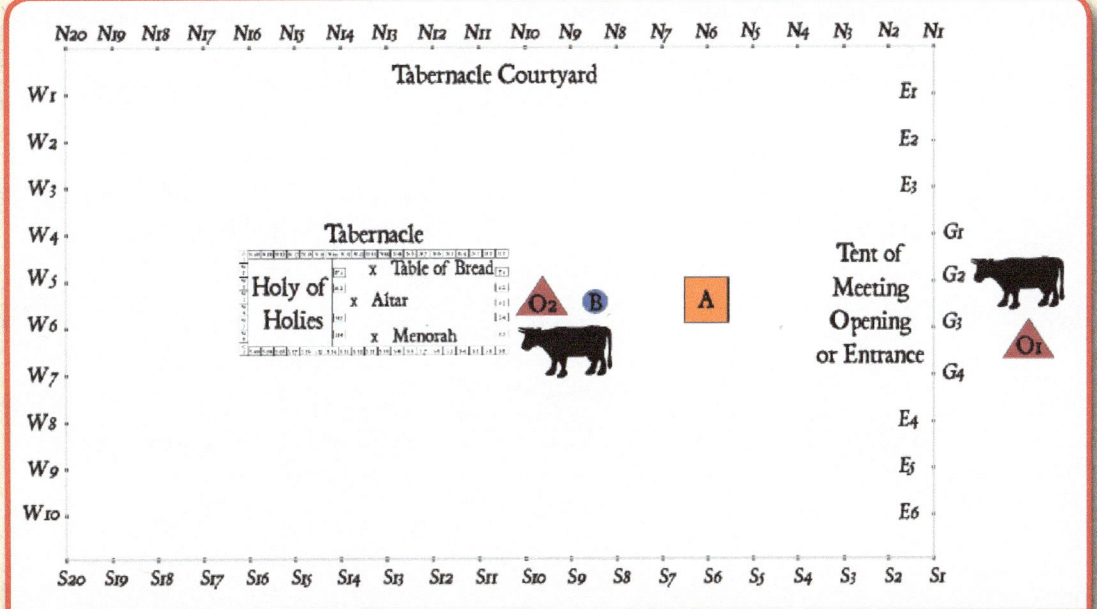

Traditionally Assumed Sacrifice Locations are Inefficient and Make the Courtyard Unclean

be slaughtered at the tent opening (O1), the parts dedicated to the altar would need to be transported to the middle of the courtyard. Obviously, if animals are slaughtered near the Tabernacle (O2), it would be impossible to keep that space "holy" as animal excrement and byproduct remains would be tracked into the Tabernacle, even after the priest would wash himself with water from the copper basin. Furthermore, if permitted inside the courtyard (serving as a corral), the animals would prove to be a threat to the courtyard, which is typically depicted as being tethered to the ground via ropes and pegs, which would create tripping hazards for man and beast alike. Courtyard traffic and congestion would also be a problem, as the gate size and courtyard space are limited.

Environmental Design Comparison

Design Element	Round Tabernacle Rating & Basis		Rectangular Tabernacle Rating & Basis	
Rain & Dew	Excellent	• Domed roof is conducive to watershed. • Surfaces are exposed to air to allow for evaporation and drying.	Poor to Fail	• Many models assume flat roofs. • Loose roofs would allow water ponding. • A-Frame is not viable with listed parts. • Leather roof material layers are prone to capturing or retaining moisture.
Wind	Excellent	• No ropes or tethered anchor lines are required to secure freestanding frame. • Wind loading is uniform in all directions. • Dome faces produce little drag as they are not perpendicular to wind. • Vertical and cylindrical courtyard curtains deflect and diffuse wind. • Copper courtyard posts are embedded for maximum shear and bending resistance.	Poor to Fail	• Asymmetrical panels require tethering. • Vertical / perpendicular panels are subject to higher wind loads. • Distance gap between courtyard and Tabernacle reduces courtyard wall wind block effectiveness. • South and north courtyard edges have poor east-west bracing. • Unsecured courtyard post bottoms are subject to movement in high winds.
Sun	Excellent	• Materials exposed to direct sunlight are also cooled as they are uninsulated and benefit from natural convection / cooling.	Poor	• Unventilated materials exposed to direct sunlight would reach higher temperatures and would be subject to reduced life expectancy.
Sand	Excellent	• No joints sit in or on sand as all joints are located above ground level. • Roof slope and height would result in minimal sand collection.	Poor	• Sockets and bases would wear and jam due to sand abrasion and intrusion. • Large horizontal roof surfaces are conducive to collecting sand.
Snow & Manna	Excellent	• High roof slopes prevent accumulation. • Higher winds & roof displacement prevent accumulation of material on upper layer.	Poor	• Accumulation would lead to loose roof collapse. • Flat roof designs may need to be cleared manually to prevent overload.
Animals	Good	• Courtyard walls provide a good visual deterrent but are not indestructible.	Poor	• Scavengers and unclean animals would be attracted to the Tabernacle if courtyard is used for a temporary corral and place for sacrifice.

God's Dwelling Place Reconsidered

Enduring the Elements

Although weather is not formally listed as Tabernacle design criteria in the Exodus texts, it is obvious that the structure was intended for four seasons and would need to endure the elements in the Sinai desert and Israel. Ironically, the need for Tabernacle repairs is never listed, whereas repairs to Solomon's Temple are described over the course of two periods, during the reigns of King Joash and King Josiah (2 Kings 12&22).

Environmental Design

Much like sacrifice activities are "eco-friendly" processes—whereby organic materials that came from the earth are returned to the earth via natural processes—similar things could be said of the Tabernacle structure itself. Long before so-called "sustainable buildings" were added to engineering or construction industry jargon and so-called "green standards" were added to manufacturing mandates and commercial marketplace buzzwords, the Tabernacle design was specified to be made with 100% renewable and recyclable materials—regardless of the structure's final shape.

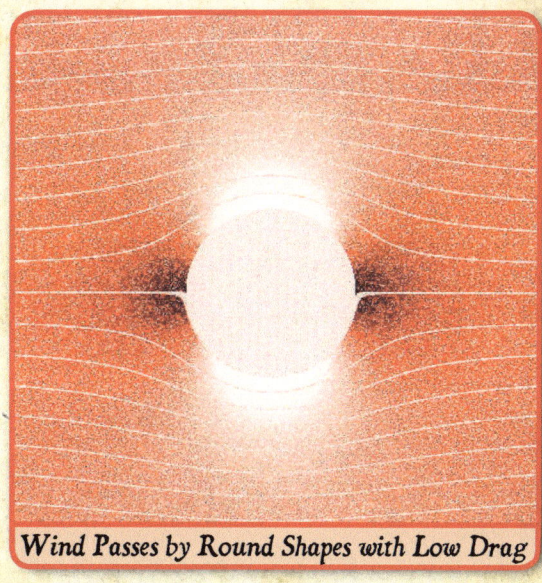

Wind Passes by Round Shapes with Low Drag

However, this is not to say that both round and traditional rectangular Tabernacle designs are equal in their ability to stand up against all environmental conditions as extreme desert conditions might demand. Demonstrated in the Tabernacle Environmental Design Comparison Table, the round Hebrew Tabernacle outperforms the traditional rectangular model in every criterion used for comparison. In the case of the Tabernacle, basic environmental design factors include moisture, wind, sun, scavengers, livestock, sand, snow, and even falling manna!

The superior performance of the round Tabernacle should come as no surprise to those familiar with nomadic architecture. For good reason, the majority of indigenous cultures have opted to build circular structures according to ancient traditions that have been handed down unto present day. Regardless of regional, ethnic,

How to Build an Igloo, © 1949 National Film Board of Canada. All rights reserved.

~ 186 ~

Ergonomic Design Comparison

Design Factor	Round Tabernacle Rating & Basis		Rectangular Tabernacle Rating & Basis	
Ventilation	Excellent	• Fabric walls are permeable to air. • Single layer roof allows for infiltration. • Large interior allows for natural convection and dissipation of incense smoke. • Top roof & east wall may be opened to vent. • Gate screen allows airflow to altar fire. • Fresh air flows past interlocking loops.	Poor	• Solid wood walls create dead end and trap air. • Four layer roof prevents ambient air exchange. • Small tent interior and partition curtain limits natural convection and traps incense smoke. • East opening is only access and vent point. • Tabernacle air quality may be poor if courtyard area and tent entrance is the slaughter location.
Temperature Control	Excellent	• Upper roof layer and east wall might be opened or closed to help control temperature. • Uninsulated walls would help the interior reach moderate morning temperatures. • High sloped ceiling allows hot air layer to rise and draw cool air through fabric walls.	Poor	• Only east entrance fabric screen can be adjusted to control temperature. • Insulated walls and roof would trap oppressive summer heat and reduce overnight heat dissipation. • Airmass trapped in dead end partitioned chamber would reach extreme afternoon temperatures.
Lighting	Excellent	• Single leather roof layers would provide filtered light and shade from bright sun. • Upper roof layer might be opened to allow more sunlight inside. • Menorah would provide light in the evening.	Fair to Poor	• Four of the five exposed tent sides would have multiple layer coverings, blocking all light. • Morning (east sunrise) could light structure, but evening (west sunset) would be dark. Holy of holies area would always be dark. • Light would leak past cracks in between wood wall beams if curtains do not cover wall exterior.
Access	Excellent	• Gate access taches are at accessible levels. • Slaughter location is close to altar and water.	Poor	• Courtyard rope and stakes are tripping hazards. • Altar, water, and sacrifice are all separated.
Aesthetic	Excellent	• A formidable structure intimidates enemies. • The dome could be seen many miles away, creating a landmark in the midst of the camp.	Poor	• Decorative layers are hidden. • The boxy structure is neither intimidating nor very visible from a distance.
Sanitation	Excellent	• Taches metals are antimicrobial. • Water is close to door; animal waste is not.	Poor	• Layered roof would be conducive to mold. • Animal waste is close to Tabernacle entrance.

God's Dwelling Place Reconsidered

Designed for the Senses

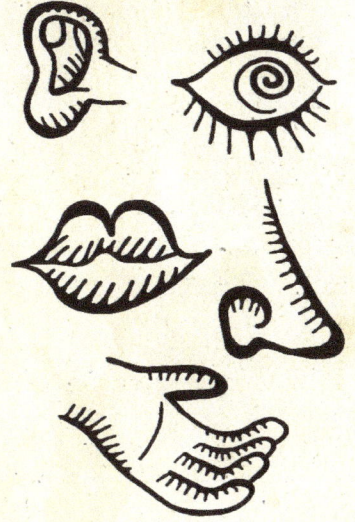

Ergonomics is a design discipline or field of study that is focused upon human interaction with equipment in a given application or environment, accounting for the five senses and other human factors in the design of products, structures, systems, or processes. Simple factors such as aesthetics, odors, textures, motion, comfort, etc., are all accounted for as they can impact human behavior and performance in the workplace.

or linguistic distinction applied, and regardless of each culture's command of mathematics, many different round designs have survived without fail or significant revision for thousands of years. Whether people build huts, teepees, igloos, wigwams, or yurts, it's clear that round is reliable.

Ergonomic Design

Needless to say, the Tabernacle design must account for human factors, as it was created not only as a place for God, but also as a place for him to meet with his creation. In ergonomic design, the form and function of the human body is taken into account, as are all the five senses.

Why is ergonomic design important in the context of the wilderness Tabernacle? Obviously, factors such as human safety and comfort effect human attitudes and behavior. People tend to avoid working in an environment that is hot, cold, loud, pitch dark, stinky, smoky, cramped, slimy, slippery, unsanitary, ugly, buggy, dangerous, and inefficient. As a rule, people obligated to make a living in such environments often begin to look for other places to work where "creature comfort" can be improved upon. Even something as seemingly petty, such as the shape of a handle, the fit of a uniform, the smell of a chemical, or the sound of an alarm can be a distraction, create dangerous conditions, or drive the worker to want to bring about sudden and lasting change. In the case of the Tabernacle, some of the key ergonomic factors include ventilation, temperature, lighting, equipment access, aesthetics, and sanitation. Because most of the ergonomic factors are rooted in environmental ones, once again, the round Tabernacle configuration proves to be superior on many levels.

"Vitruvian Man" - da Vinci, 1490
Ergonomics Accounts for Different Body Proportions

Material Utilization Comparison

Material	Round Tabernacle Rating & Basis		Rectangular Tabernacle Rating & Basis	
Fabric	Excellent	• Linen is a high strength material that creates strong tensioned Tabernacle wall barriers which prevent excess Tabernacle frame stress by controlling the Tabernacle frame geometry. • Linen is used as a secondary visual barrier. • Linen is a cool and conductive material that "breathes" or allows air to pass through walls. • The courtyard is made of wool, which creates a durable weather resistant barrier.	Poor	• Linen is not used structurally or as primary physical barriers. Linen does not reinforce frame components. • Obscured linen is used in a decorative capacity. • Linen is assumed to be part of a four layer roof where it would act as a marginal insulator. • The courtyard is assumed to be made of linen, which is not very weather resistant. • Wool is not exposed to weather but is assumed to be a roof layer and would act as an insulator.
Leather	Excellent	• Two leather types are used as single layer barriers covering unique frame section.	Poor	• Two leather types cover a common area as a double layer, performing a redundant function.
Wood	Excellent	• South, north, and west wood beam lengths and cross sections are sized as would be expected for dome frame application and structural loading. • Two "corner ring" sections form a compression ring and join opposing beams in a practical way. • South, north, and west vertical bars bear ring and rib frame weight, and would also be used in frame setup. • Holy of Holies posts are used to stabilize structure and support "thigh" braces. • Entrance (east) posts bear ring and rib frame weight and entrance curtain and would block east entrance wind.	Poor	• South, north, and west wood beam cross sections are enormous (or partially undefined) given the arrangement and the beam length, building height, and roof weight. • Two "corner ring" sections do not bear vertical load, do not join lower frame members, and are not configured to add bracing or stability. • South, north, and west horizontal bars carry almost no vertical load, would be difficult to install, and could not control geometry. • Holy of Holies posts are used only to support fabric curtains and leather roof sections. • Entrance (east) posts carry minimal load of fabric and leather roof and entrance curtain.
Metal	Excellent	• Silver "controllers" are structural elements (rods) used to control and balance wood frame. • Copper "controllers" are rods used for spanning and hanging curtains.	Poor	• Silver "sockets" are oversized and could not effectively anchor vertical beams to ground. • Copper could not be used as "sockets" as copper posts and rods are required to hang curtains.

God's Dwelling Place Reconsidered

Material Waste & Misappropriation

It is not only fitting to use materials suitable for an application, but also to avoid non-essential material use. Using thick beams for a tent wall might be compared to opening an egg with a hammer, which would work but take more effort, make a mess, and waste the egg. Likewise, the use of four coverings on rectangular models is a misappropriation of fabric and leather. Designs that do not offer evidence of purpose or intelligence are not esoteric, mystical, or divine—some designs are simply mindless.

Who Uses a Hammer to Open an Egg?

Material Utilization

When it comes to fabricating physical parts or erecting real-world structures, materials must be selected in a way where their properties match the application. For example, underwear is not made from wood, car tires are not made out of silver, windows are not made from leather, and electrical wire is not made from linen. Apart from proper material selection, proper appropriation of sizes and quantities is also good practice. T-shirts have just two holes for arms, not seventeen holes. Cars typically have four tires, but the tires do not measure twelve feet in diameter or weigh over a thousand pounds each. Furthermore, shape and orientation also play a role in design. It goes without saying that car tires belong between the car and the road, and would serve no purpose a car's roof. At times, material selection might be governed by availability. A rubber wheel might be superior to a wood wheel, but wood has been used for wheels since antiquity and was used predominantly before the advent of rubber refining technologies. Design is an iterative art, balancing design factors such as load, temperature, size, technology, and availability against material properties such as strength, density, hardness, ductility, opacity, permeability, flexibility, scarcity, workability, and cost. While divinely mandated, the Tabernacle was not exempt from such design realities.

Dual Purpose or Material Misappropriation?

In comparing the round Hebrew Tabernacle to the traditional rectangular variants, it is clear that the round model is superior in material utilization in every way. Fabric, wood, metal, and leather use is efficient and multi-faceted assuming a round or decagonal configuration; in contrast, the application and arrangements of traditional rectangular components leave a student with more questions than answers. In assuming the rectangle, material is appropriated wastefully, redundantly, foolishly, and in ways that are simply not credible. Nevertheless, dismissing prudence, those advocating the traditional rectangular models must desperately defer to explanations dependent upon esoteric symbolism and mysticism, as the traditional rectangular model is little more than bad dogma and religious fantasy.

Specification Explanation and Compliance

In the Exodus text, there are approximately 80 imperative Hebrew commandments given to specify the Tabernacle assemblies and furnishings therein. In order to derive an understanding of the Hebrew wilderness Tabernacle from these texts, any viable model must offer an answer or explanation for—and comply with—each and every requirement.

As explained and illustrated throughout the prior four sections of this book, there are two distinctive ways to interpret Tabernacle texts: round and according to the Hebrew text, or rectangular and according to English translations and religious traditions. As traditional model assumptions and problems are more closely examined, it becomes clear that the round Hebrew-based model is in far better compliance with the Bible texts, even when the biased English translation is used as a basis for comparison. While this book is not intended to fully represent every single possible rectangular Tabernacle variant, it becomes clear nevertheless that the rectangular explanation and models repeatedly fail in offering a complete and accurate representation of what is described in the Bible text, even in areas where all rectangular models are in agreement with one another. Because the quantity of information covered in prior sections and illustrations is substantial, the four sections have been distilled down to four pages of tables that bring out most of the basic Tabernacle specifications on a verse-by-verse basis. As indicated in the tables, in a few cases the rectangular models do offer an explanation that has merit. Conversely, in some cases they seem to offer no explanation for the Exodus specification, and in others the explanations themselves are either undermined by logical contradictions (expounded on in prior chapters) or have no basis by which to substantiate very questionable assumptions.

Moses on Mount Sinai - Jean-Léon Gérôme, 1900

The House Completed

"According to all that I shew thee, after the pattern of the tabernacle, and the pattern of all the instruments thereof, even so shall ye make it."

~ Exodus 25:9, KJV ~

On Mt. Sinai, Moses received specific plans for the Tabernacle and its furnishings. Some might suggest that Moses' account in Exodus 25-27 was not complete or accurate, but it is probably more appropriate to say that the details contained in Moses' record have been overlooked, distorted in translation, or obscured by tradition for centuries.

"Thus was all the work of the tabernacle of the tent of the congregation finished: and the children of Israel did according to all that the LORD commanded Moses, so did they."

~ Exodus 39:32, KJV ~

While the Tabernacle and the furnishings were first commanded in Exodus 25-27, a second record in Exodus 36:8-38:31 describe how the Israelites made the Tabernacle exactly as it was first specified.

God's Dwelling Place Reconsidered

Bible Specification Explanation Comparison

Verse	Specification		Round Tabernacle Explanation?		Rectangular Tabernacle Explanation?
Ex 26:1	10 Linen Curtains	Y	Ten curtains form decagonal structure wall. Curtain quantity correlates with wood beams, wood bars/columns, and silver pins/rods.	?	Curtain quantity unrelated to other hardware. Assumed 40 x 28 roof assembly fits over frame.
Ex 26:2	4 Cubit Wide Curtains	Y	Dimension is fitting for wall height. Dimension matches courtyard wall height.	N	Four cubit width is not needed in the design. Size may be practical in loom and to handle.
Ex 26:2	28 Cubit Long Curtains	Y	Wall length defines the structure's perimeter.	N	Overhanging curtain ends attach to nothing. Curtain distance from ground is not critical.
Ex 26:3	Join into 2 Sets of 5	Y	Structure is symmetrical and made in halves.	?	Holy of Holies location inferred at split.
Ex 26:4	Blue Loop-Joints	Y	Defines curtain color stratification and sizing.	N	Joint color detail not incorporated in design.
Ex 26:4	2 Short Edge-Joints	Y	Defines lengthwise attachment arrangement. Demands a circle or polygon curtain assembly.	N	Incorrect edges are used to join curtains. End curtains fail to connect to adjacent unit.
Ex 26:5	50 Loop-Joints	Y	Defines cord size and curtain thickness.	N	Spacing leaves large open gaps between joints.
Ex 26:6	50 Gold Taches	Y	Antimicrobial metal buttons used for entrance.	?	Holy curtain hanging at some taches.
Ex 26:7	11 Wool Curtains	Y	Eleven curtains form courtyard perimeter. Curtain quantity relates to circumference.	N	Curtain quantity unrelated to other hardware. Assumed 42 x 30 roof fits over linen curtains.
Ex 26:8	4 Cubit Wide Curtains	Y	Forms a reasonable courtyard wall height. Dimension matches Tabernacle wall height.	N	Four cubit width not incorporated in design. Size may be practical in loom and to handle.
Ex 26:8	30 Cubit Wide Curtains	Y	Length & quantity define courtyard perimeter. Length matches court post spacing & quantity.	N	Overhanging curtains attach to nothing. Curtain distance from ground is not critical.
Ex 26:9	Set of 5 and 6 Curtains	Y	Sets form two courtyard halves & gate barrier.	N	Split does not connect or relate to other parts.
Ex 26:9	6th Curtain Fold	Y	Folded curtain reduces circumference to 315. Fold may function as insulation or heat shield.	N	Fold does not correlate with other hardware. Fold bunches up irregularly on west side.

The House of El Shaddai

Bible Specification Explanation Comparison

Verse	Specification		Round Tabernacle Explanation?		Rectangular Tabernacle Explanation?
Ex 26:10	2 Short Edge-Joints	Y	Defines long axis wool curtain assembly. Demands a circle or polygon curtain assembly.	N	Incorrect edges are used to join curtains. Two end curtains are only joined on one end.
Ex 26:11	50 Copper Taches	Y	Antimicrobial metal buttons used for entrance.	N	Spacing leaves large open gaps between joints.
Ex 26:12	Fold Curtain Remnant	Y	Remnant is folded on back part of east gate.	?	Remnant is folded over back of structure.
Ex 26:13	1 Cubit End Overlap	Y	Overlap of ends reduces circumference to 314. Length accounts for curtain loop joint overlap.	N	Adjustment not incorporated consistently. Assumed to define wool assembly location.
Ex 26:14	2 Leather Roof Layers	Y	Lower layer covers lower frame section. Upper layer covers upper frame section.	?	Roof is redundant and is two layers thick. Lower leather is colored but concealed.
Ex 26:15	"Standing" Beams	Y	"Standing" rib-like beams are leaning inwards.	?	Beams stand perfectly vertical.
Ex 26:16	Beam Dimensions	Y	Wood beam dimensions are 10 x 1 x 1/2. Beam length corresponds with frame perimeter.	?	Beam thickness is 1-1/2 x 1 or 1-1/2 x ? Beam length (10 cubit height) is arbitrary.
Ex 26:17	2 Feminine "Hands" on a Beam	Y	"Hands" are sleeve features in beam ends. "Sleeves" relate to male silver rods/pins.	?	"Hands" are male "tenons" at one beam end. "Hands" relate to female silver "sockets".
Ex 26:18	20 Edge Beams South and Rightward	Y	Boards are arranged south and clockwise. 20 Beams relate to curtain and bar quantity.	?	South edge runs along linear east-west axis. 20 beam quantity defines building length.
Ex 26:19	2 Silver Parts / Beam	Y	Silver parts fit in sleeves and govern motion. Quantity relates to curtains, beams, and bars.	?	Silver "sockets" anchoring vertical beams. No reason for 2 sockets / beam is offered.
Ex 26:20	North (2nd) "Rib"	Y	Second "rib" mirrors first and is rib-shaped.	?	Rib is a "side" but is not like a "rib".
Ex 26:21	40 North Silver Parts	Y	North side silver parts mirror south side parts.	N	Oversized vertical anchor function assumed.
Ex 26:22	6 Westward "Thighs"	Y	Thighs are crotch-like beams & west of origin.	N	Thighs are made into the west "side" wall.
Ex 26:23	2 "Corner" Beams	Y	"Corner" ring segments join thighs & ribs.	?	90 degree "corners" join S, N, and W walls.

Bible Specification Explanation Comparison

Verse	Specification		Round Tabernacle Explanation?		Rectangular Tabernacle Explanation?
Ex 26:24	Head Coupling "Ring"	Y	Wood ring joins opposing rib beams at head.	?	Traditional reasoning is not consistent.
Ex 26:25	16 Silver Parts / 8 Beams	Y	16 silver rods pin together 8 wood beams.	N	16 silver "sockets" are west beam bases.
Ex 26:26	5 Bars for 1st Rib	Y	5 bars are vertical & support first (south) rib. 5 bars correspond w/curtain & beam quantity.	?	5 bars are horizontal & secure south beams. Bar quantities are unrelated to other hardware.
Ex 26:27	5 Bars for 2nd Rib; 5 for West Rib and West Thighs	Y	5 vertical bars support second (north) rib. 5 vertical bars support west rib & "thighs". Sets correspond w/curtain & beam quantity.	N	5 horizontal bars secure north beams; 5 horizontal bars secure west beams. Bar quantities are unrelated to other hardware.
Ex 26:28	Middle bar End-to-End	Y	Beams in middle of frame run contiguous. Defines "thigh" brace beam orientation.	?	Middle bar runs full length of Tabernacle or through beam centers, or is a ceiling spine.
Ex 26:30	Mountain-like Erection	Y	Tabernacle resembles a mountain.	?	Pattern Moses saw at Sinai are not recorded.
Ex 26:32	4 Silver Parts, 4 Gold Pegs & 4 Pillars	Y	Silver parts form a single ring. Gold pegs join ring to pillars. Pillars support the ring.	N	4 posts free-stand vertically via 4 silver "sockets". Gold "hooks" are not detailed.
Ex 26:33	Veil Hung from Taches	Y	Taches formed on silver ring hang the curtain. Veil surrounds Ark of the Covenant.	?	Curtain is hung from or at some of the 50 taches. Veil blocks Ark from only one side.
Ex 26:36	Screen for Tent Opening	Y	Screen acts to diffuse wind.	Y	Screen acts as east side barrier.
Ex 26:37	5 Pillars, 5 Copper Parts, and 5 Gold Pegs	Y	5 east pillars mirror 5 west bars. 5 copper parts are 5 curtain rods. 5 gold pegs connect 5 curtain rods to 5 pillars.	N	Quantities are unrelated to other hardware. 5 copper "sockets" assumed to stand posts. Gold hook configuration is not detailed.
Ex 27:1	5 x 5 x 3 Cubit Altar	Y	Altar is "quartered" and 5 cubits in diameter.	Y	Altar footprint is a 5 cubit square.
Ex 27:9	100 Cubit South Edge Toward the Right	Y	South courtyard edge is a semicircle section (spanning from east origin toward the right or clockwise) with a 100 cubit diameter span.	?	South courtyard edge is a linear span measuring 100 cubits. South and southward Bible language is redundant without reason.

The House of El Shaddai

Specification Explanation Comparison

Verse	Specification		Round Tabernacle Explanation?		Rectangular Tabernacle Explanation?
Ex 27:9	Frame to Hang and Court Fabric for First Edge	Y	Only a courtyard frame half is introduced. No new fabrics are created; wool curtains are used. Courtyard frame is specified in two halves.	?	New fabric pieces are created for courtyard but with no dimensional specifications. Courtyard is specified as 4 walls.
Ex 27:10	20 Copper Posts, 20 Copper Controllers, 20 Silver Joints	Y	20 south posts, rods (controllers), and joints correspond to 5 wool curtain subassembly and partial (150 cubit arc) circumference.	?	20 copper posts are often depicted as wood. 20 copper controllers are depicted as bases. 20 silver joints are decorative post top spheres.
Ex 27:11	North Edge Hangings Quantity 20/20/20	Y	Hangings are frame elements, not curtains. Hangings are made "to court" wool curtains.	?	Hangings are extra fabric curtains made for the court along with metal parts.
Ex 27:12	50 Cubit West Edge with 10 Posts	Y	The north courtyard has a west edge that has 10 posts and measures 50 cubits from the head of the structure.	?	The west edge may or may not include south and north courtyard posts and measures 50 cubits from corner to corner.
Ex 27:13	50 Cubit East Edge to Origin	Y	The north courtyard has an east edge that measures 50 cubits from the head to the structure's eastern / sunrise origin.	?	The east edge eastward Bible language is redundant and without reason and makes no reference to the structure's point of origin.
Ex 27:14	3 Posts / Hangings for First 15 Cubit Flank	Y	All courtyard posts span 30 cubit wool curtains into two "flanks" measuring 15 cubits which are each spanned by 3 posts 7.5 cubits apart.	?	Gate "flanks" and/or all courtyard posts are spaced 15/3 or 5 cubits apart. A fourth post is assumed to be in the 15 cubit flank span.
Ex 27:15	3 Posts / Hangings for Second 15 Cubit Flank	Y	The second 30 cubit wool curtain half is described to have the same span measurement.	?	The second "flank" is assumed to be positioned relative to the gate.
Ex 27:16	20 Cubit Gate	Y	Gate curtain is arranged as an arc.	Y	Gate is linear and measures 20 cubits.
Ex 27:16	4 Posts to Gate	Y	Four posts join court halves and support screen.	?	Gate post spacing is subject to debate.
Ex 27:17	Court Posts Around	Y	Text alludes to a circular courtyard.	?	"Round about" post layout is rectangular.
Ex 27:18	Court Height 5 Cubits	Y	Court posts are 5 cubits but embedded 1 cubit.	?	Posts are free standing in bases with ropes.
Ex 27:19	Copper Court Pins	Y	Court posts pinned into the ground.	?	Extra copper parts are used as pegs in ground.

Heavenly Curtains

"Who coverest thyself with light as with a garment: who stretchest out the heavens like a curtain:"

~ Psalm 104:2, KJV ~

The Psalmist compares the heavens to a curtain using the same Hebrew word used in the Tabernacle instructions. During the daytime, ambient daylight would permeate through the single layer linen curtain wall which is stretched out on the horizon.

~ The Subjective Perspective ~

Apart from strictly analyzing the proposed Tabernacle solutions from the standpoint of technical and literal "quality control" criteria, the two radically different models of God's "dwelling place" might also be compared on a more subjective basis.

As first alluded to in the introduction, the historical precedent for round tents is significant. Indigenous peoples and nomadic cultures of every continent have used round mobile dwellings for thousands of years. Rock art dating back to the Bronze age depicts round yurts being used in Siberia. Formal records of yurt usage in Asia dates back to the 5th century BC, per the Greek writings of Herodotus. While the etymology of yurts or "gers" are thought to be of Turkish origin, it would appear that there is some Hebrew connection, as "ger" is the word for "sojourner". In contrast, no culture of record has independently created portable housing to the rectangular Tabernacle specification—with 3 walls heavy and thick enough to stop a 9mm bullet.

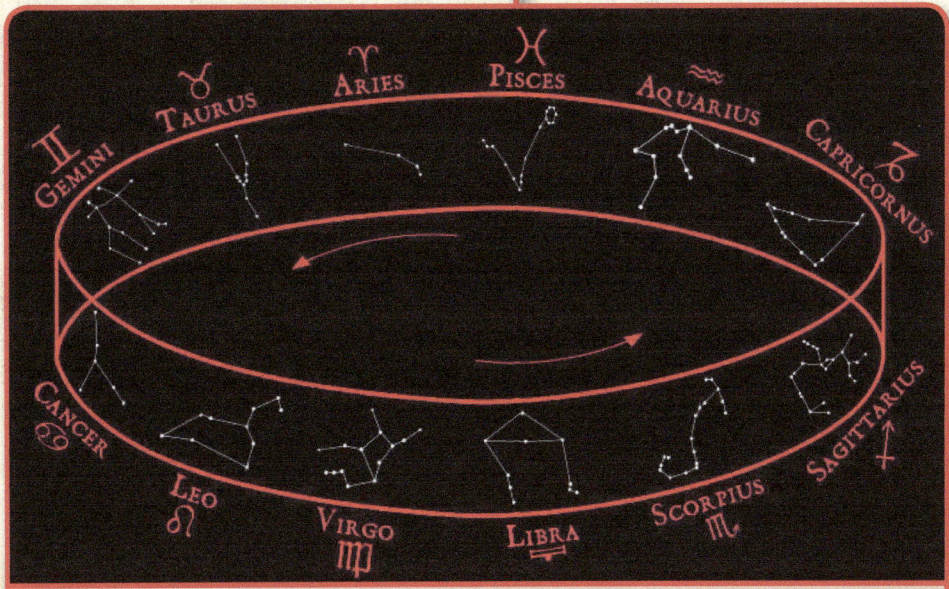

The Zodiac has been Represented in Circles and Cylinders for Thousands of Years

In nature, there are virtually no 90 degree corners or right angles, whereas the anatomy of almost every living thing seems to incorporate round shapes. Virtually all trees and plant life forms have round vines, round seeds, round fruits, or round flowers. Likewise, eggs are round, much like the birds nests which shelter them. Even though the comb is hexagonal, bee hives are often round. Bubbles are round, as are water droplets. Round is naturally occurring because round is efficient and is indicative of environmental equilibrium. Why wouldn't the house of the creator somehow resemble the creation?

Considering that the Tabernacle curtains are arranged in a 360 degree ring or cylinder shape, all Bible references comparing the Tabernacle to the heavens or vice-versa begin to make more sense. After all, in observing the heavens from earth, they are perceived to begin at the

Planetariums Show Constellations on Dome Interior

horizon, and they encircle the observer in every direction, barring obstructions from things like mountains or trees, of course. The biblical heaven-curtain and the heaven-tent analogy are far more reasonable than any preferred or imagined rectangular Tabernacle arrangement, where curtains would be visible only directly overhead and to the east, assuming the tent's interior is the point of reference for the analogy. Moreover, curtains installed on rectangular models typically fall short of reaching ground level, which is yet another disconnect in the curtain-heaven comparison. While there may be several different cosmological models debated in scientific circles, not a single one of them is likely to feature a rectangular sky.

Assuming that the Tabernacle roof also qualifies as a "tent" barrier, the heavenly tent analogy offers another layer of similitude. Resembling a planetarium, the Tabernacle's dome interior would probably admit small points of light in the leather stitching and imperfections. Depending upon leather thickness, treatment, and opacity, the leather layer could very much resemble the stars overhead shining brightly in the night sky.

The House of El Shaddai

Finally, there is the name of "El Shaddai." The name "El Shaddai" is most often translated as "God Almighty", however the Hebrew "Shaddai" is also associated with land or a field. In the context of the Tabernacle, it makes sense that such a large and majestic structure towering over the Sinai landscape would be a suitable house for a "God of the land". Furthermore, the ancient Hebrew did not have numerals, so letters would be used in the place of numbers (e.g., a=1, b=2, c=3, etc.). With the Hebrew El Shaddai having a three

Starry Ceiling

"It is he that sitteth upon the circle of the earth, and the inhabitants thereof are as grasshoppers; that stretcheth out the heavens as a curtain, and spreadeth them out as a tent to dwell in:"

~ Isaiah 40:22, KJV ~

Isaiah wrote that God sat over the "circle of the earth" as he spread out the heavens as a tent. It is impossible to compare this to a rectangular structure.

Hebrew Zodiac Mosaic - Beit Alpha Synagogue

God's Dwelling Place Reconsidered

El Shaddai and the House of π

Doorpost Mezuzah

"And these words, which I command thee this day, shall be in thine heart... And thou shalt write them upon the posts of thy house, and on thy gates."

~ Deuteronomy 6:6 & 9, KJV ~

$$314 = שדי$$

Jews mount small mezuzot on their door frames or gates to keep the Deuteronomy 6 commandment. This is a remarkable correlation, as the mobile Tabernacle had a 314 cubit courtyard, whereas these door boundary markers spell "Shaddai", which is numerically equivalent to 314 in Hebrew.

letter spelling of shin-dalet-yud, the gematria or numerical equivalent of Shaddai is 314—the near perfect multiple of the π constant. Clearly, given the 314 Tabernacle courtyard dimensions, this correlation is highly unlikely, statistically speaking.

Could it be a matter of mere coincidence that the God without beginning or end would want to be associated with a circle, the only shape that has no beginning or end? Furthermore, could it be a matter of random chance that given all the ancient Hebrew names for God, that Jews have affixed the sacred "Shaddai" name to their doors for generations? Could it be by accident that the Hebrew letters used to spell Shaddai so closely resemble 3-1-4? Clearly, our God is one of 314; El-Shaddai is the God of PI.

Expanding the Tent Paradigm

When the rediscovered pattern of God's dwelling place is compared to the Scriptures and other typology found throughout nature, the "what difference does it make" response begins to sound pretty ridiculous. Through systematic study, anyone truly motivated by intellectual curiosity will begin to see many differences. Unfortunately, the same question is often posed rhetorically, cloaking a spirit of skepticism, sarcasm, and intellectual apathy. However, in between these two extremes, this ancient Tabernacle study also solicits a wide variety of very personal feelings and emotions, especially if an audience is left feeling duped or blindsided as a result of this unexpected, uninvited, and radical paradigm shift. Intuitively, many people sense the implications of this discovery, as it calls

Hebrew Gematria - שדי			
Hebrew Letter	Letter Name	Ordinal Value	Absolute Value
א	alef	1	1 or 1000
ב	biet	2	2
ג	gimmel	3	3
ד	dalet	4	4
ה	hei	5	5
ו	vav	6	6
ז	zayin	7	7
ח	chet	8	8
ט	tet	9	9
י	yud	10	10
ך / כ	kaf	11	20
ל	lamed	12	30
ם / מ	mem	13	40
ן / נ	nun	14	50
ס	samech	15	60
ע	ayin	16	70
ף / פ	pei	17	80
ץ / צ	tzadi	18	90
ק	kuf	19	100
ר	reish	20	200
ש	shin	21	300
ת	tav	22	400
10+4+300 = י+ד+ש = שדי			

other status quo religious views into question. After all, if traditional paradigms portray God's dwelling as something ancient, crude, and even benign, what other religious dogmas need to be seriously challenged? Proper rendering of Exodus 26-27 resulted in God's dwelling place increasing thirty times larger while using half of the material traditionally assumed. Could greater improvements be attained if the balance of the Bible texts (i.e., other than Exodus 26-27) were reexamined rationally and apart from dirty and distorted lenses of religious tradition? What if the domed Tabernacle is just the tip of the theological iceberg, whereby untold volumes of truth is submerged deep beneath the surface, hidden from those too blind to see the proverbial tip?

For obvious reasons, nobody *likes* to be deceived. But for reasons far less obvious, nobody *wants to believe* that they have been fooled or misled, especially when the legitimacy of trusted and deeply revered things are undermined or even questioned. Because people establish their identities, sense of self-value, and sense of morality by means of familiar scriptures and religious traditions, people can take great offense as they are often overwhelmed by feelings of embarrassment, vulnerability, ignorance, insecurity, and perhaps even misappropriated shame when they are simply told that they have been deceived. Since overcoming these emotional barriers are a prerequisite to making even small course corrections, a proverb often attributed to Mark Twain rings true, as "it's easier to fool people than to convince them that they have been fooled". Unfortunately, so many people can't handle the first stage of introspection, and thus many subconsciously choose to remain slumbering in a cocoon of denial rather than trying to escape a web of deceit.

In addition to the challenging personal introspection, it follows that victims of deceit must also reconcile some sense of injustice or betrayal. This entails discerning the responsibility and intentions of the deceiving party, followed by deciding to whom blame should be attributed. In the case of bad religious traditions and Tabernacle mythology, fault can hardly be ascribed to a single individual. In fact, the prophet Jeremiah prophesied a loss of truth in epic proportions, predicting that Gentiles scattered abroad would awaken to the folly that they inherited. After all, by means of language manipulation and convoluted theologies, western religious institutions have subtly taught leaders and congregations to think using terms like "Tabernacle" for scores of generations, while departing from the true purpose and pattern of the "dwelling place". Surely, every design detail of God's dwelling place testifies to Jeremiah's insightful prophetic claim, whereby substandard religious conditioning can be equated to an inherited legacy of lies.

Truth Lost in Exile

"O LORD, my strength, and my fortress, and my refuge in the day of affliction, the Gentiles shall come unto thee from the ends of the earth, and shall say, Surely our fathers have inherited lies, vanity, and things wherein there is no profit."

~ Jeremiah 16:19, KJV ~

Nearly 90 percent of an iceberg remains submerged beneath the water's surface.

Icebergs are Analogous to Hidden Truth

God's Dwelling Place Reconsidered

> ### Houses of God or Houses of Men?
>
> *"For a day in thy courts is better than a thousand. I had rather be a doorkeeper in the house of my God, than to dwell in the tents of wickedness."*
>
> *~ Psalm 84:10, KJV ~*

The Great Synagogue - Jerusalem, Israel

Traditional religious facilities do not use circular courtyards; neither do they resemble God's dwelling place as defined by the Scriptures. The Bible does not command the construction of buildings for religious assemblies.

God's Dwelling Place Reconsidered

Each year, people spend billions of hours in attendance and dedicate private fortunes to the operation, maintenance, and construction of brick-and-mortar religious buildings with the presumed intention of getting closer to God. In contrast, only an infinitesimal fraction of religious people have attempted to create full scale Tabernacle models, despite the fact that the pattern to God's dwelling place was literally given under the authority of divine mandate, never rescinded, and never replaced or superseded by new commandments to build new religious structures. How can this contrast in behavior be explained?

Westminster Church London, England

After many generations have passed, it seems that man's ideas about God's dwelling place have drastically departed from the pattern of God's dwelling place as divinely revealed through Moses. In dismissing the "thus saith the Lord" mandates, man has reduced God's dwelling place into a crude Tabernacle shack. Likewise, since the Tower of Babel dispersion, man's religious approaches have changed very little—with the dwelling places designed primarily with human habitation in mind, whereby man has a place to sit and reach toward heaven. Ironically, God's dwelling place is not designed for elevating man to heaven, but rather for making a place whereby God might dwell on earth in the midst of his people.

Could it be time to reconsider God's dwelling place? What if God's people endeavored to build a house in God's image and according to the pattern shown to Moses in the mountain? Could it be possible that God still wishes for his people to have a festival in the wilderness that is dedicated to him, whereby he might once again come to dwell in their midst? Maybe it's time to abandon the traditional Latin-based *Tabernacle* idea that has crippled religious thought for thousands of years. After all, God liberated and instructed the Hebrews so they could make the *Mishkan* or *dwelling place*—so that he might dwell among them...

May the Tabernacle of tradition become a distant memory, and may this work forever remind Israel and the nations of the world of the majesty and splendor of God's true dwelling place.

~ About the Cover ~

In August of 2016, Breaking Israel News published an article about Andrew Hoy's earth-shattering round Tabernacle discovery. The article featured a picture of two combined images—Andrew's revolutionary domed tabernacle model superimposed over W. Dickes' familiar 19th century etching entitled, *The Tabernacle in the Wilderness*. Since "a picture is worth a thousand words", the compilation image allowed Andrew's research results to be instantly contextualized and compared to the traditional rectangular model. As the article circulated, the image made it to the first page of Google's image search engine results, which demonstrated the image's public appeal. For the book, it seemed fitting to add an image of Moses from Rembrandt's famous painting, which shows Moses lifting the commandments overhead. Adding Moses to the cover not only reinforces the Exodus context, but also hints to the dichotomy of the subject matter. Is Moses raising commandments to break them, or holding them overhead to boldly proclaim them? One tabernacle design is the result of breaking the commandments, and the other design is realized by lifting them up.

~ About the Author ~

As a Wisconsin native, Andrew attended the Milwaukee School of Engineering, where his father taught engineering for over four decades. Since graduating in 1994, Andrew has worked in a variety of industries (food/service, refrigeration, coal/gas/nuclear/diesel/hydroelectric power generation, power transmission, air conditioning, industrial controls, and maritime) and served in a number of different professional capacities (intern, field service engineer, project engineer, project manager, applications engineering manager, product manager, instructor, and author).

Having a passion for Biblical Hebrew, Andrew went on to study Hebrew in Israel (Haifa University and Morasha in Jerusalem). With no particular plans to combine his language studies with his technical background, Andrew found himself at a strange crossroads after discovering the π or *Pi* constant hidden in the Bible texts. In conducting further research, Andrew came to decipher the original Hebrew Tabernacle design, and founded Project 314 and Project Betzalel, which are dedicated to Exodus Tabernacle research, education, and construction. When not working, Andrew enjoys snowboarding, cycling, in-line skating, paddle boarding, and cooking.

~ Additional Tabernacle Study Resources ~

For those wishing to share this Tabernacle study with larger audiences or to incorporate this research into an interactive individual or engaging classroom study, two additional products are recommended. First, *The House of El Shaddai—Exodus Tabernacle PowerPoint® Presentation* features over 180 presentation slides, 130+ colorful diagrams and high definition images, dozens of tables, and concise commentary, making it ideal for either classroom or independent study group presentations by means of digital video projector or large home television screen.

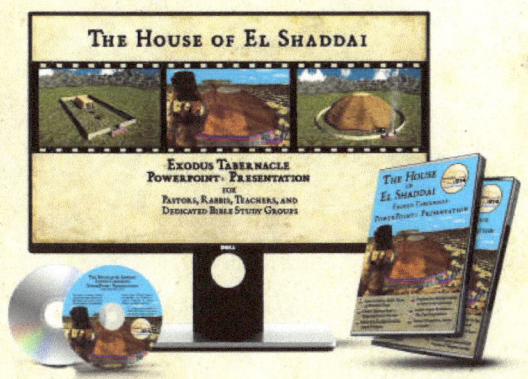
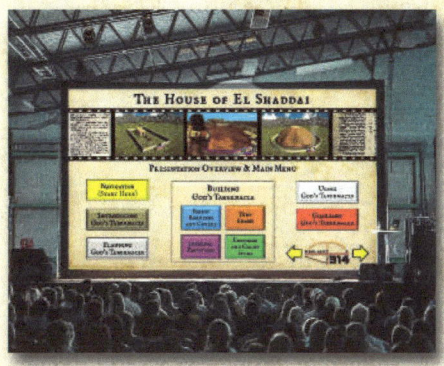

Designed for audiences ranging from 12 to adult (and ideal for incorporation into religious education curriculum or university coursework), *The House of El Shaddai—Exodus Tabernacle PowerPoint® Presentation* includes English-Hebrew Bible Tabernacle text citations, an English-Hebrew Tabernacle-specific glossary, as well as an additional quiz presentation that features 200 questions created for the purposes of subject matter review, open forum discussion, independent study, printed class handouts or assignments, or student comprehension examination.

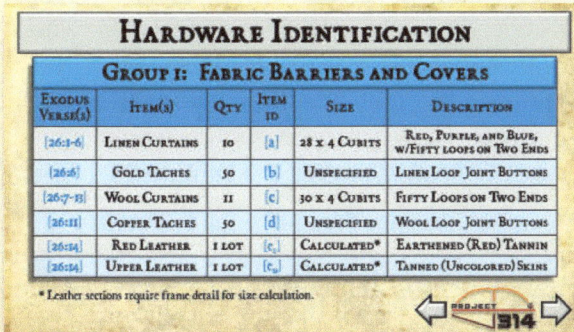

Given the wide variety of rich content and potential needs of users and students, *The House of El Shaddai Exodus Tabernacle PowerPoint® Presentation* is also equipped with links, buttons, and a site map for easy navigation for self or audience-directed studies and detailed subject matter exploration. In addition, slides are logically grouped into color-coded sections to help compartmentalize presentation content such that the subject matter may be taught in multiple class sessions of shorter durations with practical and attainable learning goals.

Although the Exodus Tabernacle presentation is primarily designed for the Microsoft PowerPoint® platform, users need not own or be familiar with PowerPoint® in order to present the material. Microsoft PowerPoint® web-based viewing tools are presently available at no charge; moreover, files are provided in formats such that PowerPoint® software or a conventional personal computer is not needed to view the presentation. While laptops and desktop computers can be used for viewing files on projectors and monitors irrespective of operating system (Windows, Mac, Linux, Android, etc.), the viewing platform flexibility extends to tablets and a wide variety of smart TV's (e.g., Amazon Fire, Android TV, Apple TV, Roku, Smartcast, webOS, etc.) via media player and familiar browser applications (e.g., Firefox, Chrome, Edge, or Safari browser platforms).

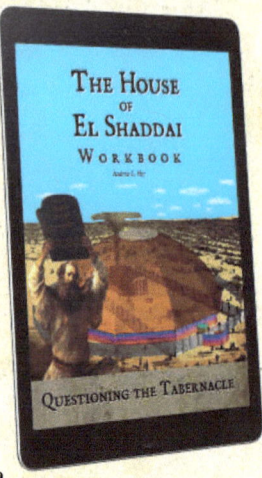
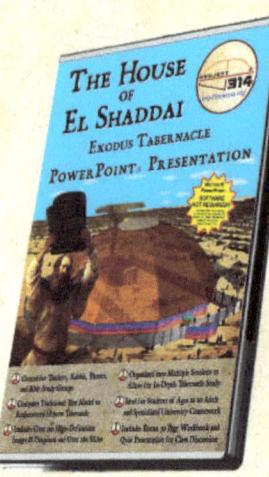

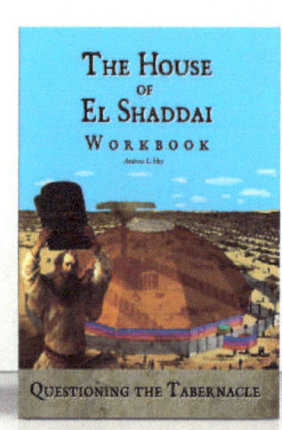

In addition to the Exodus Tabernacle PowerPoint presentation, *The House of El Shaddai Workbook – Questioning the Tabernacle* is also published independently of the digital presentation product in a perfect-bound 8.5 x 11" paperback format for teachers and students preferring to use traditional "hands-on" resources. Although the workbook was primarily designed to supplement the PowerPoint® product (featuring complementary content grouping and color coding), the workbook may also be used independently or alternatively as a study guide with or without this book. In addition to featuring 200 Tabernacle-based questions, the paperback workbook also dedicates a section to practical drawing exercises, and also includes an intensive Tabernacle study course certificate of completion, which may be used at the discretion of a teacher or course administrator.

For ordering information or other questions pertaining to ongoing Project 314 Tabernacle research and construction initiatives, refer to the contact information contained on the copyright and credits page at the beginning of this book.

www.ingramcontent.com/pod-product-compliance
Lightning Source LLC
Chambersburg PA
CBHW050854010526

44118CB00004BA/164